POWERBOAT
DESIGN AND PERFORMANCE

POWERBOAT
DESIGN AND PERFORMANCE

DAG PIKE

ADLARD
COLES

LONDON · OXFORD · NEW YORK · NEW DELHI · SYDNEY

ADLARD COLES

Bloomsbury Publishing Plc

50 Bedford Square, London, WC1B 3DP, UK

BLOOMSBURY, ADLARD COLES and the Adlard Coles logo are trademarks
of Bloomsbury Publishing Plc

First published in Great Britain 2019

A catalogue record for this book is available from the British Library

Library of Congress Cataloguing-in-Publication data has been applied for

ISBN: HB: 978-1-4729-6541-7; ePub: 978-1-4729-6540-0; ePDF: 978-1-4729-6539-4

10 9 8 7 6 5 4 3 2 1

Designed by C E Marketing

Typeset in Symbol

Printed and bound in China by C&C Offset Printing Co

To find out more about our authors and books visit www.bloomsbury.com
and sign up for our newsletters

CONTENTS

INTRODUCTION

Ever since steam engines were first installed in boats in the 1780s, the evolution of boat design has gained momentum. Freed from the constraints of having to accommodate masts and sails, the shape and speed of powerboats has developed as designers have tried to create boats that are either more seaworthy or can go faster, or hopefully both. More recently, it has been the quest for speed on the water that has led to design developments and improvements, although economy of performance is becoming increasingly important.

There's an infinite number of variables in powerboat hull design – from the width of chines, the angle of the hull vee and the shape of the bow, to the power and propulsion – and the job of the designer is to bring all of these variables together into a cohesive whole. The boat designer is always trying to find a better compromise among all these variables, one that can combine the benefits of speed and seaworthiness, and to do this they have to first understand the sea environment.

What do I mean by 'powerboat'?
When the generic term 'powerboat' is used in this book it includes all types of boat powered solely with an engine. This includes the broad categories of slow displacement boats, semi-displacement types and faster planing boats, as well as their subdivisions, such as motor cruisers, sports boats, RIBs, trawler yachts or multihulls.

UNDERSTANDING THE SEA

The sea can be a challenging, unpredictable environment; even in moderate conditions, waves come in different shapes and sizes, changing shape when the tide turns. Nothing is settled and nothing is regular in this watery environment in which boats have to operate. This has always been the primary challenge for powerboat designers: the need to find that balance in the hull design so that it will cope with the different conditions effectively and efficiently. What works in one set of conditions might not in another, so powerboats need to be tailored, while also having a wider capability.

In my long experience, the sea is rarely calm. There are of course some parts of the ocean where calm seas can make life easy for the boat driver – where a flat sea surface means all you need to do is open the throttle and go – but these conditions are few and far between. Life would be easier for both the boat designer and the boat driver if the waves came along in regular patterns and were all the same size, but the statistics tell a different story: one wave in ten can be twice the height of the average wave, and some can be even larger.

Opposite: The author drives a gas turbine powered 3-pointer at 150 mph.

What's more, they may come from different directions, creating a very uneven pattern of waves that boats have to operate in. Coping with the challenge of these changing conditions is divided between the designer of the boat, who dictates the hull shape and the power, and the person driving the boat, who dictates the speed and direction of encounter and the trim of the boat.

In an ideal world, you should be able to change the shape of the hull to enable it to adapt to different sea conditions but, except for one type of boat, this cannot normally be done. However, there are some controls that will enable you as the driver to change the trim of the boat and the way it reacts to waves and this will give you some control and enable you to match the performance more closely to the prevailing conditions. For this reason, the aim of this book is to give you a greater understanding of hull design and propulsion and how a boat will react to different conditions so that you can optimise the performance of the boat accordingly. We will also look at all the options open to both designers and operators of boats, which should help you to find the right boat for the job it has to do, whether you are a leisure user or a commercial or military operator, the latter of whom often have much more demanding requirements.

LEISURE POWERBOATS

In the leisure sector, style is king and it is the appearance of the boat that might be the primary design factor. In this respect powerboats are very much like cars in that nearly all of the working parts, the bits that make the car perform, are hidden away largely out of sight. With boats, it is what lies below the water that counts when it comes to its performance in waves – the shape of the hull below the waterline and the propulsion system – but it is often the style above the waterline that sells the boat. Performance tends to be taken for granted and few operators seem to realise that hull design can have a considerable influence on it. The interior is of course also important and here the designers are challenged to squeeze in as many smart fittings and fixtures as possible in the limited space available. For this reason, what I would term the 'bulbous look' – whereby it looks as though the

This stylish Azimut S6 is typical of the modern breed of sports cruisers today.

envelope of the boat's shape has been inflated with a bicycle pump – predominates since it creates maximum interior space, even though this approach can affect the boat's performance.

One of the main functions of a boat designer these days is to come up with a compromise that meets the requirements of the discerning owner. This raises many questions. Can I perhaps compromise on the seaworthiness of the hull in order to gain more interior space? Can I raise the sides of the hull to create more interior space without compromising the stability? Can I change the shape of the hull bottom to reduce the amount of power needed to reach the design speed? Is draft an important consideration? Most of these questions can be answered by considering the type of conditions in which the boat will put to sea. A leisure powerboat is used for pleasure and an owner probably won't think that there is much of that to be found in going to sea in adverse conditions. For this reason, they will likely be seeking a boat that performs well in moderate conditions.

With this in mind, it might make sense to design a leisure boat with an emphasis on fine-weather performance. However, what happens if the boat is caught out at sea when the conditions have changed for the worse? Trawler-type boats, for instance, often embark on longer voyages, the latter stages of which may take place so far in the future that there are not accurate weather forecasts to cover the whole voyage. For these and other reasons, every boat needs a certain level of seagoing capability and reliability to cope with adverse conditions, because you can never be quite sure when you might need them. I am concerned to find that improved weather forecasting has made some boatowners think that they can rely on the forecast and thereby never encounter bad weather. Doing so means that they fail to take into account the changes that can occur when strong tides or shallow water influence the sea conditions, rather than the weather, and this can be dangerous.

The author tests a Dell Quay Dory designed for rescue work.

We see the same thing happening regarding the weight of the boat. For a planing powerboat, the weight can be critical to both performance and fuel economy. This gives rise to the question: how much weight can you add in the interests of comfort and facilities on board without compromising the performance? It is also worth remembering that weight can have its advantages in adverse conditions as it helps to reduce the influence of the waves and therefore the motion of the boat. The designer has to find a balance – a process that has been helped considerably by the development of relatively lightweight and economical engines and more efficient propulsion systems. Powerboat design is a constantly evolving and developing cycle of progress.

COMMERCIAL AND MILITARY BOATS

For commercial and military craft, the design emphasis changes. These boats have a job to do and style does not come into the equation, or if it does, then it is a long way down the list of priorities. However, even here there have to be compromises in the design, not least because the boat and crew are likely to be operating in more challenging conditions. Can the crew stand up to the pounding of a fast boat in rough seas or are there ways to mitigate this? Reliability – though also important in the leisure-boat sector – will come much higher on the list of the designer's priorities, too, because a commercial or military boat that is out of commission can lead to considerable financial penalties in some cases, or could have knock-on effects in a major operation.

The shape of tradition, one of the classic Riva sports boats on display.

The striking angular design of the 65-knot Wally Power 118 where the author was trials skipper.

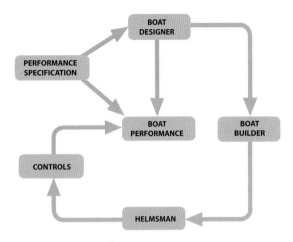

The factors that contribute to the performance of a powerboat.

The Recreational Craft Directive

The EU has determined standards for powerboat design and construction with their Recreational Craft Directive. This allocates boats a category in which they are deemed safe to operate. The highest, Category A, is the ocean standard; boats with this rating are deemed suitable for operating way offshore in adverse conditions. However, when I look at some of the boats, and their operators, that have been awarded this standard I have serious reservations about their suitability for such conditions. This illustrates one of the pitfalls of trying to set standards in the design and construction of boats without considering the experience and capability of the person driving them. The ability to safely operate a powerboat lies with both the designer and the driver, not just one or the other in isolation.

A RANGE OF STYLES

There are considerable differences in the powerboat concepts that different countries favour. In the USA, for instance, buyers fall in love with the Italian styling but usually end up purchasing something much more conservative because they know it will sell when the time comes to upgrade or downsize. They have their Downeast and trawler yacht styles, which are not generally found in other parts of the world.

In Europe, it seems that style is king, especially when it comes to interiors, but there is a nod towards good seaworthiness, particularly in the workboat designs, reflecting the more challenging sea conditions found in Northern Europe. Recent changes include bow shapes and the advent of large side windows, the latter of which in the eyes of many purists has destroyed the look on modern boats. In Australia, there is a great fondness for catamaran hulls and new concepts and styles seem more acceptable.

It is evident, then, that there is great diversity, which is good for the boating world, but everywhere there is a reluctance to adopt new technology such as hydrofoils and air support. The tried-and-tested solution is the best in most peoples' eyes and change comes very slowly.

FIT FOR PURPOSE

Over my many years of boating experience I have driven hundreds of boats of all shapes and sizes. I am frequently asked which is the best one I have ever driven and I have no hesitation in saying it is *Cesa*, the racing powerboat designed and built by Fabio Buzzi in which we won the World Championship in 1988. This was a dedicated high-performance offshore racing boat designed and built for one purpose: to win that championship. The result was superb and shows what can be achieved if you set out to put together a boat for a specific task.

I also have a soft spot for the RIB, having been involved in the design and development of the very first boats of

Modern styling on this sports cruiser.

this type. Again, it was a case of designing a boat for a job and trying to solve some of the problems with the existing inflatable boat concepts by thinking outside the box. Today, I find that many, if not most, of the RIBs on the market have strayed a long way from the original concept, mainly I think because designers and drivers do not fully understand what that concept is and also because they are focusing on style rather than performance.

It is evident, then, that powerboat design is constantly evolving and along the way there will be some backward steps as well as a lot more that move forwards in the right direction. It is a challenging world, but I hope this book can help to guide you along the right path to powerboat progress.

My choice for the best powerboat in the World is Cesa which proved unbeatable in offshore racing in the 1980s.

This F-Line 33 is the latest in sports cruiser style.

1

DISPLACEMENT AND SEMI-DISPLACEMENT HULLS

There are two types of displacement hulls: full-displacement and semi-displacement hulls. The former sit comfortably in the water and should give a reasonably comfortable ride if they are not pushed too hard. They are quite popular in the leisure sector for owners who want a slower pace of life and tend to be used in the commercial sector for heavy-duty workboats, such as tugs, diving boats and construction vessels. The semi-displacement hull is a compromise concept that was a popular alternative at one time – a sort of halfway house between the displacement hull and the planing hull. It is perhaps best described as a planing hull without the hard edges. This means that it has a flat run aft in the bottom of the hull but instead of the sharp edge at the turn of the bilge where the bottom meets the sides and where there can be a flat chine, the semi-displacement hull has a round bilge that is designed to take some of the harshness out of the ride. The idea is to combine the merits of the full-displacement hull with the ability to operate at higher speeds in what might be termed a semi-planing mode.

FULL-DISPLACEMENT HULLS

There was a time when all powerboats were based on full-displacement hulls: hulls that go through the water rather than over it. Initially, this reflected the fact that virtually all of the early powerboats were based on hulls that were similar to the full-displacement ones of sailboats. These sailing-boat concepts would often feature a hull shape that had slack bilges – ie where there was no sharp turn at the bilge as it tapered down into the keel. This has changed in most modern designs, however, and it's more common to see a relatively wide beam and a sharper angle at the turn of the bilge. Look at modern fishing boats, for example, which need to provide as much deck space as possible, a good, stable, seaworthy hull and plenty of internal volume all within a relatively shallow-draft hull. The resulting designs demonstrate what can be achieved with a full-displacement hull to meet specific requirements.

Another factor that is taken into account during the design process is the safety rules that are dictated by the length of the boat. This means that many owners want a short boat to avoid having to meet these challenging regulations, and the result is what might be termed a short, fat boat. These have been shown to work and could meet the requirements of a leisure owner for a trawler yacht, but they do not always look very pretty and for the leisure owner, appearance can be an important factor.

SHALLOW-DRAFT VS DEEP-DRAFT HULLS

To most people, the full-displacement boat reflects the concept of a sound seaworthy boat that can handle rough seas – boats typified by the traditional lifeboats and fishing boats that were built to cope with everything that the weather could throw at them. These

Opposite: The steel hull of a displacement fishing boat with a minimal bulbous bow.

13

A displacement hull being driven hard in lively seas.

particular boats were termed double-enders, meaning that the stern shape virtually matched the shape of the bow and where the sheerline, the line of the deck, was a deep curve that reflected the shape of the waves. They were also often limited in their draft because they might need to operate in shallow water on rescue missions.

The best seaworthy full-displacement hulls, however, have a deeper draft that takes the lower part of the hull away from the water turmoil that can affect the top layers of the sea, allowing it to operate in more stable water conditions as well as providing a more comfortable ride, particularly in following seas. The downside is that the deeper draft can affect access to some ports and harbours. For this reason, boats with a shallower draft tend to rule these days, especially since few owners or operators of boats with displacement hulls are looking for the ultimate in seaworthiness.

Classic displacement design: the Norhavn trawler yacht cruising through calm seas.

The impact of improved weather forecasting on boat design

Seaworthy full-displacement designs, such as for lifeboats, were developed at a time when weather forecasts were short-term and not particularly reliable. This meant that boat operators couldn't be sure about the weather when they went to sea, so boats had to be designed to cope with everything and anything, just in case. Today, we rely more heavily on much more accurate weather forecasts, and this has had a significant influence on boat design. In recent years, more what I would term 'fair weather boats' have been produced – boats that are designed to operate only in fine and moderate conditions. This is especially true in the case of modern planing boats of which more later.

SPEED VS POWER

To understand and operate full-displacement hulls you need to know a little about how they work. Because they are going *through* the water rather than over it, a full-displacement hull has a limited top speed that

The shape of tradition, a classic small fishing boat hull in wood.

is largely dictated by the length of the boat: a longer boat can travel faster in displacement mode than can a shorter boat. Typically, a 10m (33ft) full-displacement boat would have a maximum speed of around 8 or 9 knots; no matter how much power you install in the boat it will not go any faster. For this reason, full-displacement boats tend to have an engine with quite a modest power installed, so that a 10m (33ft) boat might have just a 60hp engine, which might give a speed of 6 knots. If you double the power installed then you might get the speed up to 8 knots. As you can see, that last bit of speed demands a lot more power and you don't get very much in return for the greatly increased fuel consumption and the much larger wake that the boat will create. A change in trim will occur when the extra power is applied, with the bow lifting, but there is never enough power and the hull shape is wrong for the boat to subsequently lift on to the plane.

There are two main forces that tend to dictate the speed potential of a powerboat:

» One is frictional resistance, which is the resistance caused by the water flowing past the boat that is in contact with the hull. At displacement speeds up to

about 10 knots this frictional resistance is relatively low and it only really affects fast planing boats.

» The other type is wave-making resistance and it is this that largely dictates the speed of a displacement boat. As a boat travels through the water it pushes the water aside to make way for the hull to move forwards. Technically, these are called pressure waves and their size is directly related to both the speed of the boat and the speed/length ratio. For a 15m (48ft) boat, the wave-making resistance will increase by about 50 times between a speed of 6 knots and a speed of 11 knots, which is why you can quickly get to the point at which any increase in the engine power will have little or no impact on the speed.

A motor-yacht with a displacement hull at cruising speeds creating limited wake.

The waves generated by the hull, which we see as the wake or wake waves, vary in size according to the speed. The crest of a wake wave is at the bow of the boat and as the speed is increased, the next wave crest astern will move away from the hull and be some distance astern. It is possible to see the effect of this wave-making resistance because as this aft wave crest moves further aft, the stern of the boat moves into the hollow of the wave trough of the wake wave, causing the stern to sink and creating a significant change in trim. This change in trim is generally the point at which adding more power will have little or no effect on the speed.

A heavier boat will have a greater wave-making resistance and so will reach its maximum speed at a lower level. It sounds complicated, but to simplify things, when you get to the point at which you notice a significant change in trim, with the stern dropping, then you are close to the maximum hull speed.

The ultimate long, thin hull for minimum wash when running at speed.

A blurring of lines

Since the power required for a full-displacement hull is a lot less than that needed for a planing hull, the former tends to be a more economical solution if speed is not important. For this reason, virtually all long-distance cruisers tend to be full-displacement boats, which have the fuel capacity and low consumption appropriate for long-range operations, although some designs are blurring the line between displacement and planing hulls. The double-ender concept that was used as the best solution for seaworthiness is disappearing and has been largely replaced by a transom stern, which is used primarily in the interests of creating more internal space and a more useable boat, with a cockpit in the stern area.

You can get higher speeds from a full-displacement hull if the boat is long, narrow and light. This was the concept used for earlier fast boats, for which it proved possible to get faster-than-usual displacement speeds if the length/beam ratio of the hull was in the region of perhaps 6. Of course, the penalty here was the lack of interior space and perhaps reduced stability, so long, thin hulls were restricted mainly to the early racing boats and some military applications. One application where long, thin hulls remain in use, however, is in multihull powerboats where displacement hulls can reach speeds of 15–20 knots with appropriate power (see Chapter 5).

The traditional full-displacement hull was full of curves, with hardly a straight line in sight, which must have proved a challenge for the boatbuilder before the advent of composite moulded hulls. They had to deal with this issue, however, since well-rounded hulls were considered the optimum for an easy passage through the water. Today, by contrast, many displacement hulls are based on a hard chine shape, and the deep-vee hull that is used almost exclusively for modern planing boats can operate very well as a displacement hull (although the bow shape might not be the optimum for low speeds). So, we are seeing the distinctions between displacement hulls and planing hulls becoming less clear, with the

A long, thin displacement hull designed for economical cruising.

A modern displacement hull with a hard, almost chine-like shape at the turn of the bilge.

main differences now being the power that is installed, the weight of the boat and the propulsion system that is used.

PROPELLER PLACEMENT

A significant difference between the displacement and planing hull is that, with the former, the propeller is almost always contained within the depth of the hull. On boats with a single engine, the propeller will be on the centreline and operate in a space created between the hull and the rudder with the hull shaped into a skeg to allow a good flow of water into the propeller. With twin-screw boats, the propellers are located each side of the narrow-shaped skeg at the stern so that, again, there is a good flow of water around the hull into the propeller for maximum efficiency. In both cases, there is a long, straight keel that ends in the lower rudder support – a concept that means that if the boat should ground for any reason, there is every chance that the propeller(s) would remain undamaged. Displacement boats with a transom stern often feature a different layout, with the propeller more exposed, but the general principle – with the central skeg in front of and running under the propeller – is fairly standard in displacement hull designs. This layout also allows the propeller shaft to have a near horizontal angle for greater efficiency.

A lifeboat hull showing the spray rails designed to deflect the spray at the bow.

BILGE KEELS

Traditionally, displacement hulls would have bilge keels attached to the hull at the turn of the bilge. These were longitudinal strips of wood or metal, depending on the hull construction, which were designed to reduce the rolling of the boat in a seaway. These strips would offer a small increase in the resistance with the boat moving ahead through the water, but when the boat was rolling in a seaway then the sideways resistance of the bilge keel would help to reduce the rolling. On many displacement leisure powerboats these bilge keels have been replaced by active stabilisers, which are much more effective at reducing the rolling, or even with internal gyro stabilisers. The bilge keel, however, can also be effective at helping to keep the boat upright if the boat is designed to take the bottom in ports with limited depth of water, although the keels alone are rarely deep enough to keep the boat fully upright in this situation. With the advent of moulded composite hulls, the bilge keel is disappearing because of the difficulty in moulding this feature.

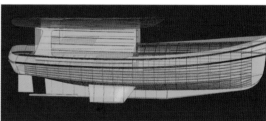

A computer generated image of a Kasten Marine hull with deep bilge keels so that it will sit upright if taking the ground.

BOW SHAPE

The shape of the bow of a full-displacement hull can affect the performance. Here, the designer has to find a delicate balance between a fine entry to cut through the water and avoid generating lift and a fuller bow shape that will ensure that the boat lifts to oncoming waves and does not try to plough directly through them. Because of the demands to increase the internal volume of the hull, we often see full bow shapes on full-displacement boats, which can lead to a more lively motion in head seas. The benefit might be seen in following seas, where you want the bow of the boat to lift readily rather than bury itself into the next wave, although in most cases, at displacement speeds the waves will be overtaking the boat so this is not a major problem. Having a vertical bow was part of traditional design and was probably largely used because it was easier to incorporate into the construction of a wooden or steel hull. Today, fashion is still dictating the use of a vertical bow shape, which tends to work well on full-displacement hulls, though a raking bow would give a softer entry in head seas and a more comfortable ride.

as you would find in a sailboat. The entry is fine at the bow and there is a distinctive chine running from high in the bow along the turn of the bilge to the stern. The intriguing aspect of this chine is that it is what I would call a 'deflecting chine', which, rather than being horizontal, is angled upwards at around 45° so that as well as generating lift to reduce the risk of the bow stuffing in following seas, it also serves to deflect spray and water away from the hull. This hull is so easily driven that the designers' claim that this 85 footer will only require 15hp to travel at 7 knots and it will have a 7,000 mile range at 8 knots.

An unusual hull shape for a displacement boat with a long, deep keel.

The Arksen displacement cruiser with its pronounced deflector chine to prevent the bow stuffing.

One solution to this dilemma is to have a fine entry at the waterline and then have the bow sections open up as it rises towards the deck. This is called flare. A hull with a generous flare at the bow can be a good compromise so far as seaworthiness is concerned – depending on the conditions that the boat is being designed to operate in – but once again, it will tend to reduce the internal volume. Despite its advantages, however, flare seems to have almost disappeared from hull forms these days.

Just when you think there is nothing new in boat design, Humphreys Yacht Design has come up with an interesting displacement hull concept while developing a long range explorer yacht using many sail boat design techniques. Here the beam has been narrowed from convention and the keel line has a distinct rocker such

A relatively new feature on larger displacement hulls is the addition of a bulbous bow: an extension added to the hull below the waterline at the bow. This was developed for ships and works well on smaller hulls down to perhaps 15m (49ft) in length. It effectively increases the waterline length of the hull without increasing the overall length, thereby increasing the efficiency of the hull. At the same time, the bulbous bow can help damp out some of the pitching motions of a hull as well as being effective in providing additional buoyancy at the bow in following seas. This is a design device that has been applied to some fishing boats, which I've seen fitted with a type of slimline bulbous bow, although it is less common in the leisure sector, perhaps because of the extra challenge for builders in engineering them even with composite moulding.

The advantages of a bulbous bow

A list of the advantages of a bulbous bow on displacement hulls down to about 12m (39ft) in length has been produced by designer Patrick Bray, based on results from extensive tank testing of a wide variety of displacement hulls. He claims that a bulbous bow:

» *starts to work most effectively once you approach hull speed (the speed at which a displacement hull does not need excessive power to drive it forwards) and will be even more effective in reducing resistance once you get above hull speed*

» *reduces the trim angle by about 1 degree*

» *reduces the pitching motion, which in turn will significantly increase comfort and seakeeping*

» *lowers the height of the bow wave, thus reducing water on deck and the environmental impact on narrow waterways*

» *increases the range of the boat by 12–15 per cent because of the reduction in fuel consumption, which in turn can result in a smaller engine and/or smaller fuel tanks being required.*

WEIGHT DISTRIBUTION

Weight distribution can also affect the performance of a displacement hull. The location of the heavy items in the hull, such as the engines and fuel tanks, should generally be located amidships; you can often find the engine just aft of amidships on boats with a relatively long propeller shaft. If you move the engine and fuel tanks aft, perhaps to make more useable space for accommodation, the boat can become unbalanced with the weight aft reducing the chances of the stern lifting to a following wave. This tended to be more of a problem in old boats that were fitted with heavy slow-revving engines, however. Modern diesels are relatively lightweight, so this weight distribution consideration is not such an important factor, although the fuel tanks should still be located at or near the centre of the hull.

STERN SHAPE

In the design of any reasonably seaworthy full-displacement hull there needs to be a balance. You don't want to match a fine bow to a full stern or vice versa, otherwise the stern might lift when there isn't a matching movement at the bow. A balance between the two ends of the boat will hopefully give the boat a relatively easy motion – something that could certainly be seen in the traditional type of double-ender where the bow and stern were nearly matching shapes.

The thinking behind having a tapered or canoe stern is that it will work well in a following sea, with the shape

A bulbous bow can improve both performance and sea-keeping to give a smoother passage.

A displacement hull with a skeg to help directional stability and performance.

of the stern dividing the waves overtaking from astern and letting them run up each side of the boat, thus reducing the possibility of the boat broaching. This was the traditional lifeboat style before planing lifeboat hulls were introduced and it is still perpetuated in the design of ship's lifeboats that are used to abandon ship.

The transom stern, by contrast, can be more vulnerable in following seas because of the amount of lift that can be generated by the waves, causing the bow to dip unless it has a full shape. However, since today fewer and fewer designs are developed to operate in more extreme conditions, this is less of an issue.

SEMI-DISPLACEMENT HULLS

Simulated clinker planking is used on this displacement cruiser.

A deep skeg on a deep-vee semi-displacement hull.

Semi-displacement hulls are often a compromise between the displacement hull and the planing boat, trying to get the best of both worlds. In my experience, earlier models in particular tend to lose out on both fronts, although some modern versions have refined the compromise. What's more, many modern deep-vee hulls have a performance at lower speeds that allows them to match the semi-displacement hull in the speed range between, say, 12 and 20 knots, for which the semi-displacement hull is designed to come into its own.

Semi-displacement hulls that I have driven have high fuel consumption once speed rises and they get out of displacement mode. This can rise quite sharply once you get above about 15 knots, which can be a handicap for both commercial operators and leisure users. They also often operate at these speeds with a considerable bow-up attitude – as though they are trying to get over the hump and on to the plane but are just not quite making it.

Finally, again from my experience, they often give a very wet ride with lots of spray flying everywhere. When evaluating a 40-year-old semi-displacement hull as the basis for a lifeboat, for instance, I found that the boat worked fairly well in rough seas as long as you found the right speed for the conditions, but there was so much spray that you had to slow down to see where you were going! This was caused by a combination of the fine entry needed to cut a path through the water and fuller bow shapes above the water that generated the spray but then left it with nowhere to go except to fly back into the windscreen.

A semi-displacement hull running at speed.

A semi-displacement hull at speed showing the spray that is generated.

However, semi-displacement hull design has been refined considerably since those days, including the fitting of various formats of spray rail or chine to try to control the spray problem and to help generate more lift when they run aft. The hulls are used quite a lot on larger craft, say 25m (82ft) and above, where the extra length gives the designer more scope to refine the bow shape and the beam/length parameters to improve the seagoing performance. As a result, there are some interesting variations on the semi-displacement hull with varying underwater hull shapes designed to improve both low- and high-speed efficiency, though none that I have tested have really overcome the spray problem.

The promoters of semi-displacement hulls will claim that their concepts are more seaworthy than a planing hull and that they operate better in the 10–20 knots speed range, where a planing hull might not be so happy. This should allow a semi-displacement hull to operate more comfortably at the slower speeds that might be demanded in adverse conditions. However, the fine bow does make them susceptible to burying in following waves and generally the modern planing hull will fare just as well. Fitting flaps to a semi-displacement hull can allow the trim to be matched to the conditions and can also help to reduce the bow-up attitude, but they do not appear to be used to any large extent, which seems a missed opportunity to give these hulls more flexibility in the way that they can be operated.

Don't get me wrong about semi-displacement boats, though: they can play a significant role in providing a boat that can operate at both slow and relatively high speeds. To this end, they have been widely used as pilot boats where open-sea performance can be important, and perhaps the spray and poor visibility is something that you have to live with to get this performance. However, from a personal point of view, the design of planing boats has improved so much that I would prefer to be out in a deep-vee rather than a semi-displacement boat in rough conditions.

Pushing the limits of semi-displacement performance in calm water.

A return to traditional styling

Semi-displacement hulls have been around for a long time and were a major feature of work and fishing boats on the east coast of North America, where they were classified under the Downeast style. In recent times, there has been a considerable new lease of life for this style of semi-displacement boat as traditionally styled boats for the leisure sector, and we can see examples of this in the work of Doug Zurn in his designer section. Dutch designers and builders have also followed similar lines, but with a lot more of the traditional styling. This has created some of the most beautiful boats on the market today with the emphasis of curves found around the stern and in the flare of the bow. They bring joy to the heart of anyone familiar with this traditional styling.

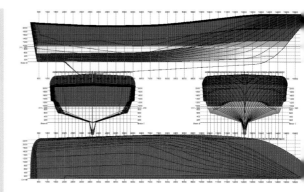

The hull lines of a semi-displacement hull with a sharp entry and full shape aft.

A planing boat running at displacement speeds creates a messy wake.

RECENT HULL INNOVATIONS

There have been other attempts to develop hull concepts based on semi-displacement hulls, whereby an operator has taken the basic hull shape and then added various modifications to the shape to solve various issues. This trial-and-error approach to hull design has its advocates, and in Holland a concept called the Slide Hull is claimed to have vastly improved seaworthiness and speed in conditions in which a conventional design might have to slow down. Here the Vripack design team, took and developed an original design by a private owner (see page 38) for what is essentially a modified deep-vee with embryo side hulls at the stern.

In Iceland, designer Össur Kristinsson has developed his Ök hull, which features a deeper centre section in the hull bottom amidships with the hull bottom curving outwards from this to a chine line. Judging by the speeds obtained, this could well be classed as a planing hull, although the focus of the design is around the seaworthiness, which is claimed to offer a significant reduction in slamming in waves. I have not had the chance to try this patented design but, if the claims stand up, then it could be a significant development in hull design.

Another concept along these lines is the hull used on the Greenline range of boats, where the vee is much flatter to give efficiency for their hybrid versions, although the concept of the central 'keel' remains.

Clearly, then, the design of semi-displacement hulls is ripe for development and new ideas. What's more, there are no hard-and-fast boundaries between semi-displacement and planing hulls; one merges with the other at around the 20-knot mark. There are hard-chine semi-displacement hulls and there are planing boats that retain many of the characteristics of the semi-displacement hull. Most of the innovation comes in the shape of the underwater sections of the hull, which is often modified to accommodate softer rounded lines, and keels or semi-keels that are claimed to offer a smoother flow to the water passing under the hull and that help to break up the flat surfaces that can add harshness to the ride.

A lifeboat semi-displacement hull developed by Damen Shipyards for lifeboat operations.

Computational Fluid Dynamics (CFD)

You would think by now that all of the various shapes and forms would have been tried, but new concepts are evolving. One of the aspects that helps this process is the ability to do model testing or even use Computational Fluid Dynamics (CFD) to assess new hull forms without the high expense of building full-size versions. Even so, objective testing of new concepts is difficult because sea conditions are never the same, so direct comparisons are difficult to achieve.

CONCLUSION

In light of the fact that fewer and fewer owners and operators are concerned with the seaworthiness of a boat and instead focus more on its comfort and economy, in my view the days of the semi-displacement concept are numbered. Instead, the world of powerboats tends to be divided into two sectors: the full-displacement hull for those who want a more leisurely approach to boating or a more rugged type of craft that will cope with arduous duty and seaworthiness, and faster boats that meet a need for speed either to save time or for the thrill of it. The latter requirement of speed is well covered by the planing type of hull, which we will cover in the next chapter.

This semi-displacement Magellano 53 is the modern interpretation of a cruising yacht.

PAT BRAY, BRAY YACHT DESIGN

Bray Yacht Design is located on the west coast of North America and as such, our cruising grounds are the Pacific Ocean. People here love boating, and like to cruise to the remote areas, some even as far north as Alaska and as far south as Mexico. Once away from the protection of the islands, you are in open ocean even if cruising just a few miles offshore. Although we design for an international marketplace, it is this Pacific Northwest experience and perspective that comes through in our designs. They must be practical and they must be sturdy. So, logically, we have become known for our long-range cruisers.

I have developed the following opinions from our work over the past 45 years, and the sum of my own experiences and those of the captains and owners we have worked with. Reducing fuel consumption and adding hull efficiency saves money and time for boaters. Finding ways to do this is one of our main goals at Bray Yachts. My baseline concept of a long-range cruiser is a vessel that can do transatlantic passages economically at a displacement speed, 8–10 knots, but then do semi-displacement speeds of 14–16 knots locally once it has arrived. To do this efficiently and economically requires a specific hull form – one most frequently found on smaller Lobster boats and motor sailers.

From our discussions with yacht captains all over the world, and correlated to our own experience, it is apparent that it is very difficult to do more than 10 knots

in the open ocean with any kind of comfort. Even if you could afford the fuel cost, the tankage required to go faster is enormous. Once you reach hull speed the horse power (and therefore fuel) required almost doubles for each additional knot in speed. Slowing down even a knot or two therefore produces a huge increase in range, with a corresponding reduction in fuel usage. So, slow down a little and save on fuel and reduce pitching as well for added comfort on a long passage.

Regardless of how efficient your hull is, a bow bulb will reduce fuel consumption, increasing cruising range. It will also reduce pitching motions, which increases comfort. To my mind, every offshore vessel with a cruising speed of under 20 knots needs a bulbous bow regardless of vessel size. We have retrofitted them to more than 60 boats from 50ft (15m) to 150ft (46m) and designed and model tested them up to 20 knots, all with great success. Generally, our hulls are 30 per cent more fuel-efficient because of our hull technology, improved even more with bow bulbs, and we are now looking at increasing that efficiency with other fuel-saving appendages, such as midship bulbs, stern bulbs and stern foils.

A bulbous bow will:

» be even more effective in reducing resistance once you get above hull speed. People think of bulbs only for displacement hulls whereas in fact a bulb starts to work most effectively once you approach hull speed, and bulbs reach their highest effectiveness above hull speed

Running tank tests to verify the design of a bulbous bow.

One of Patrick Bray's classic sports fishermen.

» *reduce your trim angle by almost 1 degree, improving visibility*

» *reduce your pitching motion significantly, increasing comfort and improving seakeeping*

» *lower the height of your bow wave, reducing water on deck and environmental impact*

» *increase your range under power by 12–15 per cent*

» *reduce your fuel consumption by up to 20 per cent, depending on the vessel speed*

» *mean that in a new-build vessel you can fit an engine with 20 per cent less horsepower and have fuel tanks 12–15 per cent smaller and still reach your contract speed and range.*

Note that these numbers have been proven not only in model tests and CFD, but also in results from vessels in ocean waves.

STYLING VERSUS SEAKEEPING

A yacht is a floating piece of art, a visual statement of the owner's personal taste, which means that good looks are important, though they should not take precedence at the expense of seakeeping. A high bow with a lot of flare is important to keep a dry boat. Sharp bows and reverse stems may be the fashion but be aware that they generally provide a very wet ride. Having a sharp bow is great for cutting through the waves and maintaining speed, but at the expense of more water on deck, as the vessel tends to go through the waves rather than over them. By having that sharp bow below a good-size spray knocker, a reasonable speed can be maintained and water can be kept off the decks in a sea of up to 3–4ft (0.9–1.2ft). We have found it best if above the spray knocker the hull has a lot of flare.

When out at sea, once the conditions worsen and it is time to slow the vessel down, let the bow form take over, keeping the bow from plunging too deep. Although there is an increase in pitching motion as the bow rises to meet each wave, with this hull form there is a lot less water on deck. Interestingly, the addition of a bow bulb to this hull form dramatically reduces this pitching. Every time the vessel tries to rise up or plunge down there is a large mass of water to be displaced by the bulb. Given the leverage arm that the bulb has at the very extreme end of the boat, it can provide a considerable amount of force. It also has a dampening motion to stop the pitching quickly rather than have it continue on hobby horsing.

STABILITY

Also frequently overlooked in a review of a vessel's capabilities is its range of stability. The minimum stability criteria required by class authorities are exactly that: the bare minimum. A really stiff vessel feels good when you are walking around at a quiet anchorage but its high initial stability will throw people off their feet when the rolling starts. A low initial stability is necessary to give a soft, easy motion that leaves the plates on the table, but this needs to be coupled with a long range of positive righting arm. Generally, if a boat has very stiff initial stability then it will have a very short range of positive stability, meaning that it will feel very stable at rest, but will have a higher tendency to want to overturn at very low angles of heel. To me, this is the worst kind of stability because it gives you the feeling of security and

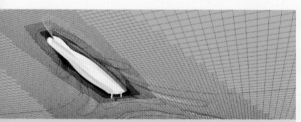

CFD can be a great tool to validate designs.

confidence when in fact as soon as things get bad it will make the situation far worse. It is not that uncommon in many vessels for the maximum stability to happen as low as 35 degrees of heel and from that point on there is less and less resistance to overturning, until at 60 degrees of heel the vessel turns turtle. Having a long range of positive stability means there is a longer period during which the vessel wants to return to upright rather than losing stability early and having more stability when upside-down than upright.

STABILISERS

Active stabilisers will reduce roll but do not provide actual stability. Instead, they produce dynamic forces that resist the rolling motions induced by waves. Generally, in most

stabiliser systems these hydrodynamic forces can only be created with forward speed and typically 8 knots is used as the minimum speed for complete stabilisation. The slower the forward speed, the less forces that are developed to counteract the natural rolling motions. If there is no speed underway, then there are no dynamic forces. The exception is the zero speed stabilisers, which work very hard moving back and forth very quickly to develop water flow over their surfaces.

HULL FORM

The Lobster boat hull has shown us that a vessel can operate efficiently at low speed but still have a high top speed. This hull form uses tight round bilges and a shallow, broad transom. A well-designed, chined hull with these same characteristics can be just as efficient. This has been proven in model testing and CFD work, as well as confirmed in many completed vessels. In addition, a

One of Patrick Bray's trawler yacht designs under construction.

chined form will reduce rolling motions and allows more floor space on the lower deck. If a round bilge is a must-have in a metal boat, then a radiused bilge build system should be considered. In this system, the bilge radius is kept constant and can be pre-rolled in large sheets.

The aft skegs of a twin screw trawler yacht.

STRUCTURE

We have found boats to be most effective when the interior structure is framed longitudinally. This is a system of widely spaced transverse frames and closely spaced longitudinal stringers, used most often in composite construction but also for aluminium builds. Even in steel construction, it is stronger for its weight and produces a form that is inherently fair from the start. Frames are labour-intensive so their numbers are reduced and, once in place, the stringers can be quickly laid in to align and hold the framework together. The long curves support the plating, producing smooth, fair surfaces.

Regardless of size or build material, if a vessel is going to head out on anything other than a calm day for a few hours, it should be designed with many of the safety and structural features found on commercial vessels and required by international classification societies. As a minimum, these should include a watertight forward collision bulkhead, watertight engine room bulkheads with a watertight (or at least weathertight) door. Door sill heights on the main deck forward of amidships should be at least 1.8m (6ft) high to keep water on deck outside, where it belongs. Freeing ports on the main deck need to be large to get water off the deck quickly before the next wave lands aboard; loose water on deck has a very dramatic and negative effect on stability and should be taken very seriously.

A spacious interior is lovely but there have to be sufficient places to put lots of handholds. Large open-plan rooms with a big main salon are nice for entertaining in harbour but it is important to think about how you will manoeuvre through the room with a bit (or more than a bit) of a roll on. Overhead handrails are a common solution but the same can be achieved with a few well-placed counters and chairs (assuming they are fixed in place).

Turning the steel hull, showing the way the bulbous bow runs well aft.

A planing hull at speed with just the aft half of the hull in the water.

THE UBIQUITOUS DEEP-VEE HULL

Probably about 75 per cent of modern boats are based on a deep-vee hull in one form or another and it works for all sizes at least up to about 30m (98ft). The deep-vee comes in many shapes and sizes, from the high-performance offshore racing boat at one extreme to the modern all-weather lifeboat at the other. It is a hull design that can perform across a wide spectrum of sea conditions and speeds and meet the requirements of a wide range of applications, and it is this versatility and capability that has made the deep-vee hull so popular among designers and builders.

EARLY DEVELOPMENT

In terms of motorboat history, the deep-vee hull is relatively new. American Ray Hunt is credited with its development, and if you go back through some of his early designs you can see the first signs of the deep-vee coming to life. For instance, Hunt designs developed just before the outbreak of World War II show a vee hull but with a rounded bottom rather than the sharp vee angle – meaning this would probably technically rank as a semi-displacement hull – but the concept was there.

Putting a vee in the bottom of the hull was not new even then, however; in the 1920s and 1930s, most planing boats had a vee in the hull but with a deadrise of perhaps no more than 5 degrees. The most efficient planing surface for the bottom of the hull of a fast boat is a flat surface, which would be fine apart from the fact that a flat surface lacks any directional stability – ie the ability to maintain a course without constant correction – and it also slams in waves. Adding a shallow vee in the hull was deemed the solution, and in many cases, including the Hunt designs, a skeg was also added for directional stability. The addition of the shallow vee helped directional stability and when it was combined with a fine entry at the bow, the slamming in waves became acceptable, although it certainly made it necessary to reduce speed in lively seas. You have to remember, though, that at that time engines tended to be heavy and with reduced power compared with modern engines, so designers wanted the most efficient planing surface for performance. If this resulted in a poor ride in waves, it was judged to be an acceptable compromise.

The requirement for fast boats during World War II did a lot to progress the development of higher-performance and lighter-weight engines, factors that after the war enabled Ray Hunt to both improve performance and enable a deeper vee to be incorporated into the hull to enhance the seaworthiness. This was also a time when better construction materials, such as composites, allowed for a lighter, stronger hull to be used. And so the deep-vee was born.

A classic deep-vee hull running at speed with just the rear of the hull in the water.

VARIABLE DEADRISE HULLS

Strangely, we are seeing a return to the sort of shallower-vee hull design that Hunt initially used with what is termed a variable deadrise hull. This comprises a deep vee at the bow and then towards the stern it flattens out so that the vee at the transom is maybe only 10 degrees. This type of hull is found on some production boats and tends to compensate for the quite heavy loading caused by accommodation and equipment that modern boats are required to have, though it does detract from the seaworthiness.

such as the Humphree interceptor system, can prevent the boat from then spinning out by ensuring that the boat turns in a more controllable way.

The full bow shape found on many modern deep-vee hulls to increase the internal space.

The deep-vee hull with narrow spray rails and wider chines matched to a full bow.

This reducing of the deadrise angle at the stern has to be done carefully because if the hull is flatter here then it will lose its grip on the water when turning and tend to slide sideways, with a loss of control. This can be corrected by fitting a fin or fins close to the transom, which will ensure that the hull has some 'bite' on the water. In a similar way, you can get this flat surface aft when a hull with a considerable deadrise heels over too far in a turn so that it is virtually planing on the flat surface of one side of the vee. Automatic trim systems,

Deadrise

Deadrise is the angle between the horizontal and the bottom of the hull on each side of the centre and is usually measured at the transom. A 5-degree angle of deadrise is very close to the horizontal, so is almost flat. The average deadrise that is found on a motor cruiser these days is likely to be between 12 and 15 degrees, which helps to cushion the ride and give directional stability. These boats are not designed to fly out of the water so this deadrise is adequate for most practical purposes. For an offshore racing boat, however, the deadrise might be between 24 and 28 degrees, which allows the boat to be pushed to the limit and reduces the chance of it leaving the water, while also cushioning the ride when it does. Deciding on the deadrise is one of the major decisions for a designer because the lower the deadrise, the more efficient the hull, but the higher the deadrise, the more the ride is cushioned in waves and the better the directional stability.

A deep-vee lifeboat at speed with a secondary chine in the topsides to help deflect spray.

DEEP-VEE RACERS

Some of those early deep-vee hulls were used in the new sport of offshore powerboat racing with considerable success, though I still look at photos that show the boats always flying out of the water, which looks very dramatic, and wonder about the moment of the boat landing back in the water, which I can assure you must have been very painful for the crew and tough on the boat. There were two lessons to be learned from studying those pictures of early race boats: first, if the boat leaves the water you are not going anywhere fast because the propeller(s) is out of the water; and second, when the boat re-enters the water it will take some time for the boat and crew to recover and to get moving again. The aim when driving a deep-vee hull, or for that matter any design, should at least be to keep the boat in contact with the water and thereby maintain both propulsion and control.

That aside, the use of the deep-vee hull in offshore powerboat racing demonstrated its potential and, with

The pinnacle of traditional powerboat design, a Cigarette 35 in which the author navigated.

improved comfort and performance, this soon filtered down to the leisure sector – first to smaller sports boats, where it offered a dramatic improvement in performance when combined with the more powerful outboard motors then available, and later into the motor cruiser sector, where it is now pretty much the standard type of hull for all planing boat applications.

Just on the plane, showing the whole hull still in the water with considerable spray generated.

CHINES AND SPRAY RAILS

Other modifications to the early structures included the use of chines and spray rails, which are now standard features on deep-vee hulls. The chine is the flat surface introduced at the point where the bottom of the hull changes into the vertical side panels. It serves two purposes:

» it deflects water away from the hull and stops it riding up the sides of the hull

» it provides extra dynamic stability by generating additional lift if the boat heels over to the side.

Getting the shape and width of the chine at its optimum is one of the main challenges facing a designer because it can have a considerable impact on both the performance of the boat and the ride comfort. An easy solution is to use a wide chine, which will help to generate maximum lift so that the boat rises easily up on to the plane, but the flat surface of this wide chine can impact on waves when the boat is pitching into a head sea, generating high-impact loadings. Taking the wide chine up into the bow on a rising curve can improve performance in head seas and reduce the chance of the bow burying into the back of an approaching wave, and it can also help to deflect the spray to give a dryer boat, but this can also impact on the ride comfort in head seas.

In an effort to generate the maximum lift from the chine, some designers therefore introduced a reverse chine – one that was angled downwards, forcing the water emerging from the hull into quite a dramatic change of direction, which was good for lift and stability but produced even higher impacts when running in waves. A version of this is found in the Slide Hull developed by Vripack, for which the reverse chine starts out being very narrow towards the bow and then widens and deepens towards the stern, ending as almost embryo side hulls. I am a great believer in offering the water emerging from under the hull as smooth a flow path as possible in the interests of a softer ride, and most reverse chines are a step too far, but Vripack seems to have found a good compromise.

Calm seas and high speed are a perfect combination for enjoying powerboating.

The effect of wide chines was seen very clearly on the Atlantic record-breaker *Virgin Atlantic Challenger II*, the hull of which had very wide chines to generate the lift required for the boat to get on the plane with a 12-tonne load of fuel. We felt every square inch of those wide chines when the boat was running in waves, which was most of the time on the three-and-a-half-day crossing; the pounding was intense.

Spray rails do much the same job as chines but are generally much narrower so that they do not have a major impact on ride comfort. The main purpose of spray rails is to deflect the water away from the hull at the earliest possible moment as the boat rises on

to the plane, in order to reduce the wetted surface area of the hull. When a powerboat is travelling at speed, the wave-making resistance of the hull that applies to displacement hulls has much less influence on performance; it is for the most part the friction developed between the hull surfaces and the water that takes over. This friction is largely proportional to the area of the hull in contact with the water, so the smaller the area in contact, the better the performance. This is where the spray rails come in, peeling the water away from the hull at the earliest possible moment. Running fore and aft, the spray rails also help to give the hull directional stability, keeping the hull running in the desired direction with no yawing so that the steering is stable.

Different designers have different ideas about the number and the length of spray rails, with some running from high in the bow right aft to the transom and others stopping short in order to reduce the turbulence of the water approaching the propellers. With water-jet propulsion, it is usually recommended that spray rails are kept well away from the area of the jet intake so that there is no aeration in the water entering the jet.

A deep-vee hull with multiple spray rails showing how they deflect the water away from the hull.

BEAM

The beam of the boat can have quite an influence on the performance of the deep-vee hull. The early deep-vees tended to have a wide beam, which had the effect of concentrating the lift in the aft sections of the hull. With the lift focused here, the centre of gravity needed to be well aft as well so it would balance the lift, which was fine for the sterndrives and outboards mainly in use at that time, although these hulls were also sensitive to pitching because of the relatively short length of the hull in contact with the water, whereby a small change in the trim angle could make a significant difference in the lift being generated. This sensitivity to pitching can be seen in the dramatic photos of some of those early race boats, in which the boat is entirely out of the water and both the crew and the boat would consequently be subject to high impacts when the boat re-entered the water.

For racing boats, the solution to this was found by introducing narrower hulls, which had the effect of spreading the lift over a greater length of the hull to give better pitching stability. This was not a good solution for leisure versions of the deep-vee, however, where internal volume was important in order to maximise the accommodation space, but then leisure boats tend to operate at lower speeds and are heavier size for size, which means they already have an acceptable amount of hull length in the water.

Modern planing hull design with two steps and a vertical bow shape.

HULL STEPS

Introducing steps into the bottom of the hull is another design technique that can improve the performance of fast deep-vee hulls. Transverse hull steps were used in some of the earliest planing boats, which had nearly flat hull bottoms, and it was recognised that this could reduce both the area of the hull in contact with the water and the pitching, because the hull was in contact with the water surface at multiple points. It took a long time, though, before the concept of a stepped hull was extended for use on deep-vee hulls. As far as I know, the first deep-vee hull to have steps was the wide-beam monohull that we used to win the second Round Britain Powerboat Race, which was powered by four heavy diesel engines. When designer Fabio Buzzi found that the boat was struggling to plane because of the weight of the heavy diesels, he cut a step in the hull, which helped to move the centre of lift further forwards. Following this modification, the boat had an outstanding win against strong opposition in this tough race and there was a noticeable reduction in the pitching motions.

The same hull cutting through the active wake of the photo boat.

Hull steps are now widely used on performance deep-vee hulls, mainly those with narrower hulls and that reach speeds of more than 40 knots; it is rare to find them on production motor cruisers unless these are designed for speeds over about 35 knots. Although they offer the benefits of reducing resistance and pitching motions while at the same time increasing speed by perhaps a couple of knots on a fast boat, they do have a downside and can cause a boat that is a bit more sensitive to spin out around the lift point of the forward step.

Some designs feature two or more steps, and they vary in angle – some being straight across the hull while others are angled aft from the chine line. Different designers also have different ideas about the depth of the step and whether there should be scope for air to be drawn in just aft of the step to help lubricate the planing surfaces.

The use of steps still seems to be a work in progress, then, with little in the way of objective research being carried out, although their effect can now be quantified more clearly when using CFD methods of design. Certainly, you tend to only find steps in composite hulls, partly because introducing them into wood or metal hulls adds considerably to the complication of the construction. Furthermore, steps will not work when water-jet propulsion is used because the air introduced under the hull will enter the jet intake and cause unwanted cavitation.

not be used in adverse conditions. Time will tell whether the vertical bow endures, but it is certainly being used on a wide selection of standard production hulls these days.

A sports cruiser running at speed with a well-deflected spray line.

A stepped hull taken to extremes and combined with an unusual bow shape.

BOW SHAPE

Another area of hull design that has shown considerable change in recent years is in the bow shape, where there has been a move back to the vertical stem. There are benefits in using a vertical stem because it will increase the waterline length of the hull, and it creates more space inside the hull. However, this is usually at the expense of the performance of the boat in rougher seas, where there will be a greater tendency for the hull to broach or bury in following seas.

The use of the vertical stem can thus be seen in many cases as a fashion statement, part of a trend that sees designers of leisure craft ignoring the seaworthiness aspects of hull design on the basis that leisure craft will

The angled or raked bow, in contrast to the vertical one, gives a softer entry into waves in both head and following seas and is still the preferred shape for most boats where the accent is on performance, either for high speed or for improved seaworthiness. In the quest for more internal space within the hull, designers are matching this shape to full bow cross-sections – a combination that does give good lift but that can make the hull more sensitive to responding to wave movement, thereby producing a more lively ride and generating more spray.

Flare in the bow cross-sections, which can give the considerable benefits of a dry ride and more gentle motions in a head sea, seems to be disappearing except in some of the more traditional US sports fisherman designs. In some high-performance designs where the fine entry can risk the bow burying in following seas, a wider bow shape or even a squared-off bow close to the deck level has been used to reduce this risk of the bow burying. Another solution has been to use short fins extending out on each side of the bow – what are known as anti-stuff fins.

I am a great fan of the use of flare in bow shapes, not only because of the way that it allows a fine entry at the waterline to be combined with a steady increase in lift if the bow does bury, but also because it can help to deflect spray. Another bonus is that it looks good and

A large deep vee with surface drives powering onto the plane.

shows a respect for tradition, which admittedly may not appeal to everyone. Nevertheless, flare in the bow combines both good looks and good seaworthiness so should be considered.

DECK HEIGHT AND SHEER

The height of the deck is another variable that the designer can exploit. The higher the deck at the bow, the less risk there will be of the bow submerging. However, the deck height is more likely to be dictated by the need for good headroom inside the hull. It is much the same with the sheerline, and a reverse sheer is now the norm to gain more internal space. I do worry that with the increased freeboard found on many modern designs, the ability to recover somebody from the water could be a considerable challenge. The argument is that the swim platform can be used instead, but this doesn't take into account the significant fact that just underneath this platform are the propellers.

This sports cruiser hull has an accentuated chine that makes it almost a triple hull shape.

The cathedral hull

Over the years, there have been a number of concepts that use the deep-vee hull as the basis of the design but with variations in the shape. We have mentioned the use of reverse chines – a concept that has been taken to extremes with the cathedral hull, for which embryo side hulls extend out from the main centre-vee hull. These became very popular many years ago in the form of small practical sports boats, such as the Boston Whaler and the Dell Quay Dory. These designs, with their squared-off bow and good stability, were a very practical solution as tenders, and their load-carrying ability and good stability made them ideal family sports boats. However, the bow shape, with its three hulls in this area, tends to slam in waves because the water is trapped between the hulls, causing vast showers of spray when pushed hard in following seas. Larger sizes of cathedral hulls have been used mainly in the fishing boat and workboat sector, and again they work fine up to a certain point but may struggle in rougher seas. For the leisure sector, where looks matter, it has also not proved easy to make such designs look appealing.

ADJUSTABLE HULLS

There has been some discussion about developing boat hulls with a hull deadrise that can be varied. Variously known as a morphing hull or an adjustable deadrise hull, such a concept would have a lot to offer: a shallow vee in slight seas and a deeper vee in rough seas, so that the boat could be tuned to the prevailing conditions. It would make for a much more efficient and, hopefully, comfortable-riding boat, but the technical challenges are considerable and any benefit is likely to be offset by an increase in weight.

We know from experience that the ability to change aspects of the boat is useful. When we developed the first RIBs, which combined a rigid hull with an inflatable tube, one of the benefits was that the tube could change shape under wave impact, effectively giving us a form of variable geometry hull. There is more about this in Chapter 4. Certainly, the ability to change hull shape or at least change the lift characteristics is a possibility: lift and the angle of trim can be varied by the use of flaps or interceptors and, while not a fully morphing hull, this at least gives the driver more control over how the boat behaves in varying sea conditions.

The problem with modern designs

Apart from introducing a wider-than-normal beam to the hull, modern designs are also expanding upwards with higher freeboards, which gives more headroom inside but can make getting on and off the boat in a marina something of a challenge. It also makes the boat less able to cope with any sort of emergency. In response, the boatbuilder/designer will argue that the swim platform gives both easy access to the boat in the marina and allows recovery or access to the water from a much lower point.

One area where the need for internal volume does show is in the bow sections of some designs. Instead of the fine entry that seaworthiness should dictate, we are now seeing quite a full section on the waterline at the bow, even when it has lifted on to the plane. This becomes noticeable when you see some photos of these boats at speed where the spray, instead of sweeping outwards and aft in a clean line, is actually being projected forwards. This can't be efficient either in terms of fuel consumption or performance and it must increase the resistance considerably, yet it seems to be an acceptable solution.

The full bow shape of this deep-vee makes hard work of planing with the spray being thrown forwards.

WEIGHT

The performance of a planing boat will be very much dictated by its weight. For this reason, a designer will carefully calculate the projected weight of the boat when doing his or her sums about the anticipated performance. The trouble is, though, that virtually all planing boats come out heavier because the designer has only added in the weight of the boat and its fittings and has not made allowance for all the extras, such as the crew themselves, perhaps the tender, all the stores carried on board, maybe bicycles, and even possessions such as pictures and books. These things all add up. I remember doing a weight assessment for one owner who was concerned that his boat had lost a lot of its claimed design performance. I went back to him afterwards and said: 'Do you want to go faster or do you want to live well? You have 12 tonnes of wine on board!' This was perhaps an extreme example and it was on a larger yacht, but it does show how weight can be added without anyone accounting for it. I am sure this is why you see quite a few motor cruisers being advertised as doing 28 or 33 knots; originally, the design speed was probably 30 or 35 knots but extra weight had reduced the actual performance.

Weight can have its part to play in improving seaworthiness. When you want a boat to give the highest speed possible – as would be the case with a racing boat – then the simple solution is to pare the weight back to the bone and perhaps use exotic construction materials. That is the normally accepted route to performance, but there is another way, as we proved back in 1988 with the Class I racing boat *Cesa*. *Cesa* was a 46-footer that was powered by four high-performance Seatek diesels to give an installed power of close to 4,000hp. The racing rules of the time allowed a higher engine capacity for diesel power and *Cesa* exploited this to the full. Because she was a heavy boat she was much less likely to leave the water when running in head seas and this allowed her to travel at considerably higher speeds than the petrol-engined opposition, so none of the other race boats could touch her. She won the World Championship convincingly.

INNOVATIONS IN DESIGN

There have been many and varied attempts to introduce subtle tweaks to the basic concept of the deep-vee in an effort to improve performance. These have been largely aimed at improving the seaworthiness of a hull rather than the speed, perhaps to soften the ride or to reduce the pitching – such as the cathedral hull. Reducing pitching, is the aim of the 'beak' boat, to which the designers added what looked like a short bulbous bow coming out from the forefoot of a deep-vee hull. This was a slim, angular projection rather than the normal carefully rounded one found on displacement hulls, and, by adding more buoyancy at the bow of a planing hull, its aim was to reduce the effect of advancing waves and also to increase the waterline length. It has since been used with some success on pilot boats and patrol craft that do not have the option of turning back when conditions get difficult.

Another innovation has been the ragged chine, which is rather like an clinker-built hull in reverse with the lower edges of the 'planking' creating a series of lifting surfaces rather than having one wide chine. I have done quite a few trials with ragged-chine hulls and it does seem to soften the ride, but this is at the expense of having a much more complex shape to mould or construct as well as a considerable number of sharp edges, which can be vulnerable to impact. None of the trials were direct comparison trials, however, which are really the only way to see if changes work, since these can be a challenge to organise.

A simpler variation of much the same thing is the stepped chine. Instead of having one wide chine along each side of the hull, the stepped chine features the same horizontal area but divided up into two or more steps so that wave impact is slightly staggered and does not all occur in one go.

Another concept for chines that is widely used on commercial boats is to introduce a secondary chine higher up the topsides that allows the hull to widen out, and at the same time, helps to deflect spray away from the hull.

Yet another variation that was tried was the Very Slender Vessel or VSV. Originally developed by designer Adrian Thompson, the VSV had a length/beam ratio of around

A close up of a deep-vee hull step extending out to the side of the hull.

This multi-chine hull should offer a softer ride but the hull shape is very full which is likely to increase pitching.

8, meaning that it was very narrow in relation to its length. The aim was to create a hull that would tend to go through waves rather than contour over them, and that would allow rapid progress into head seas. The narrow hull did not have much of a planing surface, so to generate additional lift and reduce the wetted surface area, a well-defined chine started narrow at the bow and widened as it ran aft – a feature that also helped to stabilise the hull and reduce rolling. It required a fully enclosed wheelhouse to protect the crew.

It was an interesting concept aimed mainly at the military markets, where its 50-knot speed in adverse conditions would give it an edge over more conventional designs. I did trials with it with the Special Boat Service people in rough seas and the performance was quite remarkable as it produced a more or less level ride. The main problem, however, was that you could not see where you were going because there seemed to be solid water coming over the deck most of the time. Subsequent to this, the designer went on to produce a 75-footer as a long-range cruising boat, which was a lot more successful, offering a lower speed but a dryer ride.

The deep-vee lifeboat

It may surprise you to know that the hull shape of an all-weather lifeboat is very similar to that of many leisure craft, and almost all are based on a form of a deep-vee hull these days. There may be variations in how the propellers are protected, but the main difference is that the lifeboat is designed and equipped so that nothing fails, even in extreme conditions.

BART BOUWHUIS, VRIPACK

"HUMAN CENTRED DESIGN

The emphasis on placing the client's needs and satisfaction at the heart of the designs is essentially the secret of Vripack's success. Before sketching a single line, the naval architect team needs to spend as much time as necessary familiarising themselves with the client, for it is they who will be sailing out to sea on the design, manning the vessel in all kinds of weather conditions, and sometimes sailing so far out that the reassurance of safety becomes paramount.

Every client expresses him or herself in a different way. Therefore, it is important to ask the right questions to understand the personality of the client at the first meeting. Most of the time, clients already have an idea of what they want and it is up to the naval architects to find out where this comes from. The design team is looking for the perfect boat for each client, and when bringing out the wishes of the client it can appear that they are always in conflict with each other. Making concessions involves a process of finding the right balance in the puzzle that needs to be solved.

As for the making of any object, the finer the crafting, the harder the going gets. The family-owned firm of Wajer Yachts was still in its first generation as boatbuilders when they dropped by the Vripack's studio and painted a vivid picture of their ideal dayboat. Vripack's first design was summarily rejected. As was the second, and the third, at which point it became patently clear to the team that they were facing one of their biggest design challenges to date. Everything about boat design was up for discussion, including the question of how one goes about designing an icon. By now, nearly everyone in the studio was working on the project. While the designers pored over every facet of the design with the level of attention normally associated with diamond cutting, the naval architects were rising to a challenge of their own, namely to create the first-ever European-built boat fitted with the revolutionary new pod propulsion system. After months of interaction between both parties, a finely balanced composite-moulded hull was ready for its unveiling.

A HOLISTIC APPROACH

A good design is more than meets the eye: it is also a question of how well the design works and feels at sea. Therefore, Vripack believes in a holistic approach, viewing every project as a whole and not as a part of something. Every project involves a multi-disciplinary team that is brought together specifically for that project from the day of commission. In practice, it means that while a naval architect is drafting the curve of the hull at the point where it meets the waterline, a designer will already be contemplating the interior layout that might best suit the other side of the curve.

The Wajer, which was a classic design from Vripack.

The Amethyst *based on a Slide Hull by Vripack.*

A good example of this holistic approach is the result of more than 500 Doggersbank yachts that have been built in a multitude of different versions, such as power and sail, and in metal and composite. Arguably, Doggersbank is Vripack's strongest brand within the yachtbuilding industry. Doggersbanks are known for their ocean-going comfort, low emissions, clean engine rooms and equipment that will run forever. The sturdy equipment on board ensures reliability during offshore voyages. It features straightforward systems and extremely good seaworthiness. The masculine exterior styling has its origin in the way that vessels behave in seagoing conditions, resulting in the high flared bow and typical backward bulwark that provide a safe working deck for crew in all weather conditions.

The tight integration of the disciplines – yacht design, naval architecture and engineering – in achieving a holistic approach allows the team to think laterally every step of the way, the results of which are much richer ideas and better designs, achieved with greater efficiency.

DESIGN PROCEDURE

When tools are used correctly, there is enough space to lead the design in the right direction without being inhibited because the alternatives have too many consequences. While searching for the compromise, it is important to minimise the disruptive consequences of change, and to be able to change as much as possible at the right time, while never taking shortcuts in the design spiral.

Regarding the hull design and the human-centred design mentioned above, a good approach tool to help the naval architect is to create a design comfort matrix. With a tool like this, the best compromise between different hull design features and the client's requirement list can be reached by simply scoring any item following the client's order of importance. The output of this tool is the development of the balance between the best performance, comfort and seaworthiness fulfilling the client's desires.

Many of the hulls of Fairline Yachts have been developed following the use of this tool. Listening carefully to how the brand wanted the boats to ride on the water and the feeling and the behaviour they wanted to achieve, a careful balance of low dynamic trim and high manoeuvrability in addition to ride comfort and fuel efficiency was performed on those yachts, confirming the functionality of this tool.

INVESTMENT, IMPROVEMENT AND INNOVATION

The life of the designer is a non-stop learning process, creating new ideas and analysing them until a good result is found. It was as a result of this work that the Slide Hull, a patented hull designed by Vripack, was developed.

The realisation of this invention is as unique as its outstanding performance. Driven by a passion for performance and comfort, the client tirelessly worked on the optimisation of the hull of his existing vessel; literally cutting the shell and reshaping her, over and over again for nearly a decade. By pure trial and error, he made off-the-book discoveries and shared them with Vripack's naval architect, Peter Bouma, an incident Bouma remembers well: 'What he told us couldn't work and at first we didn't actually believe him. No formulas, algorithms or white paper supported anything he claimed.' After hundreds of hours of research, sea trials and empirical comfort studies, the design office managed to capture the essence of the Slide Hull and improved it even further with some 15 per cent efficiency at fast displacement speeds.

The Slide Hull is a moderate-vee planing hull with a deadrise of 17 degrees, but outside this basic hull concept the vee hull has been considerably modified. When seen afloat, the hull looks conventional, with a relatively fine entry and a lower chine line that keeps low at the bow. It is the way that this lower chine line has been modified as it runs aft that gives the Slide Hull its unique characteristics. A secondary chine above helps to deflect spray and water away from the hull.

Just below the waterline towards the bow, the lower chine adopts a reverse angle. Normally, a chine would be horizontal to generate lift and to deflect the water away from the hull. On the Slide Hull, the chine is angled downwards, which would generate harshness in the ride but by keeping the chine narrow at the forward end the harshness is removed. It is only from amidships to aft that this reverse chine adopts a significant width, and at the transom the reverse chine is almost large enough to be classed as an embryo side hull. The size of this reverse chine can be judged by the fact that the effective deadrise at the transom measured from the apex of the keel to the outer edge of the chine is 13 degrees, compared with the 17-degree angle of the main section of the hull.

'This hull arrangement generates considerable lift, which accounts for the efficiency of the Slide Hull, without having a negative effect on the seakeeping,' says Bouma. 'Another factor is having the centre of gravity roughly at the midship point, which helps to reduce pitching motions. The comfort of this hull is described by her sailors "like the

A sports cruiser by Vripack.

Typical Dutch styling from Vripack.

boat is riding cushions". The damping in waves is beyond unique and prevents seasickness. 'The lines are placed such that when the vessel picks up speed, the water flows in a way that resembles how you go down a slide. The hull is specifically designed for fast displacement-hull speeds, particularly for vessels with a large variation in loads – a hull with such unique performance characteristics that she is worthy of a patent protection.'

'In addition, the fuel consumption of our Slide Hull outperforms any other vessel that I have ever seen,' continues Bouma. 'The *Amethyst* uses just 180 litres per hour at a cruising speed of 21 knots, which is really low for a 45-ton vessel. Thanks to the Slide Hull, we outperform

all other competitors in this field,' Bouma concludes.

Because of the studio's accumulated wealth of experience, its open-mindedness, its curiosity and its holistic approach, it is able to easily incorporate all the insight it gleans and techniques it observes into what it does in a continuous process of enrichment that manifests itself in the perfectly balanced yacht that makes her owners feel at home at sea.

As Bart Bouwhuis says: 'Anything and everything that is going to be designed must be fully human centred. Nothing else.'

THE MERITS OF MULTIHULLS

The use of multihulls, mainly in the form of catamarans, dates back right to the early days of boats, but despite numerous advantages they have never been the mainstream option for powerboats. Catamarans make a lot of sense for a sailboat because you don't need to carry that heavy ballast keel around to get the stability you need, but for a powerboat the advantages are less obvious. Sure, you get a more efficient hull shape that requires less power to achieve higher speeds, and you get stability, but there are disadvantages when compared with a monohull. One of the major issues is there is often quite a sudden cut-off point between viable and less viable when the wave size increases and starts to make contact with the cross deck.

A modern planing power catamaran with a low tunnel and cut off bow shape.

We therefore tend to find that power catamarans are mainly used where a specific requirement has to be met, such as the very high speeds needed in offshore powerboat racing, the large deck area that may be beneficial for a smaller leisure boat, and sometimes for a workboat, for which the requirements for seaworthiness may be less demanding.

DISPLACEMENT CATAMARANS

Like all boats, power multihulls come in a wide variety of shapes and sizes, but the main difference is found in the side hulls, which can be either displacement or planing types. Displacement catamarans are based on long, thin hull technology with a length/beam ratio for the side hulls that support the craft being something in the order of 8. This allows them to slip through the water easily with minimum resistance, and with only moderate power they can achieve speeds that might be double that of a displacement monohull because of the reduced wave-making resistance.

While sailboat catamarans of this type tend to use just well-rounded hull shapes to give a smooth ride, on power displacement catamarans it is normal to find a chine at least around the forward sections to help peel the water away from the hull to lower the frictional resistance and to reduce the spray. A vertical bow is normal to maximise the waterline length.

Displacement catamarans capable of 20 knots are possible, but as with all displacement hulls, much will depend on the length of the hull. So, with a displacement catamaran you can get very economical cruising on a leisure craft combined with good stability, with very little in the way of rolling because of the wide beam. On a workboat, you can get a large deck area combined with the good stability, which can be a benefit in many applications.

Opposite: A small catamaran hull with a high tunnel clearance to improve rough sea performance.

A power catamaran with an embryo centre hull to reduce wave impact in the tunnel.

The long, thin side hulls on this catamaran give low wash and good fuel economy but are designed for calmer waters.

The downside can come when you try to fit comfortable and practical accommodation into the hull shape. On larger sizes, the side hulls can accommodate cabins quite easily, but even so it requires a bit of ingenuity from the designer to find a workable solution. In general, anything below 15m (49ft) in length can be a challenge, although you will have a wonderful, wide deck saloon. The viability of smaller power catamarans can be found in the large deck areas on an open sports boat version for days in the sun, but for this application speed is often a requirement of the package so a buyer would probably use a planing catamaran instead.

Good seaworthiness may not be a requirement on many leisure craft, which may only operate in fine conditions, and the displacement catamaran will usually be fine and comfortable until the waves reach such a size that they start to slam against the cross deck. Reducing speed might lessen this wave impact, and on some designs an embryo centre hull is fitted into the underside of the cross deck in order to try to reduce wave impact by splitting the wave before it hits the deck. However, the fine bow shapes do not have a lot of buoyancy so do not lift readily to oncoming waves.

The latest in modern power catamaran design with a reverse bow shape.

WAVE-PIERCER HULLS

The long, thin hulls of the conventional catamaran have been taken to extremes with some advanced designs that use very slim and longer-sided hulls to increase efficiency. Probably the best example of this is the wave-piercer hulls that were developed initially in Australia and that are now used in some enormous fast ferries. With these designs, the slim side hulls support the weight of the craft under normal running conditions while offering very little response to the passing waves, so you get a level ride. To cope with a situation in which the wave height might reach the point of impacting on the cross deck, the cross deck has been designed almost like a central deep-vee hull so that it is clear of the water in normal running but will part the waves if they get larger, thus giving these hulls a more gentle cut-off point when the waves grow larger. One of the problems with this concept, though, is that in larger waves, this centre hull diverts the water up into the inverted vee, from where it cannot find an easy escape route. This means, certainly on smaller wave-piercer designs, that slamming can occur in larger waves.

Designer Juan Moreno has found a solution for this: moulding large vent holes into the upper section of the side hulls, which gives this diverted water an escape route and helps to reduce the slamming potential. This concept has been employed on some of the increasing number of

This wave-piercing catamaran design shows the vent holes designed to relieve pressures in the tunnel.

This wave-piercer catamaran has vents in the side hulls to relieve water pressure in the tunnel.

Taking catamaran design to extremes to reduce motions in waves.

catamaran designs that are being used as support and crew-transfer vessels in connection with the growth of wind farms in the North Sea. They are required to provide a reliable service, taking technicians and stores on journeys of perhaps 50–100 miles in most conditions, so seaworthiness combined with speed is important.

The long, thin displacement hulls of the wave-piercer have been taken to extremes by some designers. In trying to increase the length/beam ratio they have used long hulls that extend way beyond the extent of the top section of the hull. In the Caribbean, Gold Coast Yachts tried this, extending the hulls out about 3m (9.8ft) beyond the main hull pod that rode well above the waves. The hulls were also wide enough to house the engines. I joined them for an inter-island journey in

challenging sea conditions and found the ride to be quite remarkably level and true.

There have also been one or two passenger ferries built along these lines, as well as some experimental craft. Nevertheless, a few major problems remain. First, the issue of where to accommodate the machinery and propulsion within such a narrow hull shape; and second, the high relative cost of the boat. What's more, for leisure craft, the ride might be smooth but the size can be problematic, since a sports boat version is about three times the size of a conventional sports boat. This pushes the marina charges sky high because of both the dramatically increased length and the wide beam. The bonus is that you ride up above the waves and the craft is certainly an eye-catcher.

The long, thin hulls of this catamaran are designed to reduce the pitching motions in waves.

Submerged side hulls help to reduce wave-induced motions on this high performance SWATH-like design.

PLANING CATAMARANS

Now we come to the planing catamaran, which also features long, narrow hulls, but these are fitted with planing surfaces underneath so that they generate lift. In its simplest form, the planing catamaran is a deep-vee hull cut in half longitudinally and with a cross deck fitted between the two hull sections. Famous designer Don Aronow used such a technique for his first catamaran hull, cutting one of his Cigarette hulls in two and adding a cross deck. The modern planing catamaran tends to use narrower side hulls than this solution would achieve,

A planing power catamaran running at speed.

and when really high speeds are required – as in racing versions – then steps and spray rails are usually introduced into the hull bottom. The racing catamaran with steps is really a very stable platform in slight and moderate conditions, riding on four points that produce good stability with reduced pitching. Leisure performance catamarans follow much the same pattern, but they may have wider side hulls to give more internal space.

The planing catamaran has outperformed the deep-vee monohull in racing mainly because of the lift that is generated by the air rushing between the two hulls, which can be quite considerable when speeds

The AV2, a catamaran with an aerofoil shape connecting the two side hulls to generate considerable lift over choppy water.

start to reach something over 129km/h (80mph). This is because the lift is not just generated by the air encountering the sloping underside of the cross deck, but also as a result of having this cross deck shaped like an aerofoil, so that the lift is multiplied.

LIFT

Air lift is an important factor in multihull performance. This can be demonstrated by the fact that these catamarans tend to go faster into the wind than they do downwind. The lift reduces the amount of hull in the water, creating a significant reduction in the frictional resistance and it is the relative stability of the craft and the reduced pitching that helps to make the air lift effective. Any pitching would affect the air lift generated and the variation in angle of the 'wing' could cause considerable turmoil and vortexes in the air flow.

With the amount of air lift that is generated by the high speeds of modern racing catamarans, there is a risk that the boat can become unstable. There therefore has to be a careful balance between the lift generated by the hulls from the water and that generated by the air passing over and under the boat. In calm waters, this balance can be relatively easy to control with the balance being in favour of the front of the boat so that it remains in position relative to the water. Where it can come unstuck is when the bow lifts to a wave, causing the angle of attack of the cross deck to be suddenly increased, with a tendency for the bow to lift

The quadrimaran with four hulls was built as an experimental military craft.

dangerously high. This is where the driver's skill can come into play because he has some control with the throttle setting.

A racing catamaran can ride a very narrow balance line at high speeds and the same applies to some of the three-pointers that are used for certain types of racing and record breaking. At anything over 160km/h (100mph), the air lift is a significant factor for the designer. Wind tunnel testing and computer simulations are used to find the balance.

The more conventional cruising planing catamarans are based on hulls that remain stable and offer good performance, but as always, this can be limited when waves start to strike the underside of the cross deck. We had this problem with the first *Virgin Atlantic Challenger* – a planing catamaran with only limited clearance under the cross deck. The result was a rough ride in many parts of the Atlantic with the pounding on the cross deck creating high-impact loadings.

OTHER TYPES OF MULTIHULL

While the catamaran is the most popular of the various types of multihull, there have been some attempts to try to replicate or even improve on the concept by adding to the number of hulls used. Leaving aside the trimaran with side-stabilising hulls for the moment, there have been trimarans with three more or less equal hulls, as

well as a quadrimaran and even one with five almost equal hulls. The aim for these was to give more useful internal volume and a wider platform for stability, as well as increased air lift. Apart from the two outer hulls, the intermediate hulls had a vee-shaped rather than a sloping bottom. None of these concepts has stood the test of time, apart from the trimaran with a main central hull flanked by two stabilising hulls, which has seen some interesting developments.

This trimaran concept follows on from that of some artisanal craft designed for efficiency under sail or paddle. There is no doubt that the concept is efficient, with its long, slim central hull, which can be designed for maximum efficiency knowing that stability is provided by the two outrigger hulls. This means that the hull can have a deeper vee than you might find on a monohull of the same size, to help give a softer ride in waves. The relatively narrow central hull does compromise the space available inside, but one solution is to bring the accommodation up on deck so that it can be spread across all three hulls. Long-distance record-breaking boats, for instance, have used quite widely spaced outrigger hulls – as in the case of the *iLAN* concept developed by Nigel Irens, which proved to be very fuel-efficient and seaworthy. This has subsequently been translated into a long-range military patrol craft in France. Other concepts, such as the *Bladerunner* from Ice Marine, bring the side hulls in much closer to the central hulls, so they are much more integrated.

An underwater view of a trimaran with minimal side hulls to give maximum efficiency.

A narrow trimaran design designed for performance.

On the downside, the trimaran does tend to incur high marina charges because the central hull extends well forward and the beam is wider. And, although the main bonus with these designs is that the fine entry can help to reduce pitching in head seas, this means that they do not work so well in large following seas where the bow can bury quite easily.

A VIABLE OPTION FOR POWERBOATS?

Multihulls, both catamarans and trimarans, do have a place in powerboat design but they usually offer advantages more for special applications rather than for the mainstream market. Catamarans are probably more widely used in the workboat and fishing markets where the large deck space and the more stable working deck are bonuses, and where appearance is not necessarily an overriding factor. In the leisure sector, though, the power catamaran has never really caught on, although there are a few builders who specialise in these designs. I think the reason for this is that leisure craft tend to be more of an emotional purchase rather than a practical one, and it has always been a challenge for designers to make a multihull look as owners expect a performance powerboat design to. For cruising power catamarans, there is less pressure on the design looking the part, but they do tend to resemble their sailing counterparts and this is perhaps a significant drawback.

I feel that some of the success of the *Bladerunner* trimaran design lay in the fact that the side hulls were closely integrated with the centre hull and this made it look more like a monohull design. Bringing the side hulls in in this way, however, does create quite a narrow tunnel between the hulls and this can lead to higher impacts if waves cannot find an easy escape route when they enter this area. I encountered this in reverse when I was in a race boat that was like an inverted trimaran, with two hulls forward and one aft. It was a very efficient concept as far as speed was concerned, and quite stable, but problems occurred in rougher seas when waves entered between the two forward hulls. At this point, the central hull that extended to a little over half

A cruising catamaran that should offer good economical cruising.

the length from aft partially blocked the exit for the water entering forward. The result was that the water literally 'exploded' between the two forward hulls and holed the inside surfaces of the two side hulls.

My design mantra
If you want a relatively easy and effective ride, when designing a hull you always have to give the water somewhere to go as it passes through or under the hull, so that it has a relatively easy path over the hull surfaces.

BILL DIXON, DIXON YACHT DESIGN

"In production powerboat design, the challenge has always been to balance the requirements of performance, stability, handling and comfort. These factors then have to be balanced against the customers' requirements for accommodation, and features such as perhaps a specific engine model.

It is ironic that as the horsepower of an engine has gone up over time for a given capacity, the weight of an equivalent boat has also gone up, thus, in many cases, negating any performance increase.

If you take a planing hull design today, and compare it to past designs, I would say that today's hull has developed due to several factors. A primary one is the constant push for extra volume for a given length. The engine is pushed further aft, and the midship owner's cabin is seen on smaller and smaller boats, resulting in higher boats. Alongside this is the high level of comfort and convenience required, leading to very high equipment standards. Two further important influences are the method of propulsion and ISO stability requirements.

Whereas in the past small boats had sterndrives, and larger boats had shafts, we are now dealing with pod drives and outboards on larger and larger vessels as well as the shafts and sterndrives. I think it is safe to say that all of these factors have been to the detriment of performance with modern boats. Our hulls today have an increased warping of the deadrise in the hull, with a lower deadrise at the transom. The waterline beam for a given length has gone up, for both volume and stability reasons. It is much easier from an efficiency standpoint to flatten the complete bottom, but this really is at the detriment of rough-weather performance and comfort. Clients get seduced by the space and comfort without considering important aspects like hull design and seakeeping.

Stabilisers and gyros have been transformative in increasing comfort levels of fast motorboats, not so much when they are dynamically stable at speed, but at lower speeds and at rest. Stabilisers increase the drag, reducing speed, while gyros increase the vessel's weight and might not be placed in the perfect LCG position.

Stabilisers also can hide some of the shortcomings of some hull designs, which only become apparent when you turn them off.

Stability is a very interesting subject, as builders and owners want to feel their boat reaches the highest category it is capable of achieving. So, for instance a Category A boat is reckoned to be capable of coping with winds up to Beaufort 10, and a 7m (23ft) significant wave height, yet I think it would need an extremely skilled seaman to cope with these conditions in reality. If the requirements from customers were to design a motorboat to operate in extreme conditions, this would require a special design. In general, we believe that the ISO stability requirements we must conform to to be challenging with today's high-freeboard, high-superstructure powerboat, but so it should be. If a boat meets Category B standards it will be a capable, stable motorboat, but will be demanding to handle in extreme conditions. This category probably applies to today's modern powerboats more than does the demanding Category A standard...

Of course, our design work is not only concerned with planing boats: there are also semi-displacement hull forms, as well as the occasional displacement form. A hull shape that has undergone continual evolution is the hull we initially designed for the Searanger 44 trawler yacht, which we now call our 'Fusion' hull. This is now widely known as the 'dual mode hull' on some of the Magellano range built by Azimut. Naturally the customer's demands and expectations do not differ from those of a planning hull.

The Fusion hull has benefited from multiple tank testing programmes across a wide size spectrum. The hull has been designed to allow it to achieve higher speeds than normal yet provide more efficient cruising in both the semi-displacement zones and at displacement speeds. The resulting hulls have gone from a raked bow to an upright bow, maximising the waterline length. Alongside the tank testing we have done testing using radio-controlled self-powered models in real sea conditions to look at the seakeeping and control.

Our latest designs have been tested totally using computational fluid dynamics (CFD), the results of which have demonstrated that CFD is now able to very accurately calculate not only resistance and trim, but also seakeeping and spray. Standout features for this hull are the performance and handling, particularly in rough weather. The bow shape gives an amazingly soft ride upwind, like the finer bow of semi-displacement hulls, but very assured handling downwind and in quartering seas. The hull also has low resistance at semi-displacement speeds, which has resulted in smaller engines, and a better range.

Hull design used to be done by hand on a drawing board. Today, however, we are designing hulls on computers, with many more tools to analyse all aspects of the hull. There are parameters that are dictated by the naval architectural requirements but, in my view, there is still an art to designing hulls; it still though comes down to the designer's judgement and skill to create the shape, and to have a vision for how the hull should perform and then to see if during the trials this vision matches the reality. We saw an example recently of how a hull shape that was designed to improve forward cabin volume can inadvertently give rise to improvements in the ride and seakeeping in head seas.

Hull development never stops, technology improves, customer requirement changes. Hybrid propulsion is something that is a 'buzzword' in our industry, with many misconceptions as far as customers are concerned. Customers have a vision, just as for their cars, of an electric-powered boat, without any idea about where the high amounts of energy required for this can be made. Yet there is no substitute for dense liquid fuels, and it is clear that this will remain the case for the foreseeable future. However, there are areas where a combination of both normal propulsion and electric power can bring benefits to customers, such as low-emission cruising in rivers and docking, energy recovery, and silent motoring for short periods. There will still be the demand for speed, but with the electric solution, the future challenge for the designers will be to make hulls more efficient at slow speeds without it having a negative impact on high speed. This will almost certainly involve some form of foil technology, not lifting the boat out of the water, but giving support to the hull at certain speeds.

Multihulls are also of consideration in this new world of boating. These offer lower drag and more efficiency

The Magellano 76 at speed.

and their development is something that we have been involved with for several years now, in step with the growing popularity of multihull powerboats. Like all different forms of hull, there are pluses and minuses to a catamaran. To really make significant efficiency gains, especially for a fast boat, weight and hull shape have a huge influence. Designers of multihulls are driven by the same customer expectations as their monohulled cousins, and the danger is that with such a large platform the design could be compromised by too much volume for its size. There must be a balance between the level of equipment and comfort and the efficiency. At the moment, I think it is fair to say that today's catamarans are selling on the basis of their space benefit, to the detriment of their performance.

4 RIGID INFLATABLE BOATS

RIBs – or rigid inflatable boats – are a relatively new addition to the powerboat repertoire; indeed, I was involved with building the first one in the world in 1963. It didn't work, but at least we set the ball rolling for what is now probably the largest category of powerboat in use today.

OUR EARLY PROTOTYPE

That first RIB was developed when we were trying to solve a problem. At the time, I was responsible for all the repairs, maintenance and development of the RNLI's inshore lifeboats and we were having issues with the inflatables in use at that time.

These 5m (16ft) outboard-powered inflatable boats did a wonderful job during inshore rescue work and were welcomed by the traditional lifeboat crews as a supplement to their all-weather but slow traditional lifeboats, but the fabric bottoms were wearing out when they were dragged across abrasive beaches, especially in the area around the wooden transom. This was becoming a major maintenance headache.

To try to overcome this, we cut out about 1.5m (5ft) of the rear section of the floor fabric and replaced it with a piece of flat plywood that was fastened rigidly to the transom. This plywood was able to stand up to the harsh treatment at the point where the wear was taking place and, as a bonus, it also improved the performance of the boats by creating a hard planing surface. This semi-RIB solution also allowed the boats to be deflated and rolled up for easy transport when a replacement boat had to be sent out to a lifeboat station, but sadly it did not solve the wear problem on the bottom fabric; the area of wear just moved forwards to the wood/fabric joint. To overcome this, we thought: 'Why not replace the whole of the bottom of the boat with plywood so that there would be a hard, robust surface to stand up to the wear and tear caused by beach launches?'

The prototype had a shape that roughly matched that of the original fabric bottom. It was probably the first full-scale RIB ever built and it worked beautifully in calm water, but once we hit waves the plywood bottom structure started to break up. We quickly realised that putting a rigid structure into a boat that was designed to be flexible meant that something had to give. Unfortunately, it was the rigid plywood bottom that gave because the longitudinal strength of the boat was now being transferred from the flexible inflatable tubes into the plywood bottom, which was just not strong enough for the job.

Opposite: Over-enthusiastic RIB driving with the props clear of the water.

The author on trials in what is thought to be the first RIB in the world.

One of the very early RIBs built as a racing boat to put these boats on the map.

PSYCHEDELIC SURFER

That might have been the end of the RIB, had it not been for the fact that one of the RNLI inshore lifeboat stations based at Atlantic College in South Wales had been facing much the same severe wear problems on the fabric bottom when launching and recovering their boats on the rocky beach. Their initial solution was to attach longitudinal plywood strips to the bottom fabric, which would flex to a degree and at the same time offer some protection to the fabric. This led to the start of a project for their senior students to try to find a long-term solution. This work was carried out in 1966 with the blessing of the RNLI, which funded some of the development work.

Like us, the first thought of the students was to replace the bottom of their sailing club rescue boat with a plywood sheet glued to the tubes. That worked, though it gave a harsh ride. They therefore persevered with the concept of a fully rigid hull bottom and, after many prototypes, ended up with a rigid deep-vee hull shape that had sufficient longitudinal strength to support the inflatable tube. The boat duly underwent trials on an RNLI inshore lifeboat station. A further series of prototypes was subsequently designed and built by the College in the years 1968 and 1969 – I think in all there were something like 15 prototypes built at Atlantic College – but it was in 1969 that the college designed and built the 6.4m (21ft) RIB *Psychedelic Surfer*, which took part in the first ever Round Britain Powerboat Race. Because the race rules stipulated a minimum length of 6.4m (21ft), the available tube had to be lengthened, meaning that *Psychedelic Surfer* became the largest

RIB built at that time, and the first one to have a twin outboard installation. It was groundbreaking stuff and to everybody's amazement, the boat went on to finish the race in good order and attracted a lot of attention.

A difficult labour

The RIB did not have an easy birth. The fact that Atlantic College had to build around 15 prototypes before they got it nearly right shows how the evolving RIB concept needed to be fine-tuned before it could be said to be a good working design. This may be because the concept was developed more by modifying the existing inflatable ideas and trying them out on the water rather than by sitting down at a drawing board and producing a design that is more or less cast in stone. It is doubtful whether any professional boatbuilder could afford the luxury of building so many prototypes to fine-tune the design, but since this was largely a student project, it was not limited by commercial demands.

ATLANTIC 21 INSHORE LIFEBOATS

Indeed, the design of *Psychedelic Surfer* formed the basis of the Atlantic 21 inshore lifeboat that was finalised and entered service in 1972, and went on to be used very successfully by the RNLI for many years, becoming the cornerstone of their inshore fleet. This was probably the most seaworthy boat for its size ever built and with minor modifications it remained in service for more than 30 years.

Part of the success of the Atlantic 21 concept was the driving position. Atlantic College had been working on the saddle seat concept, which enabled the driver to securely locate himself at the helm to leave his hands free to control the boat. That saddle seat became a necessity because with the superb sea-going capability of the boat, the crew had become the weak point of the system and there was a need to create seating that would give them a more comfortable ride and be able to locate themselves in the boat.

A self-righting system was also developed for these boats, comprising an inflatable bag mounted on an arch at the stern. This was necessary, since the RNLI had decreed that all its lifeboats should be capable of being righted after a capsize, and while the small inflatable rescue boats could be righted manually by the crew, the Atlantic RIBs were too large and heavy; thus the righting system had to be added and the crews trained for the job.

Self-righting systems

To achieve self-righting, buoyancy has to be introduced at a point where it makes the boat unstable when it is in the inverted position. This is usually achieved by means of an inflatable air bag attached to the top of an arch mast at the stern of the boat, where it largely compensates for the weight of the engine(s). This air bag can be inflated automatically if the RIB capsizes, though normally it would be crew activated so that there is time to first make sure that none of the crew is still under the inverted boat, where they could be injured when the boat rights itself rapidly.

Righting the boat this way is only one part of the system, however, because there is little point in righting the boat if the engines will not start afterwards. Engines are usually fitted with a cut-out switch that will automatically stop them before it is fully inverted. Both intakes and exhausts therefore have to have a form of sealing to prevent water entering the engine. The systems become complex and they have to be engineered in such as way that they cannot be operated accidentally. Batteries also have to be of the sealed type and fuel tanks need a breather seal. A lot of pioneering work on these

inversion-proof engines was carried out by EP Barrus, a company that has focused on developing and adapting both outboard and inboard engines for specialised applications.

Testing the self-righting capability of a RIB.

LATER DEVELOPMENTS

Commercial builders such as Avon and Flatacraft developed their own RIB concepts during the late 1960s and the RIB became a commercial success, first as a tough workboat and then as a yacht tender/sports boat. Outboards were the engine of choice but the diesel-powered RIB followed a few years later, in the early 1970s. Some commercial users were not convinced by RIBs, however, and thought that the inflatable tubes were too vulnerable in the harsh commercial environment. This led to the development of RIBs with foam-filled tubes. These comprised foam interiors that could be shaped to match the requirements covered with a hard-wearing polyurethane skin to create a more durable style. These had a small degree of flexibility so that they could absorb shock loads, which meant they worked well as fendering, but most of the variable geometry characteristics of the inflatable tube were lost.

Another 'compromise' RIB concept consisted of a structure that was made up from cylindrical fenders attached along the topsides of the hull to form a tube of sorts. The idea here was that just one of the fenders could be replaced if it were damaged, but again, there was less resilience in this type of tube and it was not consistent in shape along its length, meaning that it might get caught up alongside some structures.

A typical sports RIB with the tubes well clear of the water at speed.

A RIB all-weather lifeboat.

Rescue operations in extreme conditions by the US Coast Guard.

RIBS TODAY

When we first started building that prototype RIB 50 years ago, we were just trying to solve a problem with the existing inflatable boats. What started as a solution to this problem turned out to be what is perhaps the biggest revolution in motorboat design since Ray Hunt produced his first deep-vee hull. The RIB was never the cheapest solution, it was never the easy option, but its capabilities and its seakeeping convinced most users that this was a sound option. Today, few users need or utilise the capabilities of their RIB to anywhere near its full potential, being content to use a RIB as a sound, sensible, practical everyday boat that has a good margin of safety built in and good stability. In the commercial and military sectors, the RIB has become the boat of choice for a great many operators and even in the USA, where RIBs were very slow to catch on, it is now the boat of choice for many in every sector of the market.

Why is a RIB so much better than comparable non-RIB boats? It is a question that is often asked and there is no easy answer. What the RIB concept does is bring together many elements of boat design and merges them into a whole. It is doubtful whether any other boat design project has created such a new concept by mainly combining existing ideas and design concepts to create not only one of the most seaworthy boats for its size, but also one of the most practical and exciting.

In the development of the RIB, the main starting point was the inflatable boat, which had been around for many years by the time the RIB was developed. The inflatable had proved itself in many applications as both a day sports boat and as a rescue boat, but these applications had also shown the limitations of the concept, which were mainly in the flat-bottomed hull shape. Concurrently, the deep-vee hull was also a tried-and-tested solution for small-boat hull design. By merging these two technologies together, a craft was created that opened up a whole new era of boat design.

However, the RIB was more than just a merger of two existing technologies: it was the addition of the saddle seat and helm console, which made the relationship between the boat and its driver more intimate, that allowed the boat to be driven much harder in adverse conditions. It was also the self-draining nature of the hull and the low freeboard as well as the additional buoyancy of the tube, which allowed the RIB to operate in conditions in which conventional designs could be at risk.

THE PROBLEMS WITH MODERN RIB DESIGN

The development of the RIB saw a new design concept being introduced into boat design: the inflatable tube. This allowed for a measure of variable geometry in the hull shape. We have talked about morphing

The water flow away from a RIB hull with different tube attachment points.

hulls that can change shape, and this was something the RIB could do automatically under the impact of waves, and thus adapt semi-automatically to changing conditions. However, no one hull design is going to be at its optimum under all conditions – every boat design is a compromise to find a middle road – and while the tube on the pure inflatable could absorb some of the shock loadings from wave impact, this was largely cancelled out by the virtually flat bottom of the boat, which offered little or nothing in the way of cushioning. By combining the inflatable tube with a deep-vee hull, though, the shock-absorbing qualities of the hull were dramatically increased.

TUBE POSITION

Today, most RIB designers, builders and operators appear to have lost sight of this attribute of the RIB. Those early RIBs comprised an inflatable tube that was attached to a rigid hull bottom, whereas most RIBs now consist of a full rigid hull with a tube fitted around it. There is a big difference in this approach because with the original concept the tube had the freedom to roll in over the rigid hull, which allowed a considerable amount

of impact absorption; the hull effectively changes its shape to adapt to the waves. The system also gives a more wave-friendly shape to the hull, without the inverted vee that can be found between the tube and the hull, rather like a reverse angle chine. This can trap the water emerging from the hull rather than giving it a free exit path, which creates a harsher ride. When the tube is attached to the outside of a hull, as we see with most modern RIBs, there can be a quite sudden increase in buoyancy where the lower part of the tube meets the rigid hull, and this is not a wave-friendly shape. Alternatively, some tubes are attached quite high along the sides of the hull where their contact with waves can be quite limited and where they tend to act mainly as fenders along the hull rather than adding additional buoyancy and creating an impact-changing shape to reduce wave impact.

SIZE MATTERS

This change in the way the tubes are used is only one factor in modern RIB design. The next issue is their size. I recollect in the early days of RIBs predicting that the maximum viable length of a RIB would probably be about 10m (33ft), on the basis that this would be the size at which the additional weight of the tube and the much heavier loading would reduce the effectiveness of the tube. Today, we are seeing RIBs getting larger and larger; I have tested a 24.4m (80ft) RIB that was built as a yacht complete with three bathrooms! In this RIB, the inflatable tubes added nothing to the performance in waves, took up a lot of space and added considerable weight. This is not what RIBs were conceived for and you have to wonder at the rationale behind such a concept.

RIB designs are also being used for large all-weather lifeboats where the heavy-duty tube would struggle to deform under wave impact and where its function is mainly as a fender. This is useful, since these RIBs are used as pilot boats and the inflatable tube can help to prevent injury to a pilot if he slips during transfer and falls between the boat and the ship. However, the high-pressure inflatable tube does not make it easy to hold the boat alongside. In response to this issue, many of these larger RIBs are now using foam tubes rather than inflatable ones, which at least recognises that the

RIBs are used as pilot boats, one of the most challenging jobs at sea.

RIBs have grown in size where the tube merely performs as a fender rather than as an integral part of the design.

larger-size inflatable tube primarily acts as a fender and reserve buoyancy rather than improving performance in rough seas.

UNDER PRESSURE

Probably the most adverse change in modern RIBs is the pressure used to inflate the tubes. On the early RIBs, the tube material was not of the high quality we see today and this limited the tube pressure that could be safely used. We did a lot of trials and found that up to about 2psi, the tube will deform on wave impact quite noticeably and thus provide good impact-absorbing characteristics. Once you get above this 2psi figure, the tube starts to have 'bounce' – ie instead of absorbing the wave impact, it reacts by bouncing, which can lead to a considerable deterioration in the ride quality of the boat. Modern RIBs have tube pressures up to perhaps 5psi and I have seen RIB builders recommending tube pressure of 3.5–4psi. Inflating the tubes this hard will certainly help to take all the wrinkles out of them, which makes them look good, but their response when running in waves will be to give a much harsher ride with a much sharper response to changing wave shapes. The tube becomes like a tennis ball and will bounce off the waves rather than absorbing the wave impact. You can often see this when a RIB with high tube pressures tries to come alongside: it will bounce off the jetty or ship's side rather than easing alongside with the tube acting as a fender.

Another side-effect of having the tube pressure too high in RIBs is that it can cause the boat to bounce from side to side, first on one tube and then on the other, which creates a very uncomfortable lateral motion that is not resisted by the conventional saddle seating; I have even seen a video of one incident when the bounce became extreme and the boat turned right over, largely because of overinflated tubes. Apart from this, it can also make it harder to control the boat because this sideways bounce can reduce the possibility of subtle steering and throttle control. Since the boat is moving forwards, it is not always easy to identify this lateral bounce factor, yet it can be responsible for many of the negative comments made about RIB performance. It is interesting to watch videos of crews when they are driving RIBs in rough seas, since you can see the considerable sideways movements of their bodies and particularly their heads.

Despite this evidence, so far little has been done to either recognise this problem or find ways of dealing with it. Yet the solution is really quite simple: just reduce

Plastic covered foam is attached to a RIB hull.

the pressure in the tubes. In addition, I have often thought that there could be a strong case for being able to vary the pressure of the inflatable tube systems while at sea, and indeed I know a couple of builders of larger RIBs who have developed such systems. This could do a lot to improve the ride of the boat in varying sea conditions, but of course it is an added complication that is not always welcome.

Ride comfort in rougher seas is not such a serious problem as it may sound because very few RIBs actually have to operate under really adverse sea conditions. Rescue boats and Special Forces boats may be required to do so, of course, but for the average RIB user there is less chance that they will venture out under conditions in which the tube pressure may make a significant difference to the performance in waves. If you do start to use your RIB in challenging sea conditions, think about reducing the tube pressure to get a more comfortable ride.

User error

In the early days of RIBs, when construction materials and methods had not been refined as they are today, it tended to be the boat and its engines that were the weak point when operating in rough seas, which meant that the driver would nurse his boat through the waves. Today, however, construction techniques and materials have improved considerably and engines and drives can stand the strain, but it has become apparent that the crew are the weak point to progress. The durability of the boat and its engines means that the crew can suffer injury due to the harsh ride.

SHOCK MITIGATION

'Shock mitigation' has now become the buzzword in RIB operations, not least because owners and operators are required to have a duty of care for the crews of their boats. They therefore have to be seen to be taking steps to mitigate the shock loadings from the boat. This has led to a proliferation of sprung seats and even integrated sprung-control consoles to help protect the crews. This is something of a short-term solution, however, because with this special seating to help

reduce the impacts, the crew often simply drive their boats that bit harder, and don't get the same feedback from the boat to suggest that they should be easing off on the throttle. This seating also has a negative effect on the behaviour of the boat in waves because it raises the centre of gravity and thus can make the movements of the boat livelier.

So, we are entering something of a vicious circle of RIB development here: the performance of the boats is improving, which can create problems for the crew, but the steps taken to improve conditions for the crew can make them then capable of operating the boats faster, which in turn increases the impacts on the crew. Then we should consider the other negative impacts of sprung seating, one of which is that with the up-and-down movement of the seat it becomes harder to get the delicate throttle control that is needed for good operation of the boat in waves. We will look at these problems further in later chapters, but it is a problem that is not necessarily confined to RIBs: it is endemic in all fast boats and as boats get faster and more capable, so the crew has become the weak point in fast-boat operations.

A RIB heeling into a turn, giving a harsh ride as it lands on the flat of the vee.

TUBE LOCATION

There is more to RIB design than the tube pressure. The tube location can be important, too, and if you look around at a variety of RIBs you are likely to see a variety of tube heights. By this we mean the height when the crew and any other operating equipment is on board;

with smaller RIBs, there can be quite a difference in height if you have three or four crew on board.

The optimum should be a tube that is just above the water surface at the stern when the boat is at rest. At this height, any tilting of the boat will start to immerse the tube on the lower side and stabilise the hull, and when the boat comes on to the plane the tube should be well clear of the water so that it doesn't cause any drag.

When the tube is too low and partially in the water at rest, it could cause unnecessary drag as the boat comes on to the plane, leading to sluggish performance. Marine growth on the tube is also more likely if the boat is left afloat.

When the tube is too high and well clear of the water at rest then, of course, you lose the stabilising effect of the tube and its function becomes much more that of a fender than a stabiliser. This is especially an issue for rescue boats, since if the tube is set quite high at rest then a casualty in the water could disappear under the tube when alongside, which could make recovery more difficult.

TUBE SHAPE

On the earlier RIBs, the inflatable tubes were the same diameter throughout their whole length because the techniques of making tapering tubes had not been developed. This meant that the entry at the bow could be quite blunt even when the two side tubes met in a vee at the bow. Today, there are RIBs with a squared-off bow to create more internal space and these work fine when the bow lifts as the boat comes on to the plane and the tube is well clear of the water. Problems start when operating in waves, however, particularly in following seas when the bow can drop down after coming over the crest of a wave, and the tube immerses. The additional buoyancy of the tube is great for preventing the bow from submerging, but the resulting great spray of water that is caused by the sudden immersion of the blunt tube usually ends up drenching the people at the helm. It can also restrict progress in following seas. The modern tapering tube results in a much finer bow shape and a smoother entry in this situation, although of course there is the possibility of the bow submerging completely if driving close to the limits. We will look at driving techniques in Chapters 12 and 13 but the tube shape has to be a consideration for the RIB designer.

A solution to spray

The round shape of the inflatable tube does encourage spray to curl on board over the tube when operating in waves. You are most likely to encounter this when the boat is starting to lift on to the plane or coming off the plane and the tubes are quite low. A solution to reduce this problem is to fit along the hull rubber rubbing strips that are shaped like an inverted vee so that they catch the water rising over the tube surface and deflect it back down, akin to a spray rail. These rubbing strips only have a limited effect, but they do help.

It is possible to persuade an inflatable tube to adopt a D shape by fastening it to the rigid hull at the top and bottom, which can be an improvement, although attaching the tube to the outside of a rigid hull is not the best solution if you want maximum performance in rough seas. It is challenging to try to get a smooth transition from the rigid hull to the tube surface so that the water coming off the hull has a smoother path to follow, but a low pressure in the tube will help to allow it to adapt to the water flow and reduce the incidence of slamming and a harsh ride. With a round tube, you end up with an inverted vee in cross-section, often just above the chine line of the rigid hull where it meets the tube. The shape of the round tube attached to the vertical side of the hull naturally forms this inverted vee and this can lead to a harsher ride when waves slam up into

The beautiful lines of this large sports RIB show just how far RIB design has advanced.

A powerful military RIB with multiple seating.

this vee. Of course, the tube will distort to a degree to absorb some of this wave impact but even then the ride can be harsher than if the tube were attached in such a way as to allow the water emanating from under the hull to flow freely upwards. I've said it before and I'll say it again: with any fast boat hull, the water flowing away from under the hull needs to be given a relatively free-flowing path if the boat is going to have a soft ride.

When the water gets trapped and does not have an easy exit path, as can happen with an inverted vee, the water can react almost explosively when it is forced into a considerable change of direction. The main impact of this unhappy marriage between the rigid and inflatable parts of the hull will occur towards the stern as the boat rises and falls in the waves, but it can also be considerable towards the bow when operating in following seas. This sort of wave impact can put a particularly heavy stress on the tube fastenings to the hull, and in cases when a boat is being driven very hard in adverse conditions it has been known for the tube to part company with the rigid hull and peel off backwards over the main hull. This question of the relationship between the tube and the hull is one that often seems to get overlooked in RIB design, but careful consideration can mean the difference between a comfortable and a harsh ride.

CONCLUSION

With RIB design, the designer has many more options available than the designer working on a regular deep-vee boat. Having said that, there are very few designers who specialise in RIB design, which I think accounts for the fact that so many RIBs look as though they are just rigid hull designs that have had the tube wrapped around them. Like most things to do with boat design, if a design is going to work well then it has to be fully

integrated. Getting a RIB design right can be a lot more challenging than working on a deep-vee hull and the more I see of RIB designs, the greater the sense I get that there are only a few designers who understand and appreciate the finer points. The faults in many RIB designs probably become more apparent than they might in more conventional designs because they tend to be operated in more adventurous conditions

RIBs are becoming more and more complex to enable them to perform challenging duties.

than normal leisure craft; the military in particular have a reputation for driving their boats extremely hard. Whether you are driving a RIB or a conventional powerboat, the thoughtful driver tries to give both the boat and its crew a smooth ride and he will probably make just as much headway as the one who goes hell for leather. RIB designs have a lot to answer for in that they opened up the possibility of powerboats being able to operate at speed in adverse conditions, but in most cases they work.

MANIVANNAN KANDASAMY, CFD CONSULTANT

"Computational Fluid Dynamics (CFD) is fast replacing build-and-test approaches such as tow-tank testing, making it much easier to perform full-fledged engineering simulations on readily available supercomputers like the Amazon cloud services. CFD enables the calculation of the fluid velocity and pressure over the entire flow field around the hull by solving the Navier–Stokes equations, which are the fundamental conservation laws for mass, momentum and energy that govern the fluid flow. Unsteady Reynolds-averaged Navier–Stokes equations (URANS) provide a happy middle ground for most applications where the smallest scale eddies are accounted for using turbulence models, and they are widely used in all engineering fields. Specialised software for boat hydrodynamics tracks the free surface and the multi-directional motions of the boat to provide the entire hydrodynamic profile of the boat in any given operating condition at a fraction of the cost of model testing.

Common applications of CFD for vessels include calculation of resistance, power requirements, fuel consumption, motions and added resistance in waves, G-forces, ride comfort, motion sickness index, slam loads, green water on deck, steerability in waves and wake wash. Coupling the hydrodynamic results from the CFD with its structural analysis counterpart, ie Finite Element Analysis (FEA), allows calculation of the structural loads, deformations and vibrations. After initial set-up, subsequent changes to the virtual geometry can be easily performed. It then becomes effortless (standing on the

shoulders of the supercomputers of course) to optimise the geometry within a particular design envelope for any particular hydrodynamic property depending on the trade-off criteria.

The example applications that follow are an assortment of simulations at various stages of the design spiral for different powerboat hulls. These were simulated using FlowCFD specialised software for boat hydrodynamic calculations.

THE MOSLER TANDEM CATS

The Mosler tandem catamaran designs stemmed from Warren Mosler's deep intuitive understanding of the differences in motion between zero and long-wheel-base vehicles and preliminary experiments with tandem monohulls and cats. He deduced that tandem catamarans would have a better ride quality and subsequently designed a 13.7m (45ft) planing sports-fisher and a 30.5m (100ft) displacement passenger ferry, the latter of which was built by Gold Coast Yachts and currently ferries passengers between St Croix and St Thomas in the Caribbean.

A notable feature of the sports-fisher is its planing characteristics: the shorter tandem hulls allow for the boat to get on plane at lower speeds. FlowCFD was tasked with evaluating the initial sports-fisher design and optimising the planing trim angles. It has shown the optimal trim angle of planing monohulls to be 4 degrees; however, in tandem planing hulls, the aft hull rides the wake of the front hull and the effective angle of incidence changes. The initial design evaluation at 40 knots was carried out with static trim of both forward and aft hulls at 4 degrees. It was found out that the forward hull wake trough occurred just ahead of the aft hulls (see image

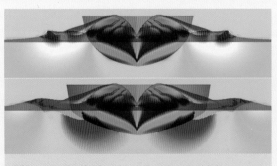

CFD analysis of a fast boat showing the high stress areas when performing.

CFD analysis of a catamaran in beam seas.

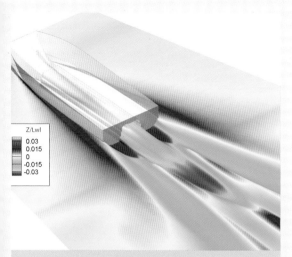

Z/Lwl
0.03
0.015
0
-0.015
-0.03

The water flow past a high-speed catamaran shown by CFD.

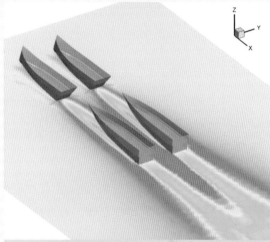

Analysis of the water flow around an innovative four-hulled catamaran design.

on the top right) and the aft hulls were encountering the upward incidence angle after the trough, making the effective planing angle much greater than 4 degrees. The geometry was then put through a particle swarm optimiser, which ran it through various configurations searching for least total resistance and converged at an optimal configuration of 2.4 and 3.1 degrees respectively for the fore and aft hulls. Taking into account the encounter incidence angle and the overall dynamic trim of the boat, this configuration resulted in a dynamic trim close to 4 degrees for the aft hulls. The hulls were then simulated in moderate to high sea states at different speeds and headings to get the safe operating envelope.

The 30.5m (100ft) QE4 passenger ferry is a tamer displacement-hull version, with emphasis on ride comfort. A notable feature of this tandem displacement cat is that it is able to overcome the critical hull-speed barrier of conventional displacement hulls by virtue of its design. At critical hull speed, the trough of the bow wave reaches the aft end, hence conventional displacement hulls squat down and trim up high, causing a sharp rise in resistance. However, since the tandem hulls do not trim about their individual LCG and provide a restoring moment to each other, they do not trim up as much and

are able to overcome their individual critical hull speed barrier. A 30.5m (100ft) conventional displacement hull would encounter this hull speed barrier around 15 knots, but the QE4 cruises along at 20 knots.

FlowCFD was tasked with calculating the fuel-consumption and seakeeping performance in moderate and rough seas. The resistance came out to be 21kN, and with an overall propulsive coefficient of 0.6, the required delivered power was 360kW at 20 knots. The fuel consumption was then calculated to be around 25 gallons/hr using the engine performance curves. Carrying 50 passengers, this consumption puts the tandem cat in the top 5 per cent most energy-efficient passenger ferries.

The design was then put through worst-case scenario testing with the boat operating at cruise speed, maximum load and maximum recorded wave heights at resonant conditions. The results indicated that the vertical accelerations exceed 1g at maximum probable wave conditions in resonant waves due to wet-deck slam, which have a less than 1 per cent probability of occurrence at any given hour along the ferry route.

Based on construction and field experience, the next-generation ferry is being designed to make the hulls more slender with a teardrop-shaped taper, which reduces both the resistance and vertical accelerations.

TEKNICRAFT

Teknicraft Design has a monohull test boat, which comes in handy for code validation and to experiment with local flow characteristics. One such test was for the resistance effects of adding spray rails. These reduce the amplitude of the bow wave compared to the bare hull but since the wave trough amplitude is also reduced along with the wave crest, the net wetted area remains almost the same as for the bare hull, which is a bit counter-intuitive. So, there is negligible difference in frictional resistance due to the spray rails, but a 7 per cent decrease in wave resistance that gives a 5 per cent decrease in total resistance.

HORIZON POWERCAT

The PC series of Horizon Powercats are highly efficient semi-displacement symmetric hulls resulting from decades of design and development by Angelo Lavranos. The latest in the series, the 22.5m (74ft) PC74 was designed with the previous PC52 and PC60 as baseline. With such a large length modification, a complex set of design criteria needed to be handled with some limitations and compromises and the L/B ratio had to

be reduced. FlowCFD was tasked with doing a study on the effect of hull separation distances on the power requirements.

The resistance of the catamaran was compared to twice the resistance of a single sponson to study the effect of wave interference between the two hulls on the resistance characteristics. At lower speeds, the wave interference had adverse effects on the resistance as the two wave troughs clash near the aft hull, causing a bigger suction region. However, at higher speeds, the wavelength is long enough and the diverging wave wedge angle sharp enough that the two bow wave crests interfere near the aft part of the hull and provide increased lift, which is very beneficial for semi-displacement hulls. Also, higher pressures aft provide a forward hydrodynamic thrust by 'pushing' the boat and less energy is lost to the wake. This effect was reflected in the hull spacing studies, which showed that the smaller hull spacing had a higher resistance at lower speeds but a reduced resistance at higher speeds due to the beneficial interference. Taking advantage of this, the PC74 design spacing was optimised for a cruise speed of 22 knots.

SETZER YACHTS

Ward Setzer of Setzer Yachts specialises in the design of custom yachts. As part of an initial cost/benefit study, FlowCFD was tasked with comparing the powering and

How the predicted movements of a fast boat can be analysed to predict the onset of seasickness in a passenger boat.

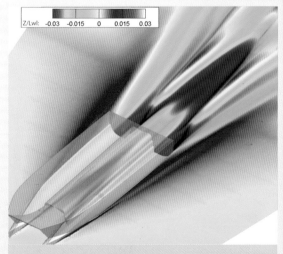

A dramatic picture of the predicted water flow past a fast catamaran hull.

seakeeping performances of two 16.8m (55ft) semi-displacement catamarans. Hull 1 was asymmetric with a vertical face in the inner tunnel and a constant cross-section from midship to stern. Hull 2 was a symmetric hull with smoother curves, a keel and a slight taper up from midship to the stern.

The resistance calculations indicated that Hull 2 had 10 per cent less drag than the Hull 1 over the speed range. The asymmetric Hull 1 has higher wave elevations in the outer hull and smaller elevation inside the tunnel due to its flat inner hull surface. The vertical chines on the inner sides cause a separation of flow behind it at higher speeds, thereby reducing the wetted surface area and frictional drag.

Hull 2 has a better pressure recovery with higher pressures aft, which provide a forward hydrodynamic thrust to the boat with reduced stern losses and a smaller rooster tail. Also, similar to the Horizon power cats, the two bow wave crests interfere near the aft part of the hull at higher speeds and provide increased lift. This beneficial wave interference is more pronounced in the symmetric Hull 2 compared to Hull 1, which has the flat inner surfaces. While this is advantageous in calm water, this increased interference wave height was found to cause wet-deck slamming in sea state 3 for Hull 2.

The seakeeping studies indicated that the roll motions of Hull 2 were lower than for Hull 1 for all speeds. However, the pitch and heave motions in head and bow waves were larger. The bow-steering tendencies of Hull 2 are less with smaller wave-induced yaw moments in bow and stern quartering seas. The smaller moments and motions in stern seas at high speeds also indicate that Hull 2 has a lesser tendency to dive.

CONCLUSION

These CFD simulations are but a few of the many ways CFD can assist boat designers. The time frames and costs for these calculations are much less than what would be incurred in tow tanks and wave basins and, for instance, a five-speed resistance curve for a catamaran can be done in less than a week, including the initial set-up time. Each seakeeping calculation at a particular speed and heading takes a couple of days after that. Changes to the

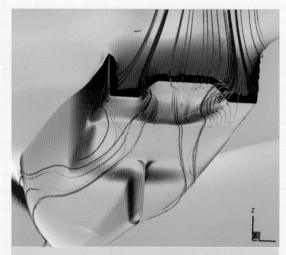

CFD analysis can also be applied to displacement hulls.

design can be easily incorporated by directly modifying the computational grid along with the integral quantities, such as resistance and motions, and local flow features can be visualised at areas of interest using 3D stream lines, pressure contours and vortex extraction methods. Designers also get a visual feel for how their design works through animations. With a certain amount of synergy between the boatowners, boat designers and CFD engineers, it is possible to arrive at an optimal hull form to best suit the statement of requirements.

5 FOILS, FINS AND FLYING BOATS

There has been an endless quest to make boats go faster, and the logical route to doing this for planing boats is to reduce the wetted surface area of the hull in contact with the water. One of the earliest attempts to achieve this was to introduce steps on the planing surfaces, but there have been a variety of other systems and techniques, all of which have been designed to actually lift the hull in the water and thus reduce the contact area.

HYDROFOILS

Probably one of the earliest of these systems was the hydrofoil, which dates back to some early planing designs. With this type of boat, the hull rides on a series of foils that are in the water and these generate sufficient lift from the forward speed to lift the hull in the water. The foils themselves are much more efficient lifting surfaces than the hull of a boat and are shaped with an aerofoil cross-section, rather like an aircraft wing, although they're generally thicker from top to bottom because of the relatively slow speed. Indeed, they generate lift just like an aircraft wing but because water is much denser than air, the wing profile has to be different.

A Russian passenger-carrying hydrofoil with submerged foils.

Given sufficient lift from these foils, the hull can be lifted clear of the water and rides above the waves. With the foils immersed in the water, the ride can be remarkably smooth. However, it does not take a lot of imagination to picture that this will only occur in relatively calm conditions; once the waves are large enough to start striking the bottom of the hull, the speed and effectiveness of hydrofoils is reduced. Consequently, hydrofoils tend to be used on fine-weather craft or perhaps those operating in sheltered waters, such as rivers and lakes. There is also the problem of increased draft when the boat is moving at a slow speed or stopped and the hydrofoils may stick out at the side of the hull, both of which can be a significant handicap.

There is no doubt, then, that the hydrofoil can offer considerable potential as a design technique for fast powerboats, but they also have disadvantages and, on balance, they have never realised their promise, particularly for smaller craft up to say 20m (65ft). Instead, hydrofoils have tended to be used mainly for larger craft, perhaps those over 25m (82ft) in length, and they have not found any significant place in the leisure sector.

Opposite: This amphibious craft has retractable caterpillar tracks for land use.

The Princess sports boat that features hydrofoil lift to improve performance and stability.

An early Russian sports boat hydrofoil craft with fixed foils.

The retractable foil fitted to the latest Princess sports boat to generate lift.

Having said that, though, we have recently seen new leisure hydrofoil sports boats being introduced as the effect and experience from the foiling America's Cup sailing catamarans has filtered down into the general boat sector. For instance, just as this book goes to press, one of the major British powerboat builders, Princess, has introduced a sports boat that has a foil stabilising system developed in conjunction with the British America's Cup team. Here, a pair of small foils can be lowered beneath the centre of gravity of the hull to generate lift and they are also adjustable, so that they can be used to trim the hull. It is a new and adventurous system that may well point the way to future use of foils. It is certainly still a work in progress, although the boat is now being marketed with this foil system so the designers must have a degree of confidence in it. The concept looks good and the foils are claimed to have a very quick response to correct boat movements, so apart from generating lift this might be the new boat-stabilising system.

FULLY SUBMERGED HYDROFOILS

In general, there are two main types of hydrofoil: those for which the foils are fully immersed and those with surface-piercing foils. With the fully submerged foils, the lift generated increases with the speed. In some cases they have been fitted with small flaps on their trailing edges to allow a degree of control over the amount of lift, and if under computer control they can give a level and controlled ride. It can be a complex system for smaller craft, however, and although submerged foils have been used on some military and passenger craft, the system has not stood the test of time. This is because although efficient, it makes for a complex and expensive craft and the fully immersed foils can be vulnerable to debris in the water. What's more, there were major problems with the propulsion system, since it can be a challenge to keep the propeller in the water as the craft lifts up on to the foils. To overcome this, steeply angled propeller shafts or complex water-jet systems were tried, neither of which were particularly efficient. Another problem that was experienced by some of the military versions when used in rougher seas was that the forward foil would come clear of the water and tend to plane on its underside rather than re-entering the water, meaning that the craft had to slow down to get it back under control again.

I do not have experience with the modern versions of fully submerged foils that are based largely on the technology used in the America's Cup sailing catamarans, but the pictures of them performing look very exciting. This new concept of submerged foils allows them to be retracted when not required, allowing the boat to revert to normal sports boat operation with the hull in the water. Accordingly, these prototype designs may herald a new generation of hydrofoils that offer effective performance at high speeds, although the problem with a propulsion system that works at varying drafts remains, and I suspect that rough-sea operations may not be as viable as those of a conventional planing hull.

SURFACE-PIERCING HYDROFOILS

The alternative to these fully submerged foils are surface-piercing foils. These have formed the basis of several larger passenger-carrying hydrofoils developed particularly in Russia and Italy. The foils are usually in

A sports boat riding on foils which can be folded into the hull when not being used.

Hydrofoils are used to reduce the resistance of this solar powered craft.

the form of a vee when viewed from ahead, with the extremities piercing the surface on each side of the hull both forward and aft. They provide relatively stable support for the hull at speed, with the lift balancing out as speed increases and the tops of the foils break the surface, thus reducing the area of the foil in contact with the water. However, there remain the issues of vulnerability with debris in the water, and the problem of finding an effective propulsion system with the varying draft, and a further handicap is the fact that the foils stick out on either side of the hull so that berthing the craft can present challenges.

These problems that face the design and operation of hydrofoils clearly demonstrate the challenges that face all fast-boat designers, whereby to achieve higher speeds or more economical operation, you have to accept penalties in terms of practicalities or a reduced capability to operate in rough seas. Hydrofoils have their place in fast-boat development but they have been largely overtaken by developments in conventional hulls, although new foil technology may see a revival.

FOILS ON CATAMARANS

Before leaving the topic of hydrofoils it is worth mentioning the use of foils with catamaran hulls. This concept was developed by Professor Hoppe in South Africa and his Hysucat technology has since been used in a variety of catamaran designs. The idea is to have foils fixed low down between the two hulls of a catamaran so that in normal running the foil remains fully submerged. These foils generate lift, which is used to reduce the area of the hull in contact with the water and give improved performance. The concept has found favour mainly in military and workboat designs and has even been used in some small catamaran RIBs where the performance claims are quite impressive.

An alternative version to the two fully transverse foils is to have two canard foils at the forward end rather than one transverse foil, which tends to be a better solution in smaller craft to help the foils stay in the water. However, like all foil systems, their effectiveness relies on the foil staying in the water and not riding over it and this can be a problem when sea conditions get more lively. The slow take-up of the Hysucat foil system is probably due to the fact that it needs a catamaran hull, and the questionable rough-sea performance, although users I have talked to dispute this.

ALTERNATIVE FORMS OF LIFT

Lift can also be generated by the air passing over or under the craft. This can be exploited to reduce the area of the hull in contact with the water but in general it does depend on using a catamaran or multihull type of hull, and because air is much less dense than water, a much larger area of wing is required to generate the lift. We have already touched on the use of air lift with high-speed catamaran hulls, whereby the lift can be improved by forming the cross deck into an aerofoil

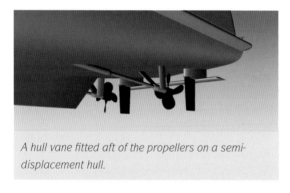

A hull vane fitted aft of the propellers on a semi-displacement hull.

shape. This works well in calm or moderate seas, but if the catamaran starts pitching – as it might in a head sea – then the angle of incidence of the foil is constantly changing, which tends to cause turbulence rather than generating lift, although high speeds might not be possible in these conditions. The effectiveness in calm water is quite impressive, though, with the boats going faster into the wind, which has the effect of a higher wind speed through the tunnel.

Wings have been tried on monohull racing boats but for different reasons. We had a wing on the very successful *Cesa* race boat that was mounted just aft of the cockpit, and that had a considerable dihedral or vee in its transverse shape – ie it formed a shallow vee rather than being directly horizontal. The reason for this was to try to stabilise the boat transversely at high speeds with

more lift being generated by the horizontal side of the wing when the boat was heeled over. It did help, but the effect was not really enough to compensate for the extra weight of the wing.

Despite this, our use of this wing and our racing success with that boat spawned a new generation of monohull race boats with wings, though these were all just straight horizontal wings – fitted in the hope of generating lift – that did nothing to increase the overall speed of the boat to which they were fitted. A much larger wing area is required to generate any worthwhile lift from a wing at speeds of around 160km/h (100mph).

A new approach to using air lift is seen with the Advanced Aerodynamic Vessel (AAV) that has been developed in France by A2V. Their prototype vessel has two widely spaced hulls in catamaran style and these are linked by an arched cross deck that forms a giant aerofoil with the pilot house located inside or just above it. The bottom of this aerofoil is virtually flat and is quite high up above the water, while the upper section follows a full curve to create the aerofoil section that tapers down at the rear. It is certainly an unusual type of craft, but following extensive trials with the prototype that was 10m (33ft) long and capable of 60 knots with a pair of 200hp outboards for propulsion, the company has received commercial contracts. One is for a passenger shuttle on Lake Leman in Switzerland and the other for a 25-person crew-transfer vessel to operate in West Africa.

The AAV exploits the possibilities of using air lift to the full with the side hulls located well apart in order to maximise the wing lift effect. The side hulls are quite narrow planing hulls with steps to reduce the wetted surface area, and when running at speed, these hulls only skim the surface. What is interesting about these AAV designs is that while they exploit the possibilities of using air lift to the full, they have a good seagoing capability, mainly because of the high clearance under the wing. This means they can operate in adverse conditions, which is the holy grail of fast-boat performance. The economical performance of these designs will obviously appeal to commercial users, but in the leisure sector they could offer the excitement of high speed in relative comfort. Perhaps the only

Significant lift is generated by this catamaran where the cross deck is aerofoil shaped.

disadvantage is that for the wing to be effective it has to be continuous, with no open cockpit, which means that all crew and passengers have to be inside the wing. Nevertheless, in my view, this new concept for high-speed craft is one of the most exciting developments in recent years.

WIGS

One step further down the line for using the air lift generated from forward motion is the WIG – Wing in Ground technology. To all intents and purposes this is an aircraft in many ways, like a seaplane, although it only flies very low above the sea because it generates its lift mainly from the close contact with the sea surface. In consequence, WIGs are now classed as sea-going craft and are mentioned in the Colregs because there is a need for them to take avoiding action from regular shipping and boats.

The WIG can operate very effectively at moderate speeds over water and it takes off and lands from the water so it has a sort of boat-shaped hull with relatively short, usually stubby, wings that are designed to generate lift at low speeds. Obviously, because they are flying they tend to be weight sensitive, so lightweight construction is essential; modern versions tend to be constructed in composites with power from lightweight aircraft-rated petrol engines. I flew one of these with no previous experience of flying as a pilot and know that they have very simple controls: steering is operated by an air rudder in the tail and to take off you simply open

the throttle and go. In the small single-seater WIG that I flew, the take-off speed was close to 35 knots and you knew when you were airborne because the steering suddenly became light and seemed to be totally ineffective. For me, it was a moment of panic because I thought that the steering had failed but then I realised that because the craft had no contact with the water there was little for the rudder to work against. You thus have to start anticipating when you want to turn and start the process early. It took a while to get the hang of it but I was soon enjoying 'flying' up the River Rhine at 80 knots just a few feet above the water. It was uncanny, but I do worry that if the concept catches on then, with development, it could lead to some dangerous situations on the water because WIGs react differently to conventional craft.

A flying RIB using hang glider technology.

HOVERCRAFT

Air lift of a different sort is found with the hovercraft concept. This has now been around for more than 50 years and when it was introduced in very basic form it was hailed as a revolution in water transport. The concept is simple: introduce a cushion of air underneath the hull and let the craft ride on it, which greatly reduces the friction between the hull and the sea surface and allows the craft to slide across the water. The air cushion vessel or hovercraft is not confined to the water, either: it can cope with beaches and other relatively flat surfaces. It is therefore easy to see why it was hailed as a revolution, although trying to translate the basic concept into a practical craft proved challenging and the

A regular RIB and a hovercraft both used for inshore rescue work.

A modern surface effect craft where the whole hull is lifted in the water by an air cushion.

hovercraft has never really lived up to its promise.

The early development faced two challenges. First, because the craft was not riding in the water but above it, it was classed as an aircraft and so it had to meet aircraft standards and specifications and the crew had to be pilots, which of course put the costs up considerably. Second, it relied on flexible skirts made from a rubberised fabric to contain the air cushion and these were subject to considerable wear and tear. Air propellers were also required for propulsion, which generated a lot of noise and with no 'bite' on the water, control could be challenging, particularly in cross winds – as for the WIG.

These pure hovercraft found a few niche applications and were particularly suitable for use in ice-covered waters and for access to remote areas. Some passenger services were operated and still continue to this day, while a considerable market for small sports hovercraft developed once the requirement to have a pilot's licence was abandoned. Indeed, the whole requirement to classify hovercraft as aircraft has been ditched, but still the pure hovercraft has only a limited market.

The sidewall hovercraft or Surface Effect Ship (SES) offered a more practical solution for many applications and this could be classed as part boat, part aircraft. It still rode on a cushion of air but this was contained within a rigid hull with 'sidewalls' along each side that extended into the water to contain the air cushion and flexible skirts at just the bow and the stern. This lent the craft many more of the attributes of a seagoing vessel,

with the sidewalls giving the craft directional stability and 'bite' on the water, while just having flexible skirts at the bow and the stern reduced some of the problems with wear and tear. With these designs, it was also possible to use marine propulsion systems, which was a big bonus. Despite this, the concept has only had limited success, mainly because of the higher expense and the need for regular maintenance on the skirts.

Moving on from this development, there were attempts to create a type of hovercraft for which no flexible skirts were required. Here, the challenge was to contain the air cushion under the hull using just rigid components of the hull. Don Burg in the USA was one of the first designers to achieve this with his Sea Coaster designs. Various prototypes were built and operated with some success as commercial craft, with excellent performance on limited power and good fuel economy; the motor for the air fan that maintained the air cushion was an added source

A prototype air-supported vessel at speed.

An air-assisted vessel built by Tuco Marine.

of fuel consumption but the overall consumption was considerably less that that of a matching conventional hull and, in moderate seas, the ride was better. What's more, with no flexible skirts, the maintenance was similar to that of a conventional craft. Operating in waves of any significance was still a challenge, however. I was invited to go to sea on one of these Sea Coasters and found the performance to be very impressive. However, the US workboat and leisure markets are surprisingly conservative and while they might show huge interest in new technology, in this case they were reluctant to part with their money to invest in it.

Instead, the concept was taken up by Effect Ships International in Norway, and with considerable research and development work, including extensive tank testing, they produced a very effective air-supported concept. This 20m (66ft) design was extensively tested in the open sea and many operators and builders showed a lot of interest, but for most, moving into an innovative

An underwater view of an air-supported vessel showing the air chamber and the pod drive system.

concept like this was a step too far when it came to investing in new technology. At the time of writing, Tuco Marine, a workboat builder in Denmark, is the only company to have built a prototype and offer this effective technology.

Effect Ships went on to get considerable EU funding to build an electric-powered passenger version using the air cushion for higher efficiency. This battery-powered craft could achieve 30 knots for short periods and it had a quick-charge system so that is could operate as a fast passenger ferry, perhaps on commuter routes, but again, despite having a prototype demonstrator to prove that it can work it is still waiting for commercial success.

SWATH

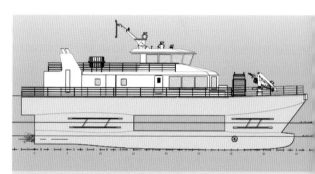

The profile of a SWATH craft showing the narrow struts that connect the top and bottom hulls.

A bit more successful, at least in the commercial sector, has been the SWATH. This stands for Small Waterplane Twin Hull and the idea here is to put the buoyancy that supports the craft below the surface of the sea with only a vertical structure with minimal buoyancy providing the link between this underwater buoyancy and the work deck or accommodation above water. This means that the passing waves will only have a small effect on the overall buoyancy of the craft as they pass the hull, which gives a stable ride. It works, and designs based on SWATH hulls have been used for a number of specialised applications, such as pilot boats and offshore passenger transport.

The downside is that the SWATH concept is only suitable on craft perhaps over 20m (66ft) or so because the gap between the lower buoyancy and the upper deck is too small on smaller craft, so waves can quickly strike the underdeck as conditions deteriorate. SWATHs are also more expensive than a conventional hull, so they can only be justified where the benefits are obvious and tangible.

Most SWATH designs have had the two underwater hulls in parallel, as in catamaran form, but another option that has been tested is to use a trimaran format. Here, there were three hulls, none of which ran for the full length of the craft. Instead, there was one forward and two aft in tricycle formation, which economised on the structure. The system worked, but again the complication of the structure and the cost did not justify the investment except in special applications.

WIND FARM FERRIES

The introduction of offshore wind farms has led to some owners being prepared to experiment with some of these alternative hull designs in order to ferry technicians and work crews out to the wind farm structures, often in adverse conditions. The passengers on board want as smooth a ride as possible to reduce fatigue and seasickness and so there can be some justification in the higher investment in alternative designs if it gives a rough-weather advantage. The standard designs all use catamarans and in most cases these provide an effective means of passenger transport in the conditions experienced. This reduces the incentive to invest in more expensive concepts that might offer better rough-sea performance or higher and perhaps more economical speeds, although recently an SES has been trialled, as have SWATHs, with some success.

AMPHIBIOUS CRAFT

Finally, there are amphibious craft, which can operate on both land and sea. These designs mostly stem from the DUKW ('Duck') amphibious craft developed during World War II and, again, here we have a craft that is more expensive than a conventional design but that will do something that the others can't – ie make the transition from land to sea or vice versa. It is easy to see the

Folding foils are used to lift this amphibious craft in the water.

attractions of such a craft but the complications involved will often outweigh any advantage in the operation.

One of the best-known types of amphibious craft is the Sealegs RIB, which has a single wheel forward and two aft, each of which is hydraulically driven using power from an auxiliary motor in the boat. The wheels are retractable; to come ashore you simply lower the wheels as you approach the beach or slipway and when they make contact with the beach, you drive ashore. The wheels and their hydraulic systems add quite a bit of weight to the boat so there is a reduction in performance, but unlike most other systems, the

The Sealegs amphibian craft with retractable wheels.

An advanced amphibious craft which has foils that deploy for water use.

Sealegs has all of the road-going parts out of the water when afloat, and propulsion is by a conventional outboard on the transom. Although the company previously built their own RIBs and sold a complete package, they are now licensing the system to other boatbuilders, so we are likely to see more of this innovative system.

Another modern system uses a pair of caterpillar tracks fitted under the boat for land transport. These units are lowered down under hydraulic power and provide good traction on softer beaches. When afloat, the tracks fold up into the hull, which adopts a more or less deep-vee shape. Apart from the extra weight, this system performs fairly well.

FLOATING CARS

There have been attempts to create cars that can operate afloat but none has stood the test of time, with the extra weight and complication required to give the amphibious quality making the craft sit low in the water and at the same time compromising the road performance. Larger versions for passenger carrying have also been developed, mostly using a water jet for the water propulsion, but again in general the compromises required are just too much for a viable craft.

Amphibious craft in their present form are therefore mainly for specialised applications and the loss in performance has to be balanced against other benefits.

One concept that appears to overcome this compromise is the Dobbertin HydroCar developed in the USA. This striking design promises speeds of up to 60 knots on the water and over 193km/h (120mph) on land. Power comes from a 725hp supercharged petrol engine and a complex gearbox allows this to be coupled to the land wheels or to the single Arneson Surface Drive at the stern, or both when making the transition from land to water. It costs over US$1 million and on the water it runs on two retractable 'skis'.

Striking a balance
The example of the HydroCar shows what can be done with enough money, although there are still compromises in terms of the seaworthiness. This is true of nearly all powerboat designs, whether they use what might be termed exotic or conventional technology, and this is where the skill of the designer comes in. Design has to be a considered balance between advanced technology, performance requirements and most of all, cost.

ANDREW LEA, NORSON DESIGN

"

Many of the hulls I was involved with at a younger age were focused on one key operational attribute: perhaps going as fast as possible, handling as well as possible, or having outstanding seakeeping performance. In short, there were extreme margins of compromise that had to be designed and engineered into such vessels to give owners close to what their key requirements were, and as such, one or two of the other primary hull characteristics would suffer. This led me to re-evaluate just what could be attained by reducing the level of compromise, looking outside the traditional box and coming up with inventive, simple solutions so that the best all-round hulls could be designed and proven to perform well.

I have always been a speed maniac, and as such, have had to train myself to evolve hull lines and features other than just to ensure stable performance at the highest possible top speeds. Using a simple hull evaluation process as well as 25 years of high-speed vessel design, driving boats, and data collection, I have managed to deliver designs of minimum compromise, which has resulted in very grateful clients.

The basics, however, are still vital. In order to create the parameters of a platform, interaction with clients and end users is critical. One needs to gain as much platform requirement information as possible relative to the method and areas of operation, and I will merge high-speed leisure, military and racing disciplines here for simplicity. Historical data can be researched and from this, such parameters as wind and wave data, significant wave height and lengths can be determined, along with an idea of what the harshest encounters are likely to be on the vessel. This is now tied into the maximum speed, range, endurance, crew, power type etc, and a vision of the end product with hull lines is established.

Regarding preliminary weight estimates based on required scantlings, powering and outfitting options as well as variable loads, it is critical at this stage that all variables are noted – not just the number of crew, fuel and water. Once a decent weight estimate and centre of gravity (CG) location have been made, the hull can be refined and propulsive calculations made using the standard empirical method merged in with known historical efficiency factors. Such a process can be repeated several times before the outcome gives the designer a decent factor of safety on everything, with perhaps the client willing to alter illogical requests that simply will not work in the real world.

Hull optimisation can now be studied together with more in-depth global CFD work and/or scaled prototype development. I tend to split the hull into three distinct sections for this effort, namely bow section, mid-section up to LCG, and then LCG to transom and beyond. Various proven optimisation features can then be examined for the base hull on their known merit and their interaction with other such features. For example, straight or reverse bows seem rather trendy at the moment but they have multiple design concerns over conventional raked bows and for high speeds can add significant surface area to planing surfaces if the vessel's trimming systems are not correct. If the LCG is optimum then ballasting systems, morphing hull control surfaces and integrated foils can help with this. The amidships to LCG area is predominately exposed to the highest slamming loads, and as such, deadrise is critical, but too much will compromise top speeds, so again this is optimised with proven solutions. Changing the deadrise in this area is a key solution and can be done with careful thought on water flow at speed and integration with steps that most of our vessels over 60 knots have. Also, some benefits with longitudinal steps have been found, as well as with single to double chines.

A Norson trimaran concept design.

An advanced fast patrol boat design with reverse bow.

We are trying to cushion the hull in this area using its own geometry and mass so that the deflected water actually softens the impacts, resulting in slamming-load reductions occurring at the source of impact, and not only from a suspension seat. The angle of attack of this centre section is very important and is tied in with the performance of the aft section. This aft section is the business end at high speed and where the rubber should meet the road if the design logic has been correct from the start. The first point of analysis is verifying calculated and/or historical trim angles of similar hulls to generate preliminary running angles and water lines at top speeds. Of course, these vary with the variable loads and extent of trimming of the propulsion system and control surfaces, so one must find a minimum or maximum or average here. With this in place, wetted surface area and trim angles can be used, once again through empirical means, to refine performance and powering predictions. Numerous optimisations can then be made to distribute high-pressure areas and deflect water to generate more lift and stability at speed. Spray rail geometry and placements are critical, as are aft step transitions and aft surface angle of attack.

In order to fully validate such optimisations, we embrace powerful bespoke CFD analysis to generate vital data that proves gains or losses from the use of perhaps unconventional hull features. At present, we are linked to a countrywide supercomputing system to enable high resolutions to be married to high-speed CFD runs. This data can be later compared to real-world sea trials and programming refined to best reflect the natural balance of such dynamically complicated systems. In addition to the hydro side, we actively look at aerodynamic optimisations and have managed to create catamaran designs with up to 50 per cent more lift compared with conventional layouts.

If time, vessel size and budget allow, we strongly suggest scaled prototype building so that real-time sea trial data can be recorded and used against full-scale CFD results and calculations, so any final alterations can be made before full-scale tooling and building is started. This gives the designer and client a hands-on feel for the vessel and enables the human interaction and handling responses to be experienced and, if needed, improved upon. In addition, accelerometer and strain gauges can easily be installed; these scale prototypes are a great step forwards and can be used to test future hull concepts.

Model testing for a long distance, powerful, record-breaking catamaran.

At the end of the day, the designer's job is to reach the best design possible with the minimum possible compromise. We know that this systematic process works and keeps improving with the more data that is generated and then cycled through the design process. It is a sad thing to compromise speed and we do not necessarily need to if we continue to think outside the box.

THE POWER BEHIND THE PLEASURE

How engines for boats have changed over the past 50 years. From outboards with tenuous reliability and smoky diesels of limited power and high weight we have now entered an era in which outboards are powerful and reliable – it is rare to find a modern engine breaking down – and diesels that are light in weight and responsive, with a high power/weight ratio.

It is this change in engines that has largely made the performance boats of today such an attractive and viable proposition, but the change has also filtered down to slower displacement boats, to the point at which it is now viable to operate in the open sea with just a single engine and feel comfortable that it won't let you down even in adverse conditions. The change has come about for two main reasons: first, there has been a much wider recognition that it was the engine systems – the systems that support the engine to keep it running – that were the cause of so much unreliability rather than the engine itself; and second, the switch from engines developed solely for marine use to engines that are based on automotive units. For the latter engine type, there was a strong accent on reliability, with plenty of funding available for research and development to ensure this, and being lightweight was also deemed important.

A typical modern engine installation engineered to ensure reliability.

Then there is the argument over whether to use diesel or petrol as a fuel. Because petrol is widely available in the USA and is low cost, there was little incentive to switch to diesel there, except perhaps on safety grounds, so petrol is still the primary fuel. In Europe and many other parts of the world, however, it is different: marine diesel is widely available even in remote areas and in many cases with reduced taxes. What's more, diesel engines are more economical, so from a cost point of view the diesel is a viable and safer alternative for marine use.

OUTBOARD ENGINES

The outboard motor started life as a very simple concept that could be clamped on to the transom of a boat to provide portable power. This type of outboard can still be found, usually for fitting to yacht tenders, and is enhanced with hand starting, which means no external electrical supply is required. This is practical for engines up to about 50hp but above that the outboard loses its portability and merely becomes a fixture bolted on to the transom.

Outboards are the odd one out in terms of marine engines because they tend to be specifically developed for the marine application, rather than being automotive derivatives,

Opposite: A diesel outboard installed on a RIB.

although some motorcycle heritage and experience was probably involved somewhere along the line. The result is a triumph of engineering. The power output of the larger modern outboard has crept up and up and today we are seeing all the major manufacturers producing engines of 300, 350 and even 400hp. Regardless of their power, they are almost universally run on petrol as a fuel although diesel outboards have now become a viable option.

A significant change during their evolution has been the switch from two-stroke configuration engines to four-stroke ones. The latter tend to be heavier and more complex, but the benefits are better fuel economy, no oil in the fuel, improved reliability and much-reduced emissions. These add up to a modern outboard that is smooth running and meets higher emission standards while maintaining a relatively light weight.

DESIGN COMPLICATIONS

It is a challenge to the designers of these complex pieces of machinery to not only get the basic engine into the compact space and to ensure that it can run with the crankshaft vertical, but also to ensure all the periphery equipment can be accommodated. This equipment includes the starter motor, the alternator, the fuel pump filter and injection system, the water pump and, in some cases of very high-power engines, a supercharger. Added to the complication is the tilt and trim hydraulic system

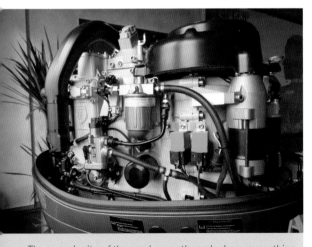

The complexity of the modern outboard where everything has to be contained inside the engine hood.

and the steering, which these days tend to be controlled by fly-by-wire systems with electrical rather than physical connections, although there are still hydraulics involved at the engine end. The control of the whole engine is by means of electrical connections, rather than the push-pull cables of old, and throttle and gear controls, which somewhat simplifies the installation. The downside to this is that the whole installation is dependent on having a reliable electrical supply, which can be a challenge in itself particularly in small craft. The engine also has to be capable of operating in the wet and damp conditions created at the stern of the boat at speed.

The weak point of many outboards has been the requirement to change the direction of the drive from the vertical to the horizontal for connection to the propeller. The gearing required for this has to be housed in a size-limited, compact hub to reduce resistance and to provide a smooth flow of water to the propeller. Modern materials capable of handling the high loadings have reduced this problem but it can still be a limiting factor.

THE ADVANTAGES OF THE OUTBOARD ENGINE

We are seeing a resurgence in the use of outboards for powering performance craft, particularly in the USA. If you ignore the high fuel consumption then the advantages of an outboard installation can be significant: the engine is mounted on the transom so it leaves the majority of the interior of the boat free for pleasure or commercial use; it is relatively lightweight, which is good for performance; and most of the engine noise and vibration are left far behind. There is a raft of new designs that make the most of these outboard advantages and it is now possible to have up to four outboards across the transom, which will make about 1,500hp available – sufficient to meet the power needs of a large number of leisure craft. It is necessary to meet very strict fuel tank and supply requirements, but that should be the case with any fuel system and with today's fire and explosion safety requirements, petrol is a relatively safe fuel for boats. Having that amount of power attached to the transom does challenge the designers, however, because it shifts the centre of gravity of the boat a long way aft, so the hull has to be designed for the job.

The modern trend is towards multiple outboard installations for larger sports boats.

The focus with outboards tends to be on the more powerful units that are fitted to performance craft, but smaller versions of these engine units are used on a large proportion of small boats, such as RIBs and sports boats. These are usually single-engine installations, a fact that reflects the reliability and the confidence that users have in a single-engine installation these days. These smaller outboards tend to be much less complex and in many cases will have tiller steering and throttle control or, where remotes are fitted, push-pull cables can still make the control connections. However, I wonder how long it will be before electrical systems take over – whereupon designers will have to meet the challenge of installing a reliable electrical system in a small open boat.

The case for multiple engines

The marine industry seems to be very conservative when it comes to the number of engines installed in a boat. Because of the reliability of modern engines, we are seeing many modern displacement boats returning to the use of just a single engine, even those designed for long-range cruising. This is probably the best and most economical solution as costs and design challenges start to increase when you

switch to two. Twin-engine installations are, however, now the norm for planing boats, apart from the new generation of outboard-powered boats where multiple-engine installations are required to obtain the required level of power on the transom.

With more conventional inboard installation, we might see a planing powerboat in larger sizes requiring perhaps 2,000–3,000hp. Once you get to this size of engine they have moved outside the sphere of the normal mass-produced truck engine and into the realms of partly hand-built ones with a smaller market. This puts the costs up considerably, which means it might be worth considering having, say, four smaller engines each on its own drive rather than two more powerful ones. Not only could this produce a cost saving, but there could also be a saving in weight and also in space requirements; four smaller engines spaced across the boat would have a shorter length than the larger engines, so it might be possible to gain 1m (3.3ft) or so of extra internal space. Then there is the added flexibility of the propulsion, with it being possible to operate on just a couple of the engines when high speeds are not required. It is certainly worth looking at these options when working on the design of a new boat.

DIESEL OUTBOARD ENGINES

Many commercial users of outboards have been concerned about the use and availability of petrol as a fuel, which has created a demand for a diesel outboard. Much of this pressure has come from the military, who do not want petrol on board their fighting ships, as well as from insurance companies, who don't like the idea of having to have petrol storage on board. The feat of connecting a compact diesel with adequate power to a lower unit that has power and torque limitations has been a challenge and for years the Yanmar diesel was the yardstick in this sector. However, its relatively low power at 35hp was not enough for most planing boats and as higher emission standards came into force, production was stopped. A number of manufacturers tried to step into the gap, with the major players, such as OMC and Mercury, producing adapted versions of their petrol outboards that could operate on diesel fuel. These were still spark-ignited engines and tended to be rather rough running, challenging to start and not particularly emission free. Next, several manufacturers tried adapting small automotive engines to act as the power units for outboards, but the high torque of the diesel proved challenging – the issue of getting the torque of the diesel to the propeller.

So far, at the time of writing, there have been two successful diesel outboards to hit the market. The smaller is the Neander Shark, which is an innovative design with twin crankshafts that produces 55hp – a conservative power output that is likely to be upgraded – but it is probable that a twin installation can provide adequate power for many RIBs and smaller craft as well as for displacement boats. Neander is now marketed by diesel engine manufacturer Yanmar, which offers worldwide servicing.

The other is the Oxe unit made by Cimco in Sweden, which is offered with 200hp and is based on a compact high-output automotive engine connected to a very innovative propulsion system that represents probably one of the most significant changes to outboard design for many years. The Oxe has a horizontal engine and uses high-capacity belt drives to take the power first to a compact gearbox mounted below the engine and then down to the horizontal shaft of the propeller drive. In this lower section, the toothed belt is guided by rollers so that the two parts are close together to create a narrow leg for the outboard, and the lower drive roller is compact to create a slim lower unit. The current model can handle 200hp but there will soon be a 300hp version, thereby allowing the diesel outboard to closely match the power of many petrol ones. Lower-horsepower versions are also being developed to offer users a wide spectrum of power.

Mention should be made here of the Cox diesel outboard, which is claimed to be the highest power-density diesel engine. This opposed-piston two-stroke unit is rated at 300hp in pre-production form after more than five years of development by a dedicated team of engineers. However, production versions of this diesel outboard are now fitted with a more conventional V8 diesel and it is about to hit the market at the time of going to press.

The handicap of the Cox engine and the other diesel outboards is their price, which is around double that of an equivalent petrol unit for the same power. What's more, they are heavier. Against this, you get much-improved fuel economy, a safer and more readily available fuel, and hopefully an engine that will have a longer life. These factors suggest that the use of the diesel outboard will be restricted to mainly commercial and military users where high operating hours can justify the greater capital costs because of the fuel savings, and for tenders of craft carried on board ships where petrol fuel is not allowed. As production rises, the cost of these diesel outboards is likely to come down.

STERNDRIVE ENGINES

The complex world of the outboard motor is matched by that of the sterndrive engine, but here the engine is protected inside the boat, so it becomes a more conventional engine installation. The downside is that the drive has to be taken through two right angles to the propeller as a result of trying to keep the lower hub size as compact as possible – as for outboards. This lower hub and its gearing has been the weak point in sterndrive design but the effectiveness of the system as far as propulsion is concerned has led to some ingenious solutions with angled and belt drives.

The compact arrangements of a diesel combined with a stern drive.

As with outboards, having a diesel engine as the power unit increases the torque and puts extra stress on the drive system, which has tended to be the limiting factor in sterndrive design. Despite this, the sterndrive engine solution is still used quite a bit – especially in the USA – because it hides the engine away in more sophisticated boat designs, although the advance and sophistication of the outboard mean that is taking over from the sterndrive.

Petrol sterndrive engines are still widely used in high-performance boats, again, particularly in the USA. Here, their attraction is their relatively low weight and high power density. There are a number of specialist engine tuners who take the basic V8 automobile block and completely rebuild and tune the engine to produce massive horsepowers in the 1,000–1,700hp range. They can include superchargers, turbochargers and fuel injection, which not only render them reliable in most cases, but also make the engines look beautiful, with lots of chrome and stainless steel. Mercury Marine is probably the only major marine engine manufacturer to produce and market this type of engine in the USA. In Europe, there is the marine version of the Lamborghini V12 engine, which is the main engine used in Class One offshore powerboat racing. This is the exotic end of powerboat engines and virtually every one is hand built.

At the more practical end of the market there is the diesel sterndrive engine that is now fitted in many motor cruisers and powerboats. Modern diesel engines bear little relation to the diesels of old, having become both sophisticated and highly tuned, following the trend in the automotive world, and they are now a close match to the power/weight ratio of petrol engines. Almost all of the ones on the market are based on automotive engines, mainly for the simple reason that the basic engines are produced in vast numbers, which keeps down the costs of both development and production; it is likely that to meet modern requirements in terms of emissions and reliable power output it would be prohibitively expensive to develop an engine solely for marine purposes, so modifying car, truck, earth-moving and even train engines has become the way to go.

The use of truck engines for marine requirements began around 40 years ago with companies like Volvo, MAN and Mercedes looking for alternative markets for their engines. In those days, the marine sector was relatively free as regards the standards for engines. As emission strictures started to emerge, however, it became more and more necessary to use these automotive engines, which had already been developed to meet these new standards. There was thus a spate of new small marine diesels based on car engines that started to transform

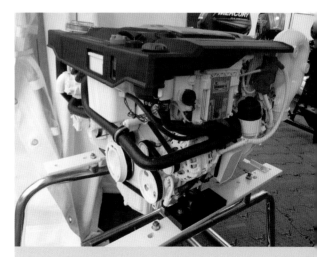

The design of modern marine engines is kept as compact as possible.

A twin diesel installation during the build of a modern sports cruiser.

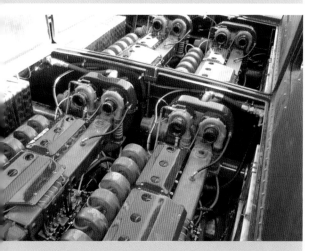

A quadruple Seatek diesel installation in a racing boat to produce over 4,000 hp.

Type of engine	Key features
Two-stroke outboards	Lightweight Higher fuel consumption Advanced electronic control Wide range of power outputs
Four-stroke outboards	Heavier Moderate fuel consumption Advanced electronic control Wide range of power outputs
Petrol inboards	Potentially dangerous fuel Lighter weight Electronic control on modern versions Higher fuel consumption
Diesel inboards	Heavier Good fuel consumption No electronic systems Very reliable Compatible fuel
Electronic diesels	Heavier Excellent fuel consumption Complex electronic systems for control Very reliable Compatible fuel

the market and edge the petrol engine out. This was because these diesels matched the power outputs of their petrol counterparts, provided higher safety standards, and used a more readily available and safer fuel. Insurance companies were probably also offering better rates for diesel installations.

Emissions standards

The challenge for engine manufacturers has been to meet the increasing demands for reduced emission standards. These are set by the EPA in the USA and by the EU in Europe, while the International Marine Organization (IMO) has set standards for shipping and boats. It is something of a confusing picture with slightly differing standards and different enforcement dates but the engine manufacturers know they can't sell engines that don't meet the prevailing international standards. Tier 3 standards have now been met – primarily by making the engines use the

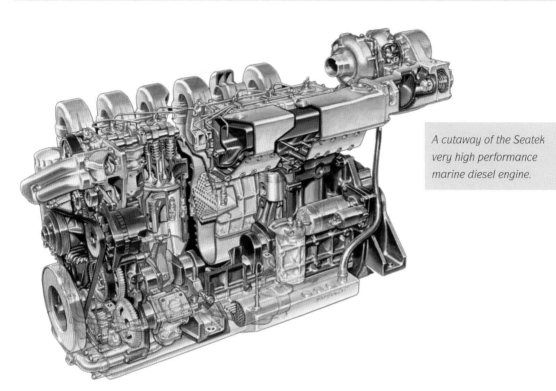

A cutaway of the Seatek very high performance marine diesel engine.

diesel fuel more efficiently. This was achieved first by introducing turbo-charging to most engines and then, more recently, by introducing the common-rail engine, which uses a more efficient, very high-pressure injection system.

ELECTRONIC CONTROL

Probably the most significant change in marine engine design that we have seen in recent years is the switch to electronic control. Again, this has largely been done in the interests of reducing the emissions but it has also led to a significant improvement in performance. The electronics come in the form of a compact computer attached to the engine, which can control the combustion process by varying the timing of the spark or of the injection according to the load on the engine. With petrol engines that are fuel-injected, both the spark and the fuel-injection timing and quantity can be controlled. For diesels on the common-rail system, it tends to be the timing and amount of fuel that is controlled. These electronic

systems are becoming highly sophisticated and are now more or less the standard.

The increase in efficiency obtained with electronic control is doubtless a significant benefit but the downside is that the engine is now totally dependent on the boat's electrical system to operate. Lose your electrics and you lose propulsion. I was brought up in a time when if anything electrical worked on a boat then that was a bonus; you did not rely on it. Today, the boat is not viable if the electrical system is not working. This has meant that boatbuilders have had to raise their game considerably when it comes to installing the electrical system and nothing short of a 100 per cent reliable one will do. This is covered in more detail in Chapter 10.

I have to say, though, that the modern marine engine is a very reliable piece of kit; I cannot remember the last time the engine itself actually broke even under the high stresses of racing. What *can* cause problems with modern engines are the additions: the systems that supply the engine with fuel, the electrical supply, the cooling water and the exhaust. The engine itself will have been thoroughly checked and tested during design

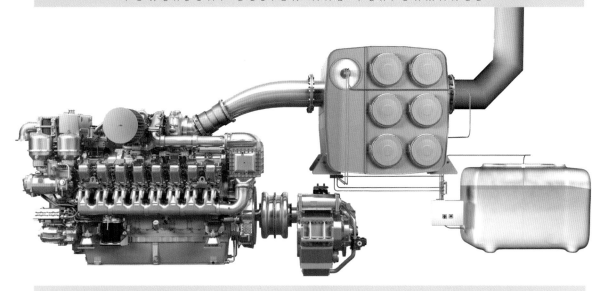

A system for cleaning up the diesel exhaust on an MTU diesel to meet the latest standards.

and manufacture but these peripheral systems will have been designed as part of the overall boat design and so will have had little or no testing in adverse conditions prior to installation. It only wants a wire to chafe against a sharp edge or a fuel pipe to vibrate and cause a leak, or maybe a cooling water hose to perish, and the engine will stop working. These are faults that even the most sophisticated electronic systems will not cure.

EXHAUST TREATMENT SYSTEMS

As far as can be foreseen, we have reached the limit of what can be achieved by making the engine more efficient, and with higher emission standards already being discussed it seems likely that it will only be possible to meet these by introducing exhaust treatment systems, which will be used to clean up the engine exhaust before it enters the atmosphere. Already, the cost of diesel engines has increased considerably because of the increased complication to meet current emission standards, though there has been a return in terms of the higher-efficiency engine. Exhaust treatment systems will not add anything to the efficiency of the engine – indeed, they may well reduce this efficiency and they will certainly raise the cost and increase the weight and size of the engine – so overall we are likely to see a reduction in performance with no corresponding return in efficiency. The increase in size

will concern designers because it will mean that more space has to be allocated to the machinery.

ALTERNATIVE FUELS

Using alternative fuels may be one way round the increasingly tight emission standards. There are several possibilities: hydrogen, liquid natural gas (LNG) and liquid petroleum gas (LPG), all of which have all been

The additional equipment fitted to a diesel engine to ensure compliance with the latest emission standards.

touted as potential boat fuels, but here we are faced with something of a chicken-and-egg situation. While there may be some supplies of these available for cars and trucks on land, as far as is known there is nothing being done to make supplies available for boats. So, no boatbuilder or owner is going to propose using these fuels until supplies become readily available.

LPG is available in steel bottles and is used for gas cooking on many boats, and has been used as a fuel for the main engine in some cases. It is certainly cheaper because of reduced taxes but refuelling involves handling heavy gas bottles – a fact that limits its application to a few small boats. LNG is being used on some ships as a means of reducing emissions but this entails giving over a considerable amount of onboard space to the gas tank, which is likely to limit its application on boats. What's more, although there are now LNG bunkering stations for shipping, I'm not aware of any that are available for boats, so this fuel is something of a non-starter. Hydrogen comes into much the same category, although again it is being used in a few cars. The future may well see changes but for now it is the lack of infrastructure that is hindering progress. The use of electric propulsion for powerboats is a major development and this is covered in Chapter 10.

CONCLUSION

Boat engines have changed dramatically over the past few years and the changes have not always been to the benefit of the user. Costs have gone up, but perhaps more worrying is the now total reliance on the electrical system for the boat to remain operational. This follows the trend in cars and trucks, though if those vehicles break down then help can be readily available; if the engines of a boat stop at sea then you are in a much more high-risk and vulnerable situation. I am therefore concerned that we are entering a time when the boats have become more reliable but, paradoxically, if something does go wrong then the crew might be helpless to fix the problem because of the high technology involved. You will probably need a computer rather than a spanner to fix the modern boat.

A triple engine installation that can save space inside the hull.

The green section is a motor/generator that can be used for electric propulsion.

FABIO BUZZI, FB DESIGN

"

People sometimes ask me, why powerboats? The answer: simply because the wind is blowing only when God wants it to, and generally in the wrong direction... Going by sea needs a lot of power; in the past, only wind and man force existed, so there was a desperate need for an alternative source of power. This was first discovered in the 19th century in the form of steam power, before shifting to petrol engines and then diesel engines, which over time have become more powerful and reliable.

The progress of powerboating is based on the progress of the power/weight ratio. This is an eternal battle between power, which is day by day more expensive, and weight, which can only increase. We could even rephrase this balance and say that powerboat progress is based on the power/dollar ratio. This means that although progress is in some ways making designing a fast boat easier, making a fast boat at a reasonable price is very difficult!

Since my early years, the weight/power ratio has been my dominant thought – so much so that when we started FB Design in 1973, our first purchase was a good set of scales! From that moment on, we have invested our whole life to this subject, creating more powerful diesel engines and lighter boats.

On the power side, big progress occurred in the 1980s with the creation of the six-cylinder Seatek diesel engine.

Thanks to this, we have won everything for many years, culminating in establishing the diesel speed record on the water at 252km/h (156.6mph) in 1992. However, time is passing and technology is improving, and FPT has since invented the common rail injection system and many other new solutions. What's more, in conjunction with FPT we have developed a new engine, based on their Cursor 16 block, a six-cylinder in-line diesel of 16 litres, capable of even 1,800hp. It was with this engine, in 2018, that we established the new diesel world record of 277.5km/h (172mph) – a great demonstration of progress in the power plant. In the future, this engine will be on the market rated at a very reliable 1,300hp.

White Iveco *in which we won the Round Britain Race. Thought to be the first stepped deep-vee hull.*

Buzzi's FPT diesel powered 3 pointer that broke the world diesel record.

However, an even bigger task was undertaken by FB Design on the weight-reduction side. This involved a big study on composites, the use of which is the only way to achieve high performances. Kevlar, carbon fibre, epoxy resins, prepreg fabrics and many new impressive materials can be mixed together thanks to the improvement of the 'composite' technology.

At this point in our story, the big drama took place!

The performances with these new materials were very good from the weight/power ratio perspective, but very poor for the weight/dollar ratio. For example, by using carbon and Kevlar prepreg composite, we could develop

Buzzi and his dog with his typical military deep-vee model.

a boat that originally weighed 2,000kg, at a cost of $20 per kilo, into one that weighed only 1,200kg, but at a cost of $120 per kilo... For this reason, we soon understood that hi-tech composite is not the way to go if we want to be successful on the market!

As a consequence, we stopped working with all those expensive composite solutions for making commercial boats and we have since dedicated 10 full years of R&D activity to creating something new, at a reasonable price. I was impressed by the commercial activity of Boston Whaler, the American company that still makes unsinkable boats, thanks to foam injection. The idea was pretty good – in fact, they are very profitable, making 60 boats a day – but these were only little boats, as foam cannot fill a big boat if it is injected from only one point, as they were doing, and without a real structure inside.

So, we started thinking about multi-point foam injection and having a real structure inside the hull that could be coupled to that foam, which can guarantee flotation. After many experiments, we patented our Structural Foam technology, and nowadays all FB Design boats use the system and are unsinkable. We asked one Navy admiral if he prefers a boat that is unsinkable over one that can sink, and of course the answer was clear: 'no one likes to sink'.

And yet, in 2012 the Costa Concordia cruise ship did exactly that, sinking like the Titanic had 100 years before,

so where is the progress? The answer: our Structural Foam, which can also be used to make cruising ships unsinkable. Of course, it involves losing some space – maybe you can carry only 4,000 passengers rather than 5,000, but in a safe way! What's more, you can still go fast: in 2018, at the venerable age of 75, I was able to set a world speed record of 277.5km/h (172mph), with a new diesel engine inside a hi-tech, unsinkable, composite boat.

A concept catamaran from Buzzi.

The benefit of our foam was clearly demonstrated when we were testing our record-breaking diesel boat. During a trial at over 270km/h (168mph), I lost a propeller blade that was turning at 10,000 rpm, which destroyed all the driveline and created two big holes as large as my head at the two prop shaft support points, yet the boat did not sink!

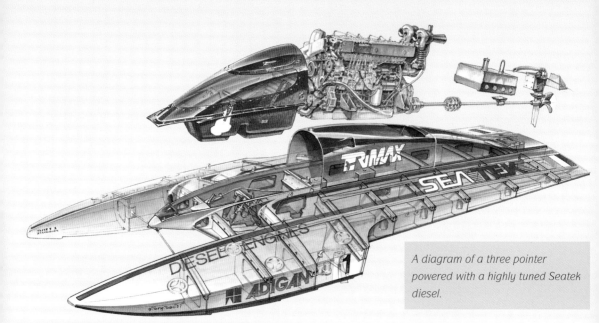

A diagram of a three pointer powered with a highly tuned Seatek diesel.

Now to keep this story short, please bear in mind that speed is a function of the weight/power ratio, but good economical sense obliges me to also remain inside reasonable commercial limits, and this is exactly the reason for the great success of our Structural Foam construction technology.

Now, let us go into some other aspects of powerboating. Of course, the shape of the hull is critical and virtually no boat model is identical to another one. This fact creates a lot of confusion, but a good skipper can choose the best boat for his typical mission.

In 58 years of racing experience, we have tested all types of boats. We started with monohulls, which give incredible advantages thank to the modern deep-vee shape, but catamarans are faster and sometimes even better in some rough waters, and we were also very successful with trimarans.

I believe Andrea Bonomi still has the offshore world race record, which he set with a trimaran called Paul Picot. Together with Antonio Gioffredi, they averaged 200km/h (124mph). Our small Class 3 trimaran has also won many races, also setting a speed record at over 220km/h (137mph). However, for some reason nothing can be better than a RIB! I won the Miami–New York race in 1994, thanks to our RIB 42' Sport; probably the best rough-water boat I ever tested. RIBs are like basketballs: they recover energy jumping on the waves. When rigid boats fall in the water, they transform their potential energy into low-temperature heat, so they lose energy, whereas a good RIB returns this energy. This is why RIBs are so superior on rough waters.

But if you really like speed, three-point hydroplanes are the answer. Why? For the simple reason that they are more stable. They touch the water at three points with the

Buzzi's Class 1 racing catamaran.

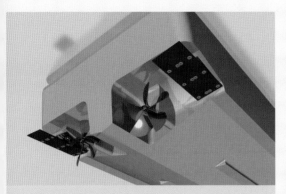

The Trimax surface drive developed by Buzzi.

CG inside this triangle, while a cat at speed is travelling with two points side by side and the pressure in the tunnel that is trying to make the cat fly, fighting against the weight that is keeping the nose down. This is why so many racing catamarans flip over.

Do you see? There is always a right hull for the right mission! But it is only experience that tells you the best solutions. One demonstration of this fact can be found in the modern family of displacement catamarans, which day by day are becoming more popular. Travelling in full-displacement mode, these boats have a theoretical maximum speed proportional to their waterline length. This means that they are superior only if they are long enough, let's say over 20m (65ft).

One of Buzzi's successful racing RIBs.

However, I believe that monohulls of 30m (98ft) are a very poor solution compared to catamarans of the same length, which can reach a displacement speed of 35 knots with half of the power of a 30m (98ft) planing monohull. And you have a lot more comfortable space on board.

So, why are there more monohulls than cats? Doctor Bonomi is the only one able to give a logical answer: most cats are really awful, because they place five decks one on top of the other, and the result is aesthetically a disaster! The future is waiting for a good architect capable of designing a nice-looking catamaran. I tried, and I believe I did a pretty good job, but in the end I was not successful.

Buzzi now focuses on commercial designs such as this RIB42 for police use.

So here we are: the eternal conflict between the cold logic of engineers pitted against the fantasy of architects. Coming from a family with 400 years of architectural tradition and being a mechanical engineer, I suffer acutely from this problem. I do love architects, but only when they are also logical. Too many make different boats rather than good boats. Just think of the reverse bow of some new megayachts. They are totally illogical as on the big waves those boats could be nosediving. And because of the reverse bow, many boats lose their directional stability at speed and sometimes need a very deep fin in the tail, increasing their draft by several metres, just so they are stable during navigation! This is a clear example of how much emotion comes into powerboat design.

The perfect balance between performance, comfort and style comes only from well-proven design. An experienced yet land-based designer seated at their drawing table will always lose against designers with real navigation experience, such as Sonny Levi, Don Shead, Ray Hunt and of course ... Fabio Buzzi!

FUEL MANAGEMENT AND ECONOMY

Fuel plays a vital role in powerboat operations, and it sounds obvious, but to complete a planned passage in a reliable fashion you need to ensure you have enough of the stuff on board. Beyond this simple supply requirement, however, are many other considerations: you may be concerned about operating economically to minimise the fuel consumption, in which you can use the fuel to help trim the boat in certain circumstances; and there are considerable rules and regulations governing 'green issues' and emissions. Either way, the question is: how can we reduce the amount of fuel that we burn but still get enjoyment for the professional, effective operations from our cruising?

CALCULATING FUEL CONSUMPTION

The main problem with reducing fuel consumption is that, on many boats today, we don't know how much of it we are using. We may know how much there is on board when the fuel tanks are filled up, because the builder's handbook tells you this, but do you have any idea how much fuel is going through the engines at any one time, and do you know how much fuel it might take to complete a passage?

Of course, you can work it out *afterwards* by checking what is left in the tanks, but for assessment to be meaningful we really want to know what the engines are burning as we go along. This can be done in a couple of ways:

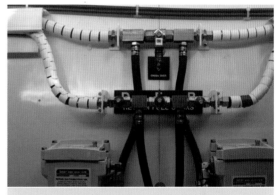

A well installed fuel system that allows either engine to run off either fuel tank.

» You can look at the engine manufacturer's charts, which will show the theoretical amount of fuel the engines are burning at any given rpm.

» With larger modern engines, there is a way to find out what the real-time fuel consumption is using the computer control that operates on many engines. This produces a read-out of how many litres per hour each engine is burning on the engine monitoring display. That is a useful figure and you can immediately see how, when you open or close the throttle, the fuel consumption of the engine rises and falls. These figures can be quite frightening if you are paying the bills, but bear in mind that they only tell you half of the story because they do not relate to the speed of the boat or the distance covered.

» What you really want to know, therefore, is not how many litres per hour the engines are burning but the litres per mile or miles per litre figure.

Opposite: Feeding clean fuel to these powerful engines is a challenge.

How to calculate litres per mile

Assuming that your boat has a modern electronic engine display that shows the fuel consumption in litres per hour, it is easy to convert this to the much more useful litres per mile figure. To do so, simply divide the litres per hour figure by your speed in knots. However, do remember that the main speed read-out on board will come from the GPS, which will show the speed over the ground and not the speed through the water figure, which is the one you want, so you may need to add or subtract a knot or two to allow for the tide influence.

It can be a good idea to spend some time on a calm day taking fuel consumption figures throughout the speed range of the boat so that you can draw up a graph of fuel consumption per mile. If you want to be fully in control of the fuel situation, you may need to do trials on different days and in different conditions to build up a full picture. This will be a valuable tool when doing your passage planning, since you can simply multiply the litres per mile figure by the length of the passage to find out how much fuel you will need when running at that particular speed. Then add on a reserve amount, perhaps 20 per cent, plus an allowance to get you to an alternative port, which could be a greater distance away than your chosen port. You should also allow for the amount of fuel in the tank that will not be accessible, and bear in mind the facts that fuel consumption is likely to increase if you have a head wind on the passage and that for a planing boat, it will also go up if you have extra weight on board.

Why is this litres per mile figure so much better than using litres per hour? It's quite simple really: it means that for every mile you travel you know how much fuel you will burn or have burned, and that is the positive indication of whether you are running economically or not. You may have a deadline to keep and need to open the throttles, but if you are just intent on having a comfortable, economical cruise then you can set the consumption to suit your mood and/or perhaps your pocket.

The external fuel filter for an outboard. The flexible piping and wiring can be vulnerable.

The litres per mile consumption figures may be slightly unexpected. For instance, running at the lowest speed may not prove to be the most economical for a planing boat. Instead, you may find that you need to get the boat on to the plane to achieve the best consumption figure per mile travelled. Either way, at least when you have that litres per mile read-out or calculation you can see the effect of all the different throttle settings and decide on the one to suit. Having that read-out also means that you can see the effect of trimming the hull and what happens when you adjust the trim with the flaps. You may be surprised to see what a difference a change of trim can make to the fuel consumption per mile at different speeds, and that can apply to semi-displacement boats as well. NB: don't look for an immediate change in the consumption when you make adjustments because the readings may take some time to settle down after a change.

One important point to remember when carrying out fuel consumption checks in this way is the effect of tide. As mentioned, GPS always measures the speed over the ground and not the speed through the water. When travelling with the tide, you will get a better mileage and when it is against you, the consumption per mile will appear to go up. These can be valid consumption figures to use when you are cruising because they represent the actual consumption at the time, but when you are trying to find the right trim and balance to optimise the fuel consumption they will confuse the issue, so try to do any fuel trials in non-tidal waters or at least at slack water.

So with these figures available you will know how many miles you are planning to travel on the planned passage and it is not rocket science to then calculate how much fuel you will need. That is the easy part: the complications set in when you try to check what amount of fuel you have on board and what level of reserve fuel you should carry. The builders of the boat will tell you how much the fuel tanks will hold but do they tell you how much of that fuel is useable? Almost all fuel tanks have the suction pipe that connects the tank to the engine, above the bottom of the tank. This is because it is not good practice to draw from the bottom of the tank because then there is no space for any water or dirt in the fuel to settle out. So, as much as 10 per cent of the fuel in the tank may not actually be available for use.

That is fine if you know about it, but then the next question concerns the accuracy of the fuel gauge. These are fitted on most boats using a variety of measuring systems. Whatever the system used, it is vital that you know first how accurate it is and second whether the amount includes the section of unusable fuel at the bottom of the tank or not. The tank gauges that simply show '¼', '½', '¾' and 'full' do not give you the level of accuracy you require and the uncertainty can leave you guessing.

Without doubt the best type of fuel gauge is the sight gauge – a clear vertical tube attached to the tank where the level in the tube matches that inside the tank – but with the tanks usually located below the deck, access might be impossible.

Talking about reserves of fuel, you should always plan to have a suitable reserve on board before departure. It's nice to imagine that you'll never have to think about using your reserve when on a passage, but I like to play it safe and have plenty of fuel on board even though there could be a speed penalty because of the extra weight. A reserve of 10–15 per cent seems to be an accepted fuel reserve level, but I think that is too low. At 10 per cent you only have another 10 miles' running on a voyage of

100 miles, which is not much if you have to detour, stop to help another boat or perhaps you need to speed up to get to port sooner. I would therefore recommend the reserve should be at least 20 per cent, and that reserve should be calculated on top of the distance to the furthest alternative port in your passage planning.

When thinking about fuel consumption and fuel reserves, on a twin-engine boat also look at what the consumption per mile might be when running on just one engine when you carry out fuel-consumption trials. This could happen if you were to suffer an engine failure when on passage and could make a significant difference to the fuel consumption. If it does happen, it is not a good idea to run the remaining engine at high rpm, since it will be operating with a propeller that is not matched to the engine and the new boat speed, and this can overload the engine. Moderate rpm will help to ensure that the remaining engine keeps going until you get to port and it is not likely to make much difference to your speed.

Diesel bug

'Diesel bug' is an organism that can grow and multiply in diesel fuel and that will eventually lead to clogging of fuel lines and filters and generally prevent the engine from operating effectively. The build-up tends to be slow and steady rather than a sudden problem, and if you clean your fuel filters frequently you may become aware of the problem because of the 'gunge' you find there, before it gets serious. Once in the fuel system, it is very hard to get rid of, although there are various 'disinfectants' that are claimed to cure the problem. However, it is much better to prevent it in the first case by using fuel from a reliable source.

EU legislation dictates that boats that operate on inland waterways and on recreational craft 'when not at sea' will soon need to operate on sulphur-free diesel fuel. Just what is described as 'sulphur-free' is not quite clear at the time of writing, but we do know that the sulphur content in fuel does help to reduce the diesel bug problem, so it seems likely that issues with the diesel bug may increase when this sulphur-free fuel is introduced. At present, sea-going boats are exempt from this ruling, but how long that will last is an open question. Another possibility in the future is the use of bio-diesel, which is also thought to be more prone to the diesel bug.

CONCLUSION

If you want to reduce emissions, then speed and hull design are two factors where the savings can really be made. It's quite simple really: as a general rule, the faster you go, the more fuel you will burn and the higher your emissions will be. So, one of the easiest ways to reduce emissions is to reduce speed. Your fuel consumption will also rise if you continually open and close the throttle, as you might when trying to maximise the speed in rough seas.

As for hull design, you might get better economy with a catamaran hull and even greater efficiency if this catamaran has the aerofoil lift wing between the hulls. For a monohull, the lower the hull deadrise, the more efficient the hull form will be, but there will be a penalty in the harsher ride. You find that many small yacht tenders have a low deadrise, which is acceptable if they only operate in harbours.

The seawater filters on the engine systems are a vital component for them to function well.

For future demands for reducing emissions and fuel consumption we may have to live life at a slower pace and adapt to change. To many, that could take away the very ethos of planing powerboats. Perhaps the trend to green boating will start at the professional end of the market where economy could have a bigger impact on operations. The use of electric propulsion may also affect fuel consumption and the battery storage could contribute to your reserves. However there can be considerable losses when sending electric power to battery storage and then taking it out again so the efficiency of hybrid systems is not always good unless you can get 'free' or cheap electric power from shore charging.

ENGINE MONITORING

With the modern electronic engines that are now almost universal in both diesel and petrol versions, one of the benefits of going electronic is that there can be much better monitoring of the engine and its performance. Almost every aspect of the way that the engine is running can now be monitored and, if you delve into the electronic computer and the display screens, you can get access to most of the intimate details about your engine(s). In theory this should allow you to get a picture of how the engine is operating in considerable detail but to do this you probably need to have quite a bit of engineering knowledge behind you. By comparing past and present readings about the various parameters of the engine, it should be possible to detect the early warning signs of something going wrong before it does.

That is the theory but I remain to be convinced that that is what happens in reality. Few boat operators are likely to have the experience or knowledge to be able to interpret the engine read outs in a meaningful way or make predictions about the future behaviour of the engine. Of course, there are some simple aspects that can be evaluated such as whether the cooling water temperature is steadily increasing – this could be a good time to check out the cooling system to identify the problem before it gets too serious. The same can be done with oil pressure – a drop in pressure can indicate wear. This is what we used to do in the past but then we did not have the benefit of a computer storing the historic readings to make a direct comparison. With the modern monitoring systems there is much more scope for analysis but it requires an expert to do this so it could pay to get a trained engineer to check out the monitoring perhaps every 100 hours of running, but certainly at the end of every season.

With this new-found wealth of information about the engine, the gearbox and perhaps also the propulsion system, there are usually a series of alarm systems built in, in case one of the readings goes outside pre-set limits. In a worst-case scenario there may be occasions when the engine automatically shuts down to prevent any damage to the engine. This is all well and good but it does not leave you with the option of keeping that engine running if you and the boat are in a dangerous situation. In my experience when an engine alarm sounds the display screen might perhaps say 'engine temperature high'. What it does not indicate is whether you can keep the engine running for a bit longer or better still how much time you have left before serious engine damage occurs.

We now have so many alarms on board that it seems almost every time I go to sea one goes off. Often I watch the skipper just switch the alarm off because it has sounded previously and he thinks he knows what the problem is. It might just be a faulty sensor, but if you adopt this approach every time then eventually something serious will end up being ignored. So alarms on boats need to be taken seriously. At the very least they indicate a course of action that needs to be taken to stop the alarm going off.

I recollect one case where both the engines just shut down when we were 30 miles from land. Nothing we did could solve the problem so in desperation we contacted the engine service centre by radio. There was no immediate solution offered but eventually they came back to say they thought it was the fuse. 'What fuse?' we said. 'The fuse in the computer.' There was no mention in the handbook of a fuse in the computer but we stripped the computer down and there was the fuse! Replacing it with a bit of silver paper allowed the engines to start again and I was very glad this had not happened in a dangerous navigation situation.

On another occasion I travelled to Holland for a boat test. It was a cold and frosty morning and the engine would turn over on the starter but it would not start. We eventually tried new batteries but again no joy and I went home very unhappy with the situation. It turned out that the engine computer would not let the engine be started unless the ambient temperature was above a certain level.

There are now alarm systems that allow the situation and/or the condition of the engine to be monitored from the shore. I was recently aboard a 65 footer where it was not only the engines that could be monitored but the whole boat's electrical system. This allowed the experts in the shipyard or from the installers to give advice to an owner out at sea provided, of course, that there was a phone or radio link. It can be a reassuring extension of engine monitoring but it can give a false sense of security, allowing an owner to think that he does not really have to get to know his or her boat and that help will always be at hand. Alarms, and the level at which they effect direct control over the engine, can be a mixed blessing and it pays to understand just what the alarms are indicating and what action to take.

DOUG ZURN, ZURN YACHT DESIGN

" *It was in the early 19th century that speeds exceeding 50 knots became attainable on the water, often in large commuter yachts travelling for the most part in protected waters. It wasn't until 1955 that sustainable high-speed waterborne travel could be accomplished in reasonably sized vessels both in protected and unprotected waters.*

My interest in powerboats began at a very early age when I was exposed to a Ray Hunt-designed Boston Whaler. However, most of my time on the water in my formative years was spent sailing. It's my experience in sailing, and understanding of what the ocean can dish out, that has been at the core of each one of my designs. Sailboats have taught us that form follows function. Powerboats should be no different if they are intended to be used and enjoyed, and not just be 'dock candy'. They must be designed for the clients' intended use and with a worst-case weather scenario in mind. Then just make them pretty to look at!

Hull design and construction are the foundation upon which everything rides and therefore require the most attention to produce exceptional performance. It is the reaction of the hull with the water surface it is travelling on that affects passenger comfort, and there are six motions we try to minimise as we design.

On high-speed planing hulls, the two motions that affect passenger comfort the most are surge and heave. Excessive acceleration and deceleration in these two directions contribute the most to human fatigue and make for an uncomfortable ride. Hull designs that minimise both can be achieved by means of a narrow chine width relative to length and fine entries. If you combine these with distributing the weight of the vessel over the area of the planing surface of the hull, in a manner that produces favourable bottom-loading characteristics, then you will generate a comfortable ride in most sea states.

Typical US styling on this quality cruising power yacht.

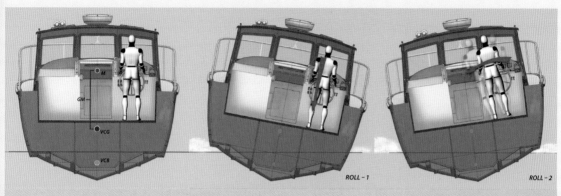

Cross section of a Doug Zurn design showing how the stability is calculated.

Roll, pitch and yaw also affect comfort. Whether the hull is designed for slower displacement speeds or high-speed planing, roll can have an adverse effect on comfort. In slow-speed displacement mode, attention must be paid to the vertical centre of gravity (VCG). The location of the VCG in conjunction with the hull's athwartships form stability set up what is known as the metacentric height (GM) of a vessel.

It is the GM that determines the hull form's roll period. The larger the GM, the shorter the roll period, which means a stiffer boat and a snappier roll motion, which is not desirable. This effect is typically found on a planing vessel.

Commercially available gyro stabilisers such as SeaKeeper were introduced to the pleasure boat market in 2008 and are an excellent solution for reducing roll by as much as 95 per cent for vessels operating at slower speeds. Roll and pitch can also affect comfort levels when vessels are on the plane, but each of these can be corrected, to some degree, with commercially available modern equipment.

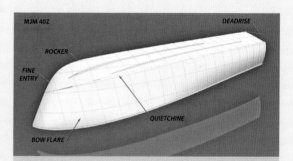

The components of a vee hull that provide quality performance.

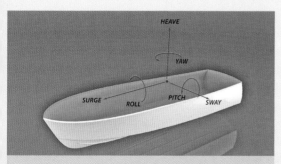

The various movements of a boat hull that have to be allowed for in a seaway.

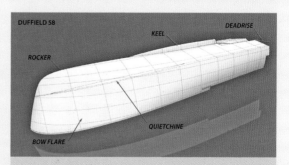

Key hull features that are designed into a production cruising yacht.

A properly designed hull for the intended purpose is still a must. A planing hull typically does not have a keel, allowing the aft end of the boat to slide out, and the boat to roll into the turn. This keeps the decks below the passenger inert and makes for a very comfortable turn. Hulls designed for semi-planing or planing speeds with keels tend to roll away from the turn, wanting to throw the passenger off the vessel.

Pitch motion may be affected by the boat's longitudinal centre of gravity (LCG) and its relationship to the planing surface of a vessel. Good design dictates that the boat's LCG remains aft of the boat's centre of lift from its planing surface. 'Porpoising' is the term used to describe the repeated pitching effect of a vessel whose LCG is further forward than its lifting surface can support. Interceptors are an effective way to reduce porpoising since they force more running surface into the water, thus moving the centre of lift back in front of the LCG. Interceptors from Humphree are available with active ride control (ARC), which will maintain a vessel's running angle while also controlling roll motions induced by waves or wind. We recommend and take advantages of modern features like these when the client's budget permits the ultimate in ride comfort.

Pitch from waves can be reduced with finer bow entries but this can also lead to a wet ride. We resolve this issue with our Quiet Chine, which incorporates a negative deadrise angle forward that transitions to a positive deadrise angle at the displacement waterline intersection, then to a horizontal orientation aft. This, in addition to reasonable bow flare, keeps spray from blowing over the bow.

Yaw and sway are the last two motions to consider when looking at the design of a vessel. On high-speed planing hulls, it's important to incorporate a moderate degree of deadrise to the bottom surface. This helps to maintain directional stability (the ability of a vessel to maintain a straight course) without compromising its ability to roll into a turn, as previously mentioned. On semi-planing and displacement vessels, deadrise angles are typically less, and small to large keels are incorporated into the design to offer directional stability. Finding the proper balance between directional stability and manoeuvrability is the key. In all cases, care must be taken not to have such a deep forefoot as to set up the potential for the bow to want to steer the vessel, especially in following seas. To prevent this from occurring, we always like to incorporate some rocker (rising of the hull when viewed in profile) into the forward sections.

We can have the best-laid plans for a successful design, but if the boat is not constructed correctly, all efforts will be in vain. Of course, budget will, in some instances, dictate to an extent material choices and construction techniques. We have been fortunate in that our clients typically have had a good understanding of what's right and what's wrong, and we design with materials that are appropriate for the task at hand. For example, for many years Kevlar was considered an exceptional material with which to build hulls, but the educated person will quickly understand that its disadvantages far outweigh its advantages. In general, it's not an easy material to laminate or repair, it is expensive, and it really doesn't

Classic Downeaster style from the Doug Zurn design.

A Downeaster semi-displacement design with a conventional sheer line.

bring much to the hull panel's strength properties. Carbon, on the other hand, is a very useful material in longitudinal stringer and deck surfaces, but its high-tensile properties are not appropriate for hull surfaces where wave impact noise can reverberate throughout the hull, unless one is willing to make that compromise. The choice of resin that holds the reinforcements together also influences performance and durability. There are three general types of resin – polyester, vinylester and epoxy – and these are arranged in order of strength and cost with the polyester being the most brittle and epoxy having the greatest elasticity to absorb impacts without fatiguing.

We discussed earlier the motions through which a boat moves and how the location of the centre of gravity (CG) has a direct impact on the effects of those motions. The CG is the centre of all weights associated with the vessel, and knowing its location ensures the vessel will perform to its designed specification. This is done by accounting for, identifying and locating all weights and materials associated with the build of the vessel.

Care must be taken to ensure the owner and builder do not exceed expectations with regards to weights and identify where compromises must be made to maintain performance expectations. In the end, the final weight of the vessel must be kept in check.

Once we have established performance goals and expectations that fall within the level of the accommodation desired, we can consider aesthetics. Aesthetics is the wrappings that initially draw us to a boat. Before we ever consider how a boat is built or what's inside, our first impressions (and the last at the end of the day) are what create the emotion within us to indulge ourselves. No one wants an ugly boat, and care must be taken to consider everything associated with the exterior of the vessel. No one thing should be out of place, for if it is, our eye is immediately drawn to it and the design as a whole is lost. There must be balance between the hull and deck surfaces, the colours chosen for those surfaces, the windows and doors associated with those surfaces, and finally, the hardware that is placed upon those surfaces. They must all function and fall together, as if one. For 25 years now we've been a resource for aesthetically pleasing yachts, bringing timeless designs to discriminating clientele in sail, and power that performs as expected.

ELECTRIC AND HYBRID BOATS

The main alternative 'fuel' to diesel and petrol for boats is electricity, and there are three main ways for small craft to operate under electric power, some more effective than others.

PURE ELECTRIC BOATS

The simplest, the pure electric boat, has been around for more than 100 years and comprises a bank of batteries that supplies power to drive the electric propulsion motor. These direct electric systems have improved dramatically since their inception in terms of practical application due to both the improvements in battery capacity and more efficient electric motors. Modern versions are starting to find favour with those who want quiet cruising over relatively short distances; with modern battery technology, it is possible to endow a boat with a range of perhaps 64km (40 miles) at low speeds. Electric boats in this category are mainly used on rivers and lakes and have been generally limited to operating at displacement speeds with close access to charging points.

The electric motor inside an electric outboard.

Speed is not impossible, however, and recent battery and motor developments have enabled some pure electric boats to reach planing speeds. Motors are also operating at higher voltages, up to around 480 volts DC, which helps to create compact, lightweight and powerful motors. Speed and weight are closely related in small planing boat design, so that the performance challenge is to install a battery pack light enough and powerful enough to allow planing speeds combined with a useful range. Hull design is also a factor and tends to be based on fuel-efficient long, thin hull designs or catamarans. With the improved technology, electric outboard-powered boats with an operating duration of about one hour at planing speeds are now viable using mainly lithium-ion batteries combined with high-voltage electric motors.

Using pure electric power on board requires a considerable change in the way you think and operate the boat; with petrol or diesel power you never really worry about running out of fuel for some reason, but on an electric boat you become very concerned when the battery charge starts to run low, because there are fewer options for recharging it: namely using shore power, and perhaps supplementing this to a limited degree by solar panels. Despite this, commercial users could see a significant future in electric propulsion and operators such as harbour authorities, whose boats only operate in a limited area and where frequent recharging is possible, could see a significant benefit in electric propulsion, though it will take some time to overcome engrained attitudes. Fast charging systems are also now

A simple electric motor inboard installation with batteries for power.

available, which could open up the electric boat market to water taxis and ferries, with charging taking place at dedicated stops.

The electric motor drive and associated wiring and control box for an electric drive.

HYBRID BOATS

The second category of electric boats uses hybrid systems. These combine diesel and electric propulsion and have the capability to switch from one to the other using the same propeller shaft; the electric motor is simply clutched in or, more likely, the diesel engine is clutched out, meaning you can go silent for short distances on battery power alone. This combination

allows the use of electric propulsion when the boat is operating in emission-sensitive areas where diesel propulsion is not acceptable. With these hybrid systems, the normal diesel engine is connected directly to the propulsion with an electric motor/generator built into the transmission. This motor/generator can be used for propulsion either to supplement the diesel power or as a standalone electric propulsion system powered by batteries, and it is also used to charge the batteries when the diesel engine is running. The switch from diesel to electric power is simple with modern control systems and much of the operation is automatically controlled. Solar panels might be added to the system if the boat design allows, to offer a free charging boost.

One of the many negative aspects of hybrids is that they add about 10 per cent to the overall cost of the boat, which could already be quite a consideration. The extra weight of the batteries required for the system can also have a detrimental effect on performance and, longer-term, there can be concern about the cost of replacement batteries. Many hybrid systems have, however, been made more effective, with diesel engine manufacturers such as Steyr and Nanni offering an electric generator/motor that fits between the engine and the gearbox. This makes for simple installation and only adds about 20cm (8in) to the overall length of the engine. Switching from diesel to electric propulsion is simple, at the flick of a switch. Propulsion manufacturers such as Reintjes and Twin Disc are also offering hybrid options with the addition of a generator/motor to their gearboxes.

A diagrammatic layout of a diesel, electric hybrid engine installation.

Despite these improvements to some modern hybrids, on a standard marine hybrid system you will not save any emissions or fuel in normal running. In special applications, such as tugs, for which there can be a wide difference in power requirements during towing and running light, the hybrid system can help with the difference, but in general, using a hybrid system could in fact burn more fuel because every time the electrical energy from the onboard generator is fed into the batteries or taken out and then used in the motor, power is lost. This makes the hybrid system generally less efficient than conventional diesel drives. If you can charge the batteries from a shore supply then you will probably get cheaper energy, but that will only last for a relatively short time, depending of course on the size of the battery bank.

Dutch hybrids at work

An example of the use of hybrid systems for workboats has come from Dutch company Waternet. Their new electric-powered multipurpose crane vessel/tug has a length of 18m (59ft) and the electrical machinery installation is contracted to Floattech. The power system selected for this vessel is a 240kW diesel generator supplying power to a bank of lithium batteries with a capacity of 13kW. Three 70kW electric motors supply the propulsion with each motor on the same common shaft.

This vessel will be used in the canals of Amsterdam for debris clearance. The designers claim that by using electric propulsion combined with the battery storage system, much better economy is possible because the generator is operating in its most efficient way. This efficiency peak is at about 85 per cent of the diesel's maximum capacity while the specific fuel consumption is up to 20 per cent more efficient than at partial load or in stationary operation. The vessel will also be a lot cleaner than its conventional counterpart and produce lower levels of emissions.

Another Dutch company, Hydrostra, has developed a combined electric motor and pod propulsion system that is being used for some tourist vessels

operating on the Amsterdam canals. This drive unit offers 100kW and provides a self-contained electric propulsion unit for simple installation. It operates on 400 volts AC and the company also has the control and power conversion systems to match.

DIESEL-GENERATED ELECTRIC POWER

The third way entails using a diesel-powered generator to provide the electrical power, which is then supplied directly to the electric motors that are the main propulsion system for the boat. This is essentially a traditional diesel electric system, but with a bank of batteries built into the circuits to offer more flexibility. With such a system there can be significant advantages:

» The generator/s can be located in any part of the boat or ship.

» A single generator could supply two propulsion motors, thereby saving on cost and space and giving design flexibility.

» A generator running at a constant speed can be more fuel-efficient than a direct-propulsion diesel, which may be optimised for a running speed different to that being used.

» You can achieve much more sensitive manoeuvring with the electric motors, which, unlike a diesel, are capable of operating from zero speed upwards.

» No gearboxes are required.

A twin electric motor installation providing power from the batteries or from a diesel powered generator.

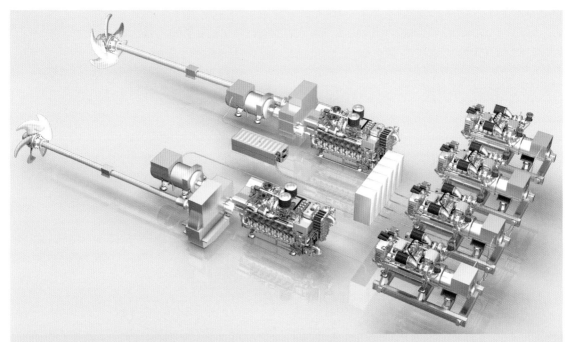

A complex hybrid electrical installation allowing a boat to be powered by diesels, electric motors and / or generators.

Just how green are electric and hybrid systems?

Electric propulsion has been hailed as the future solution for boats, but while it has its merits for some applications, it certainly is not the solution to reducing emissions that it is hailed to be. For cars, there can be a benefit to hybrids or electric drive because it allows energy to be recovered from braking and going downhill, which helps to reduce consumption. Boats, however, neither brake nor go downhill (you hope) so there is no possibility of energy recovery, so somewhere you have to pay for the energy you use. With hybrid systems, you mainly have to generate the electrical energy on board, which entails emissions from the diesel generators. With a pure electric system that only has electric motors, you have to power the batteries from shore power. Thus, while the operation of the boat itself is emission free, that shore power has to be generated somewhere, which will usually entail emissions being generated unless it can come from renewable energy sources.

Then there is the efficiency of electric systems. Every time a battery is charged, the process means about 10 per cent of the power is lost. Another 10 per cent is lost when you take the power out again, so the overall efficiency can be poor. There are also losses in the system itself through heat, and the electric motors need to be water cooled so there are more losses there. In short, don't be beguiled into thinking that you are saving the planet by going electric. It might help reduce pollution in some sensitive areas but it is not necessarily the 'clean' energy that it seems to be.

FAST ELECTRIC BOATS

For speed with electric boats there has to be a balance between weight and performance. Here, the choice is between inboard and outboard motors. Many of the more powerful electric motors used for faster electric boats have come from the road transport sector. For instance, ReGen Nautic in the USA has been a pioneer in electric propulsion and has also developed electric outboard motors of up to 300hp. These are based on existing petrol outboard motor units with the power head replaced with an electric motor. Despite this innovation, however, the business was not viable and has since closed down. Meanwhile, RIB builder Goldfish Boat in Norway has fitted one of their RIBs with a 140hp electric outboard that has reached speeds of 40 knots, combined with a practical range.

It can be a fine balance designing these planing craft, since the weight of the batteries detracts from the speed potential. The sums get better with a fully computerised control and monitoring system that should not let you run out of electric power any more than you might run out of fuel on a diesel boat. One example is the Bolt 18, built by Fairlie Yachts – a sports boat that has a 100hp inboard electric motor powered by a bank of lithium-ion batteries that give enough time on the water for pleasure and can reach speeds of 25 knots.

German company Torqeedo is offering a production electric outboard of 75hp, which could be a good match for the power requirements of a RIB or sports boat or perhaps for a rescue boat carried on board a mother ship. It hasn't been tried yet, but there could be an interesting market for an electric RIB that would have perhaps a two-hour endurance, which would be similar to the endurance of the RIB crew in rough seas. Quick recharging might be an essential characteristic, but that is possible with modern systems. This is perhaps where the future lies for electric propulsion, once the hurdles of cost and weight of the battery system stop holding back development. Another electric power development is on a lifeboat designed for installation on an offshore oil rig or platform – a concept that has now received legislative approval and prototypes are in operation.

Perhaps the ultimate electric boat so far has been developed by Cigarette Boats in the USA, working with car builder Mercedes-AMG. Their all-electric 10.7m

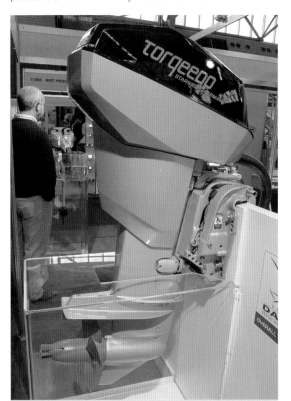

A electric outboard looks like a conventional petrol unit but here power is supplied by batteries.

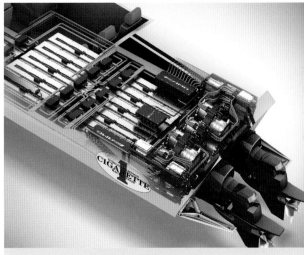

The very complex electrical installation of a Cigarette sports boat to allow 100 mph performance.

(35ft) planing sports boat can reach speeds of 160km/h (100mph) powered by electric motors totalling 2,200hp. It features six electric motors, similar to those used on the Mercedes-Benz hybrid cars, coupled to each shaft via a star-shaped gearbox and then to the sterndrive propulsion. The lithium-ion battery capacity is enough for half an hour of running at the top speed and with one hour of cruising at 113km/h (70mph), while still leaving enough power to get the boat back to harbour. The cost is prohibitive for the general marketing of a boat of this type, but this concept boat does show what is possible with all-electric propulsion, which is moving into a new world of high performance.

AC powerhouses

The secret of these electric developments lies partly in the use of electric motors that operate at around 400 volts AC. At this voltage, the motors are very compact – Siemens' 200hp electric motor, for instance, is just 50cm (20in) long and 20cm (8in) in diameter – and relatively lightweight, and require smaller-diameter wiring. They do, however, need water cooling to take away the excess heat, which can complicate the installation, but they are now a viable proposition. The AC motors can be controlled by frequency modulation, which has reduced power losses, and the whole installation is computer controlled with a read-out of power and range left at any time.

Factors to take into account are that 400 volts AC is a very high voltage to install in a boat, so the fitting has to be very well engineered for safety. The price tag is another issue in electric boat development and there are many potential owners who find it hard to justify the extra cost against somewhat vague operating benefits.

BATTERIES

Virtually all of the electric boats on the water today use lithium-ion batteries, which are lighter and more efficient than traditional lead-acid batteries. They can also be charged rapidly and do not deteriorate in the same way as lead-acid batteries, although they need to be renewed probably every seven years, depending on their use. To produce the high voltages required in modern installations, a large number of cells has to be connected in series and then the direct current from the batteries has to be converted into AC for the motor, but this is a compact and automatic technology these days.

The cost of these lithium-ion batteries has come down considerably over the past two years, largely because of competition from Chinese imports and more extensive use of them in road vehicles, where much of the development is taking place. There is a fire risk with large battery banks, but this is being overcome with built-in detection and extinguishing systems, and lithium iron-phosphate batteries are claimed to be safer.

The battery installation has to be carried out to the highest standards.

SUPERCAPACITORS

A variety of alternative battery types are under development and one promising avenue that offers an alternative to batteries for some applications could be supercapacitors. One of the first uses of capacitors in the marine world is on a 24m (79ft) French ferry – an all-electric vessel that has supercapacitors to store the electrical energy in place of the normal battery systems, with a considerable saving in weight and cost. This new ferry is designed to operate on a short route of just a couple of miles across the river at Lorient with rapid charging at either end. Its design and its innovative electrical propulsion system have been carried out under a research programme called Ecorizon R&D. Builders STX Lorient and Stirling Design International were involved in the development work.

The supercapacitor electrical storage system is an extension of the technology found in energy-recovery systems such as that used on some road vehicles and on Formula 1 cars in their KERS system. These store the energy that would normally be lost due to braking and make it available for powering electric motors when acceleration is required. On marine applications there is no opportunity for energy recovery but on the ferry application the supercapacitors can be recharged very quickly, every time the vessel docks, providing enough power for the vessel to complete a short crossing.

The capacitors are much smaller and lighter than batteries and, crucially they should not need to be replaced at regular intervals, unlike batteries. However, they are only suitable for high discharge rates over a short period. On the ferry application, solar panels are installed on the deck above the saloon to supplement the capacitor power and a diesel-powered generator has been installed with adequate power to propel the vessel, offering more operational flexibility when the vessel is used for cruising operations.

HULL SHAPE

Many electric boats are being based on fuel-efficient hulls, which is fine for specialised applications but it immediately suggests that electric propulsion is not viable for general use. One example of how hull design and electric propulsion have to be considered in tandem comes from French company Remora, which has developed an electric RIB specifically designed for harbour and marina use. Based on a 6.45m (21ft) trimaran hull for efficiency and stability, this boat can operate all day on one electric charge. The Remora also offers pollution-free operation while being completely silent, which means that it can operate in sensitive areas. Its low draft and height clearance allow it to access all parts of a marina or port. The two 4kW propulsion pods are installed in the outer hulls of the trimaran so that they allow good manoeuvrability. These are steerable pods with the motors housed in the hub of the pod.

CONCLUSION

Electric propulsion is undergoing rapid change and its use is expanding. British company Amberjack has new lithium-ion batteries under development that use nano technology to improve both efficiency and the power/weight ratio. Improved batteries and/or capacitors are

An electric motor powering a pod drive.

the key to improved efficiency and it is their weight and capacity that can often be the determining factor for electrical viability. For many workboat applications, there are also increasing demands for reducing emissions, which is helping to make electric propulsion a viable option. Cost, however, is the one factor that may deter more extensive use of electric power, especially in the leisure sector where an owner might spend large amounts on luxury accommodation but much less on going green. Despite this, increased demands for green operations, particularly in ports, could be a factor that may overcome this cost hurdle. Electric propulsion still has a long way to go, but we are seeing the momentum growing for wider adoption.

VAN OOSSANEN NAVAL ARCHITECTS

"

Van Oossanen Naval Architects, based in Wageningen in the Netherlands, are most famous for their designs of large motor yachts and their pioneering work in high-performance sailing during the last century. Less well known is the fact that the company often carries out hull optimisation studies for other naval architects throughout the shipbuilding industry, and also designs many smaller powerboats.

Niels Moerke of Van Oossanen commented: 'On our smaller powerboats, we use exactly the same rigorous optimisation process as we do on large yachts. To do this, we extensively use our in-house capabilities for Computational Fluid Dynamics (CFD). One might say this is overdone for a small motor yacht, but we believe the opposite. Very often these boats are built in series, so the accumulated running hours and fuel consumption can be much more than that of a single large superyacht.'

At Van Oossanen, about 20–30 per cent of the labour time and the CPU time are spent every year on research and development. This has led to innovations such as the Hull Vane and the Fast Displacement Hull Form, both of which are now widely used in the yachting sector and are gaining ground in the commercial sector (ferries and patrol boats). Innovation is a necessity to the company, and this also helps in attracting the right people, who combine technical expertise with curiosity. The goal is always to improve the performance of vessels, while maintaining the safety standards. Improved efficiency usually has pleasant side-effects, such as a quieter ship and improved seakeeping.

One of Van Oossanen's classic semi-displacement powerboat designs.

A semi-displacement cruiser fitted with a hull vane.

The Hull Vane is often called the 'underwater spoiler', as it very much resembles the wing on high-performance cars, albeit mounted upside down under the aft ship. It was invented by Dr Peter van Oossanen, the founder of the company, and uses the hydrodynamic lift force generated by a hydrofoil on ships and boats that are in the sub-planing speed range. Since its commercial launch in 2014, the Hull Vane has been applied on a number of yachts, ranging from 9–42m (30–138ft) and commercial ships ranging from 25–55m (82–180ft). The reduced wake and power result in a quieter ship, and the dampening of the pitching motions softens the ride in head seas. While many builders offer the Hull Vane as an option, several builders are now including it as standard on their newest series, as it allows them to reach a given speed and range with less installed power and consequently reduced tank capacity.

The Fast Displacement Hull Form (FDHF) was developed by Perry van Oossanen, son of Peter van Oossanen and now owner of the company, together with Niels Moerke. The original goal was to develop a hull form that would bridge the gap between a typical round-bilge displacement hull form and a hard-chine planing hull form. A long-term client of Van Oossanen, Heesen Yachts, had both hull types in its range, but in addition to the complexity of managing two ranges, it always posed a difficult question for clients: 'Do I want a light and fast (semi-planing) hull with more noise, less comfort in waves and mediocre low-speed performance, or do I go for a steel-hulled long range, comfortable go-anywhere yacht with a limited top speed?' Van Oossanen took that round-bilge hull form as the basis, but with extensive work in

A powerful reverse sheer on this cruiser design.

Innovative styling on this sports cruiser.

CFD, optimised it for a higher top speed. Throughout the speed range, the vessel remains in the displacement mode, which is noticeable by the absence of running trim (the bow riding up) and the absence of a hump in the resistance curve. As a result, a FDHF vessel can be sailed comfortably and efficiently at any speed within its speed range, contrary to many semi-displacement yachts, which seem to run uphill at some speeds.

Following the success of the FDHF in large yachts, the concept was further tweaked for smaller yachts, below 25m (82ft). As these typically sail at a higher speed/length ratio, this is usually without a bulbous bow, but the main characteristics remain. Most noticeable is the reduced transom immersion. Low-cruising-speed vessels with a large transom immersion drag a deep hole in the water, creating a massive stern wave. An FDHF does not rely on lift generated by the hull form, but uses trim wedges, interceptors or a Hull Vane to do this, resulting in much better half-speed performance. While FDHF seems to imply a specific hull form, the hull form is always very much adapted to each vessel, depending on its weight and speed range.

Perry van Oossanen: 'We very much believe in the custom-design and custom-build approach. More than a decade ago, it made perfect sense to use proven designs, as the performance prediction methods, including model testing, were not always accurate. Nowadays, the risk of a new design is mitigated through our very detailed weight estimates and the use of Computational Fluid Dynamics. Our clients for large motor yachts typically only find a half-knot speed margin from our predictions, even on novel concepts, such as the 70 FDHF Galactica Supernova, which has a bulbous bow, two propellers and a water jet to reach a 30-knot top speed. The new series in the powerboat segment are now also much

more diverse than before, with each series catering for clients with their own requirements for speed, range and seakeeping. This lends itself very much to our "design-for-purpose" approach. Each design is a complex mix of build material, propulsion systems, hull shape and seakeeping devices. Every choice you make inevitably has a trade-off in another area, for example a higher top speed will require bigger engines and reduced hull weight, meaning a less quiet boat. At the same time, every client has their own top speed requirement, which they find the minimum acceptable to do what they want to do.'

After the economic downturn around 2010, a number of yachtbuilders in the Netherlands saw the demand for motor yachts in the sub-25m (82ft) category picking up again. Due to the crisis, few new series had been developed, but they couldn't offer their clients the decade-old designs any more. With environmental awareness on the increase, clients wanted powerboats that could do the same (or more) with less energy consumption. Several European builders now offer FDHF motor yachts in their range, and these yachts have received industry awards for their efficiency.

Niels Moerke said: 'We are all hydrodynamics geeks in the office. When you look at the optimisation efforts done for Formula 1 cars or America's Cup sailing yachts, you see that a lot can be gained by optimising further. We continuously try to push this high-performance spirit, not only for our yacht projects, but also for the commercial ships we work on. While diesel engines are still unavoidable for most yacht projects, due to their power density and cost-effectiveness, we feel that anything we win now on resistance reduction will make a future transition to a different (more costly, heavy and voluminous) source of energy much easier.'

The typical 'rooster' tail of surface drive as the boat comes onto the plane.

PROPULSION: THE KEY TO PERFORMANCE

You can have the most powerful engines in the world in your boat, but unless that power can be transmitted to the water in the form of thrust then you are going nowhere. Put simply, the propulsion of a boat is the key to performance. What's more, if your aim is to reduce emissions and their impact on the planet then it is very important to translate the maximum amount of the engine power available into forward thrust. The propeller has been the gold standard for propulsion over the years but there are now several alternative ways of using them to increase efficiency, as well as alternative systems, such as water jets.

PROPELLER SIZE AND CLEARANCE SPECIFICATIONS

With displacement hulls, the propeller is not under a lot of pressure, and compared with planing boats, they tend to turn a lot more slowly. Much depends on the size of the aperture available in which to house the propeller. For tugs and fishing boats that have to pull heavy loads, for instance, a large, slower-turning propeller is the best solution, provided of course that there is space. On displacement hulls, draft is often the limiting factor, especially since we are seeing fewer and fewer boats with the deep-draft hulls of old. A clean water flow around the propeller helps its efficiency and to avoid interference with this, minimum clearances are specified for the aperture in which the propeller operates. The usual figure for propeller clearances is one-fifth of the diameter of the propeller, but this is often narrowed down in the interests of compact design requirements. On twin-screw boats, there is more freedom because the propellers are located on either side of the skeg and the only clearance required is between the propeller and the bottom of the hull, but again this should be as generous as possible for efficiency.

MAXIMISING EFFICIENCY

For a propeller to be efficient the shaft should be horizontal, which may be possible with a single-screw installation but not with twin-screws, for which the shaft has to emerge from the hull bottom at an angle. There is a trend towards introducing semi-tunnels into twin-screw hulls since these allow the propeller to be fitted higher under the hull and for the propeller shaft to be more horizontal. This also has the benefit of reducing the draft and offering better protection for the propellers. Because this shaft and its supports – either a P or an A bracket – are in the water flow going to the propeller, they disturb this flow. This means that whatever the installation, the propeller efficiency is a considerable way from perfect. With outboard and sterndrive installation, you don't get this shaft and support problem, but then you have the larger propeller hub to contend with, which creates its own form of water-flow interference, although in this case the design will have been fine-tuned in test tanks to optimise its shape.

A comparison between the 'cleaver' surface drive propeller on the left and the conventional propeller on the right.

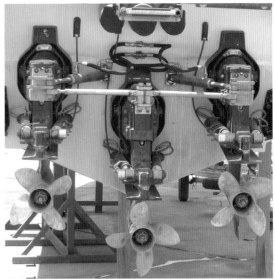

A triple stern drive propeller boat.

It is only in recent times when the focus is much more on fuel economy that the efficiency of the propeller on displacement hulls has been really considered. Much more time will normally be spent on optimising the design of the propeller itself – a highly specialised job because there are so many variables involved. The speed of turning of the propeller is one aspect, and then there's the number and shape of the blades, the diameter of the propeller and its pitch – the angle of the blades that act like a screw cutting its way through the water. All of these factors have a bearing on the efficiency of the propeller and this is a job for the specialist. Once fitted, most of these factors cannot be changed short of fitting a new propeller and on production boats it may take trials with a few different propellers to find the optimum one for efficiency.

To achieve this, it is not unknown for the propeller blades to be ground down around the leading edge to reduce the area of the blade when a propeller proves to be oversize, but this is not good practice and can lead to unbalanced propellers and vibration. Even with carefully designed and cast propellers, the balance of the propeller is not always good and the blades are not always equal in shape and pitch, although modern techniques have vastly improved the quality of propellers and reduced the chance of vibration developing. Most good propeller makers will get close to the optimum, but getting it just right can be an expensive and time-consuming job that can probably

only be justified when a run of production boats is involved. It is much easier to achieve optimum efficiency with outboards and sterndrives, for which the diameter is usually fixed, and standard replacement propellers are normally available with varying pitches, blade numbers and blade shapes.

PROPELLERS ON PLANING BOATS

These same comments about propellers apply to planing boats of course, and here the choice of propeller can be more critical. Not only do you want to maximise the top speed but you also want a propeller that can produce good thrust at lower speeds to get the boat on to the plane quickly and to provide economical performance at the cruising speed, rather than necessarily optimising the top speed. However, top speed *is* always a factor and is usually the focus for the designer and the salesman. With planing hulls, there are more options available for the propulsion systems, although the conventional shaft and propeller is still a favourite for many designers and builders.

Again, the shaft angle is important and this has to be considered along with the location of the engine and its effect on the centre of gravity. When I started powerboat racing, there was a spate of new designs for which two powerful engines were installed and connected to a single gearbox with the single propeller shaft emerging at quite a steep angle to a propeller located as far aft as possible. The thinking behind this was to keep the propeller in the water for as long as possible when the hull was flying out of the water. The shaft angle might have been perhaps 20 degrees and, if the boat were pitching into a head sea, it might rise another 10 degrees, so the propeller had a hard time developing any thrust in the required horizontal direction. Only a propeller operating on a horizontal shaft has the effective angle of pitch it was designed for, yet on these highly angled shafts there was effectively a different angle of pitch on the downward blade than that of the upward blade, which is certainly not the most efficient solution.

A common arrangement that allows the engine to be located fairly well aft is to have the drive at the front end of the engine, where the shaft line is then dropped down by a reverse/reduction vee-drive gearbox that has the propeller shaft emerging at its lower part with the shaft running back under the engine. This can reduce the shaft angle and still keep the engine weight well aft. These days, since the location of the engine weight might not be so critical, the arrangement is still used simply to place the engine aft, away from the accommodation. Many modern production hulls that offer speeds of 25–40 knots are now fitted with the semi-tunnel arrangement to accommodate the propellers more into the hull and offer a shallower angle for the propeller shaft when conventional drive systems are used.

Twin propellers where the propellers operate in semi-tunnels to reduce the draft and give a more horizontal shaft angle.

This question of shaft angle is important to propulsion efficiency and this can be judged by the fact that both outboards and sterndrive legs have a trim function that allows their shaft angle to be adjusted when underway. At rest, the shaft angle is horizontal and as the boat rises on to the plane and the trim of the boat changes, this trim adjustment allows the shaft line to be maintained in the near-horizontal plane. It is factors like this that make outboards and sterndrives a practical alternative to shaft drive for planing boats and they probably offer greater efficiency despite the added complication and the power losses of the drive shaft configuration where it has to have bevel gears to get the drive to the propeller.

Counter-rotating propellers on an outboard.

Propeller cavitation

With planing hulls, the propeller(s) are operating at a more critical level and the shape of the blades tends to be more important to avoid cavitation problems. Cavitation on a propeller is the formation of tiny bubbles on areas of the blade surface that lessen the 'bite' of the propeller in the water and reduce the efficiency of the propeller. It tends to occur initially at the blade tips and can actually cause erosion of the metal of the blade. However, with modern design and a clearer understanding of the causes, propeller cavitation is now largely under control and good propeller design allows these fully submerged propellers to be effective up to speeds of around 40 knots, which covers the vast majority of production planing hulls.

BLADES

Blade shape has changed quite considerably in modern times and there appears to be a constant refinement of their design, aided by the ability to try them out in test tanks. For instance, we are now seeing quite highly skewed blades on larger hulls, whereby the tip of one blade overlaps the blade area of the adjacent ones.

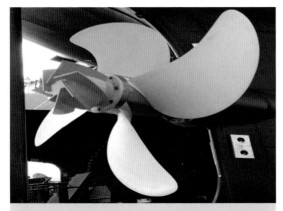

A composite propeller fitted to this displacement hull.

Other blade concepts include the rounded blade tip, a straight edge on the trailing side of the blade, and a raised ridge along the trailing edge of the blade to help deflect the water cleanly away from the blade, something that trials showed could lead to greater efficiency. A couple of boatbuilders duly adopted this latter technology, though it is not widely used.

The thickness of the blades is another factor. As propellers are required to transmit more and more power from the engine to the water as thrust, the stresses on the blades have grown higher and so there has been a need to increase their thickness to ensure they have adequate strength. Materials have also changed and the traditional bronze used for propellers is now often replaced with high-tensile stainless steel. Another new development is 3-D printed propellers. The first ones were made from a durable plastic, but the techniques have since been refined and the first 3-D printed metal propellers are under trial. Composite propellers have also been used as a replacement for metal and, again, they have worked well but have not proved a commercial success so far. The number of

blades on the propeller is changing, too, and whereas three blades was previously the standard, we are now seeing four- and even five-bladed propellers. An odd number of blades seems to be preferred, and is claimed to reduce vibration.

SURFACE-PIERCING PROPELLERS

When I started offshore powerboat racing, the first experiments with surface propellers or, to give them their full name, surface-piercing propellers, were taking place. It has long been recognised that fully submerged propellers could be operated well beyond their theoretical limits when cavitation was the limiting factor. Supercavitating propellers were thus developed, which could operate effectively well into the cavitation zone when higher speeds were required. With surface propellers, this was taken one stage further by using ones for which only the bottom blades were in the water doing the work, while the top blades were in the air, or at least in the spray zone at the water surface. The theory was that since it was the bottom blades that were doing most of the work anyway, because the flow of water to the top blades was affected by the shaft and its support brackets, why not take these top blades out of the water and let the bottom blades do all the work?

This approach required a considerable rethink of propeller design because cavitation was now not a problem and the blade shape and style could be optimised for power

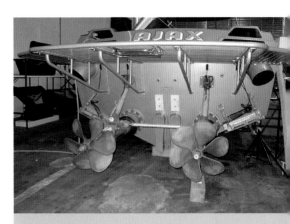

Six-bladed propellers fitted to the Arneson Drives of this Magnum.

transmission. At the same time, the stresses on the propeller were dramatically increased; you can imagine the stress when a propeller blade is transmitting several hundred horsepower while it is in the water and then transmitting no power at all when it in the air, and this load cycle happens perhaps 2,000 times per minute. Making the propeller strong enough was therefore the main challenge faced by the propeller designers. To solve the problem, not only was forged stainless steel used, but the cross-section of the blade, particularly near the hub, was also much thicker. Even then there was the fatigue of the constant loading and unloading of the blade to overcome, and shedding a propeller blade when racing was a not uncommon problem.

There was also the issue of getting the boat on to the plane. At slow speeds, the fixed surface propeller is fully immersed, so when power is applied it struggles to absorb this power because all of the blades are in the water and cannot break free. This results in the propeller being very overloaded, and this does not allow the engine to turn fast enough for the turbochargers to start working, so there is reduced power to get the boat moving.

We experienced just this when we launched the first *Virgin Atlantic Challenger* and on the first trials it would only do 8 knots! We realised we had to ventilate the propeller, introducing air in front of it, which would reduce the loading on the propeller and allow it to spin faster and get things moving. We therefore rigged temporary air inlet pipes to start with and then when

A early Arneson Drive installation with cross steering hydraulic control.

that worked, set up fixed air ventilation pipes, after which the speed went up to more than 50 knots.

These days, with fixed surface propeller installations that are integrated into the hull, it is usually the engine exhaust that is used to ventilate the propeller but this has to be installed carefully to stop the water running back up the exhaust when going astern. With articulated surface drives, such as the Arneson, you actually lift the propeller partly out of the water to reduce the loading and so get it moving and allow the engine to increase rpm as the boat comes on to the plane.

Nevertheless, surface-piercing propellers were and are used. They tend to be aggressive-looking, with very sharp leading edges and a sharp cut-off on the trailing edge, often with a lip to accelerate the water away from the blade at the final moment. It is normal to find surface propellers with an odd number of blades, perhaps three or five, as this reduces the vibration that can be associated with surface drives. With an even number of blades, one will be coming out of the water as another enters and this is what can cause the vibration; with an odd number of blades, there is a more even balance of the loadings.

SURFACE DRIVE SYSTEMS

These are usually bolt-on units rather than involving the propeller and its shaft just emerging from the transom. There are quite a few on the market today, but the pioneer was the Arneson Surface Drive. This was a complex piece of engineering that introduced a universal joint into the shaft line that allowed the final section of the shaft to be angled both vertically and horizontally, with control of the movement by hydraulic rams. The vertical movement was to lift the propeller from its fully immersed harbour manoeuvring mode so that the boat would get on to the plane and let the propeller operate in full surface-piercing mode with the hub at the water surface level. The horizontal movement allowed the propeller thrust to be used for steering, thus taking away the need for a rudder. The patent on the Arneson expired a few years ago and there have since been several lookalike systems introduced mainly by Italian firms. The best known of these though is the SDS from France Helices, which has all the controls and

Six-bladed propellers on these Arneson Drives for a performance boat.

Fixed Trimax Drives with spade rudders have proved to be one of the most reliable of surface drives.

hydraulics inside the boat rather than being exposed to the elements, as they are on the Arneson.

The Levi Drive was developed by Sonny Levi, who was involved in the early days of surface drives. It used a fixed shaft for reliability and the propeller was surrounded by a U-shaped nozzle that helped to contain much of the spray that was a feature of the Arneson Surface Drive. Its attraction was that it was a bolt-on transom unit with integral steering, but it could be a challenge to get the boat on to the plane, as we found when they were used on the second Virgin boat and she was heavy with fuel.

The Trimax Surface Drive was developed by Fabio Buzzi, and it had a subtle difference: there was a universal joint in the drive shaft and this allowed the shaft angle to be optimised for performance. Once optimised, the shaft was then locked in place and rudders were used for steering. It required a modified hull design and, in later versions, had special flaps added to assist planing. It proved to be a highly efficient and reliable surface drive system and it took the delicate task of adjusting the height of the drive shaft out of the hands of the driver.

There is no doubt that the surface drive systems are more efficient when speeds of over about 40 knots are required, but because of this and their added complication they are only a small part of the fast-boat propulsion market. In one test example, two matching 60-footers were compared: one with surface drives and

one with conventional shaft and propellers, but both with the same engines, hull design and weight. The surface drive version was some 8 knots faster at speeds above 40 knots.

A SeaRex surface drive where the drive trim is operated by the hydraulic cylinder.

CONTROLLABLE PITCH (CP) PROPELLERS

As the name suggests, the pitch of the blades for these propellers can be varied when under way. They have been used for a long time, mainly for specialised applications and only on displacement hulls. This is because the operating mechanism to vary the blade angle is mainly inside the propeller hub, so a fairly large hub is required, which reduces the efficiency. Furthermore, there can never be the same strength in the unit as there would be with a solid-cast propeller. The advantages are that they can be optimised for the load and speed, although the use of these propellers suggests that the advantages are limited and the added cost and complication cannot be justified. CP propellers for planing boats have been tried, but here the high stresses of the installation are not conducive to good reliability.

CONTRA-ROTATING PROPELLERS

Contra-rotating propellers are another option and there is no doubt that they improve the propulsion efficiency, possibly by as much as 10 per cent. However, again, there is the added complication and cost of the system and the challenge of finding the right propeller sizes for the job. Despite this, we are seeing contra-rotating propellers used on sterndrives, and integrated into many of the new pod drive systems that are coming on to the powerboat market. Getting the two propellers running in opposite directions is a simple matter of additional gearing and an extra shaft, and it is argued that the benefits outweigh this slight extra complication.

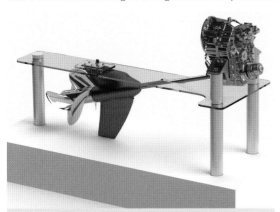

ZF's Project Disruption which comprises contra-rotating propellers on a standard shaft drive.

POD DRIVE SYSTEMS

Pod drives are gaining ground as a viable propulsion system for planing powerboats and the Volvo Penta IPS Drive has led the way here. These IPS drives fit under the hull rather than on the transom, so the propulsion point is moved forwards under the hull and the propellers are at the forward end of the drive. This has led to hull design complications. For instance, when I was testing one of the early installations of the Volvo Penta IPS drive, the hull adopted a 10-degree list when running at speed – something that the boatbuilders had tried to correct by fitting an automatic trim system, in the hope the problem would not surface during the trials. When you put propellers under the hull well forward of the transom, and with forward-facing propellers, they tend to suck the water from under the hull and I think this was what led to the instability experienced. Wide chines can help to correct this, but then of course you get a harsher ride. Nothing is simple when it comes to fast-boat propulsion. These days, Volvo Penta has hull design specifications to be followed when these drives are fitted.

Other pod drives, such as the Zeus, are transom mounted and drive in the conventional way with the CP propellers aft, and as far as I know they work well. The advantage of these pod drives is the exceptional manoeuvrability because they can rotate through 360 degrees and direct the thrust in any direction. This makes them perfect for joystick control, whereby you simply point the joystick in the direction you want the boat to move and the computer makes the necessary settings. You can get much the same excellent manoeuvrability with conventional propulsion combined with bow and stern thrusters that enable the boat to be moved very precisely even in strong winds and tides. These joystick controls are becoming very sophisticated, with the autopilot and the GPS linked in so that you can maintain a set heading and even a set position using the GPS as a position reference.

The problem is that once you have manoeuvred a boat with one of these joystick controls it is very hard to revert back to normal manoeuvring using the gears, throttle and steering, and I find it sad to think that many of these traditional boat-handling skills will be lost. However, I am sure that the insurance companies will be happy because of reduced accidents, or will helmsmen take more chances and place too much reliance on the computer systems? When you have seen the computer fail at a critical manoeuvring moment you tend to get a bit cautious about using them, but I still love them. Now Volvo Penta is amongst those developing an automatic docking system that does all the work for you, judging distances off and safe clearances so all you need to do is attach the lines...

Larger pod drive systems are coming on to the market, some of which are capable of handling power outputs of more than 1,000hp. Some of these fit under the hull while others are transom mounted; one unit produced by Rolls-Royce uses composite mouldings in its construction, marking a departure from convention.

ELECTRIC POD DRIVES

With interest growing in electric propulsion there is an alternative type of pod drive: the electric pod drive. This consists of an electric motor for driving the propeller, which is inside the hub of the unit and directly connected to the propeller – the same system that is used as a propulsion unit for some of the big

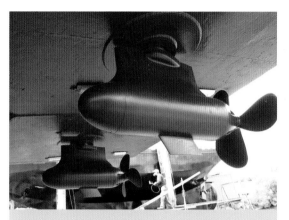

Twin fully azimuthing electric pod drives offer exceptional manoeuvrability.

cruise ships. It represents the ultimate in simplicity for propulsion systems and is both efficient and practical, and by being able to rotate through 360 degrees, it is perfect for manoeuvring as well. Furthermore, the electric motor does not need cooling as it is surrounded by water. At present, the power is limited to about 40hp maximum, which might work for a displacement hull, but they are almost certainly going to become more powerful and to be used more widely.

More powerful electric outboards are another option and are now available with powers of more than 100hp, so when we get the batteries sorted out and adequate power available, this could be the solution for the future.

WATER-JET PROPULSION

Another and very versatile option for propulsion is the water jet. First developed nearly 100 years ago, water-jet propulsion has been refined over the years but has never hit the mainstream, except as the propulsion unit for jetskis and some small yacht tenders, as well as in rescue craft and lifeboats that may have to operate in shallow water areas and where casualties might be in the water. Commercial and military RIBs also use water jets a lot, and there seems to be a very happy marriage between water jet propulsion and RIBs.

The main attraction is safety, because there are no exposed moving parts, but the water jet is never quite as efficient as a well-designed propeller system and the relatively high cost and the increased weight and

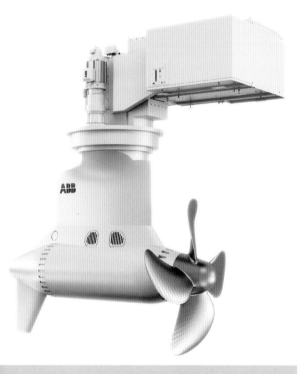

A fully azimuthing propulsion pod drive where the electric motor is contained in the hub.

complication are probably what has prevented wider use. The additional weight mainly comes about because the weight of the water contained inside the jet tunnel has to be added to the weight of the boat itself when it comes to propulsion calculations.

Where the water jet scores is its ability to cope with a wide range of loadings, so it works well on boats for which the weight of the boat varies considerably. An example of this was *Azimut Atlantic Challenger*, which was an Atlantic record boat that set out to make the record crossing without refuelling. This 80-footer was loaded with 80 tonnes of fuel when we set out from New York – twice the weight of the boat in fuel! – and would do 29 knots when fully loaded, increasing to more than 50 knots when the tanks were close to empty.

The standard water jet has the engine running in the same direction and in gear at all times when it is in use, and steering is accomplished by moving the steering nozzle to direct the thrust. For reverse, a 'bucket' or deflector is lowered over the exiting water and serves to redirect it forwards under the boat. You can engage reverse at full throttle with quite dramatic results as the bow of the boat dips considerably and the boat comes to a rapid halt.

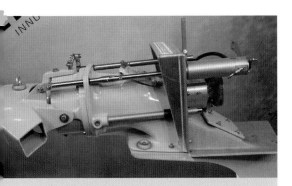

A small boat water jet unit with the operating hydraulics inside the boat.

Manoeuvring with water jets is very impressive once you understand what you are trying to do. It is the reverse that tends to confuse most people and more so when you have twin jets. Like the pods and conventional systems, most jet manufacturers have developed joystick control systems that do most of the thinking for you and allow

The water inlet on a water jet propelled hull.

you to park the boat in tight spaces. I drove one water-jet boat where not only could the jet be directed for steering and reverse but also to adjust the trim of the hull by directing the exiting water up or down. It certainly worked, but it was complicated and I found that you did not have enough hands to use this trim control effectively as well as operating the other controls.

Some outboard manufacturers offer a water-jet version of their outboards. This is achieved by removing the lower unit and replacing it with a pump that has a simple reverse bucket over the nozzle. You lose quite a bit of efficiency with this solution, but it can be a useful adaptation for perhaps a rescue boat or some workboats. Another innovation was a transom bolt-on package that comprised a compact diesel engine coupled to a water jet, which was an alternative to the diesel outboard. However, with the advent of viable diesel outboards, this solution has left the market.

CONCLUSION

As we said at the beginning of this chapter, the propulsion system is the key to performance. Given that there are so many alternative systems now on the market, finding the right system can be challenging. This is probably why certainly the major boatbuilders and most of the smaller ones tend to stick to the tried-and-tested systems of shafts and propellers. Here, I have mentioned most of the basic systems, but among those there are a large number of alternative ones developed by people who are looking for great efficiency but rarely greater simplicity. In boats in general, and fast boats in particular, keeping it simple is the solution that usually pays off in the long run.

LORNE CAMPBELL, LORNE CAMPBELL DESIGN

"High-speed planing craft, both mono and multihull, increasingly use stepped hulls. These are defined as planing hulls, incorporating one or more transverse steps across the bottom, and the theoretical advantage is that they gain speed by reducing hydrodynamic drag and improve pitch control in a seaway.

The idea of stepped hulls (and planing) was first mooted in the 1870s by the Reverend C Ramus, but remained a dream because of the high weight of available power units. In 1908, William Henry Fauber of Chicago, USA, took out a patent for a multi-step planing hull, following which a number of designers/builders started trying such hulls. These included the 40-knot World War I Coastal Motor Boats (CMB), which had single stepped hulls.

LOAD CARRYING

An important design aspect of early craft was their weight distribution. Relatively heavy engines were placed close to amidships with long shafts driving submerged propellers. This put the longitudinal centre of gravity (LCG) close to amidships so the step, also close to amidships, of a stepped hull carried most of the weight; the stern acted mainly as a trim-control surface. They could be fast and efficient at a specific designed weight, which was fine for racing but caused problems with load-carrying craft.

Hull lift depends on bottom pressure times lifting area, but pressure itself depends on the surface angle of attack

A close up of the Bladerunner hull.

and the speed (squared). Unfortunately, the central LCG of these earlier hulls caused the laden main step to sink faster than the stern, the reduced angle of attack largely offsetting the increased lifting area, so a relatively small increase in weight caused a large drag increase and performance reduction. Most World War II fast boats avoided steps to allow for a variable payload and reasonable off-plane performance.

Since the introduction of sterndrives and large outboard motors, engine and other weight has been concentrated aft, and hulls are designed around an aft LCG position that allows much better load-carrying and opening opportunities to take advantage of steps.

PERFORMANCE

A gain in performance of around 8–12 per cent can be obtained from using steps, compared with similar non-stepped hulls, by reducing hull resistance. The two main components of hydrodynamic drag are: wave-making resistance due to the water being thrown aside; and the friction of water on the hull. With speed increase, the wave-making resistance reduces as a percentage of the whole while skin friction increases. Frictional drag is proportional to wetted surface area and minimising this is of major importance, which is where steps help.

An increase of bottom pressure means less area is needed. The pressure is not evenly distributed: it is highest at the leading edge of the contact patch where water is first 'kicked down'. This only happens once with a non-stepped hull, and aft of that point water just scrapes along the bottom causing frictional drag but much less lift pressure. A stepped hull has more high-pressure 'leading edges' but less length of inefficient surface behind them. Thus, the average pressure over a stepped hull is increased, reducing the wetted area and, therefore, hydrodynamic skin friction.

With their pitch-stabilising influence, stepped hulls have increased resistance to porpoising, gaining further efficiency by being able to run surfaces at higher angles of attack than a non-stepped hull. The pressure increase of a higher angle gains a further advantage in wetted-area reduction.

Steps require ventilation to avoid suction; lack of an air feed can cause the step face to stay wetted and drag an enormous quantity of water, which kills performance. Air normally feeds from the chine, which is often opened up to encourage this. Sometimes, a craft that performs well at speed can struggle to start planing from lack of step ventilation. Measures such as trunked air to step-face outlets are then needed. Intermittent non-ventilation can cause drag to one side or the other giving erratic coursekeeping and speed.

Early craft had low-deadrise hulls – 5 or 10 degrees was common – to get the lift needed with a relatively low power-to-weight ratio. Since Ray Hunt and Sonny Levi, higher deadrise has become the norm to reduce shocks in a seaway, but this increases drag for the same lift. However, the performance advantage with steps remains.

Steps are not worth incorporating for low planing speeds. An 8m (26.2ft)-waterline hull would need to manage over 30–35 knots, for example, and the larger the boat the higher this threshold. At lower speeds, friction is less important and more bottom area is required to carry the weight, due to reduced pressure. Also, steps give higher drag when operating off-plane.

DIRECTIONAL STABILITY, STEP SIZE AND POSITION

Gaining performance through steps but maintaining safety is a compromise. Broadly, the deeper and/or further aft the step(s) are positioned, the greater the drag reduction but the less the directional stability. Directional stability requires the lateral centre of pressure (CPL) to be aft of the LCG. CPL is approximately the centroid of the wetted area of the hull looked at side on.

With a modern non-stepped hull, the planing underwater profile is a long triangle with the deepest part at the transom, so CPL is about one-third of its length forward of the transom. The skegs of sterndrives and rudders will move the CPL further aft. A stepped hull has a number of smaller triangles and the LCG of a twin-stepped hull would normally be a little forward of the aft step. You can imagine that very deep steps would largely shield the surface adjacent to the transom, thus the planing

A stepped RIB hull designed by Lorne Campbell.

underwater profile would have two largish triangles forward and one very small, or non-existent triangle, at the transom. This might give maximum drag reduction by minimising wetted area aft, but the combined CPL of the triangles could be forward of the LCG, resulting in directional instability! Trimming the drives in (as some do before a turn) worsens this situation. Compromise is necessary and there should always be an appreciable amount of aft surface, adjacent to the transom, in contact with the water.

Modern stepped hulls sometimes suffer from a bad press, with claims that they hook or spin when turning. Poor design is partially responsible – a poorly designed non-stepped hull can also spin when turning – but ignorance is another factor. Some think that a stepped hull should be treated exactly the same way as a non-stepped one!

Why? They are different beasts!

Speed from a non-stepped monohull requires a high angle of attack. Modern outboards and stern drives, as well as giving an aft LCG, are often trimmed well out to lift the bow for minimum drag. Putting the helm over with the craft trimmed thus results in difficulty initiating a turn; the lateral centre of pressure, the pivot point, being well aft, the leverage between this and the drive is small. To increase this lever, the perceived wisdom when turning is to trim drives in to flatten the planing angle and move the pivot point forwards. Trimming in hard can move CPL dangerously close to or forward of LCG and often all that is needed is a reduction in throttle to settle the craft, a gentle turn of the wheel and a progressive opening of throttle during the turn.

On one production stepped craft, there were initial complaints (via 'expert' drivers) that the boats seemed to try to hook when turning. The above advice about not trimming drives in hard was given, but to no avail. The answer came back: 'that's how you drive monohulls'! No appreciation of the difference! After some exchanges, the factory just put limiters on the drives, stopping more than a small amount of in-trim, and the complaints ceased.

RIDE AND HANDLING

If steps are not too deep or too far aft so that the aft surface is properly wetted, directional stability should be fine, as should turning. If a boat, stepped or non-stepped, has a shape that causes high heel in turns then loss of grip aft can result in a spin or hook. Also, where deadrise is low, lack of immersion aft can give the same result, on stepped and non-stepped boats.

A stepped hull has an advantage in a seaway with better pitch control making for higher speed and an easier ride. When a fast non-stepped hull meets a wave, the impact causes the bow to rise. This is accelerated as the pressure travels aft. When the pressure passes the LCG, momentum makes the bow rise but the pressure, which is now high due to the high angle of attack, lifts the stern, such that the craft leaps clear of the water with a bow high attitude. Falling back stern first, it impacts hard due to the high angle and this kicks the stern up again, while simultaneously pitching the bow down hard, which buries itself to a greater or lesser extent depending on reserve lift. If this is lacking or the bow impacts the face or back of another wave, the craft can nosedive. These violent attitude changes and impacts are very uncomfortable for both craft and crew and waste energy, and the propeller thrust is not pointing in the direction of travel for much of the time. Competent drivers can reduce these effects.

When a stepped hull encounters a wave at speed, the initial effect is the same. The bow starts to rise as the pressure impulse travels along the hull, but as it clears the first step, vertical lift ceases and the bow rise slows. The next pulse, with a twin-step boat, hits the next surface just ahead of the second step, but this is almost directly under the LCG so the boat lifts bodily (heaves) but the bow up angle does not increase. The next impulse hits the aft surface, lifting the stern and countering the previous bow lift. The net result is that the hull lifts much less and at a much more level attitude, spending less time in the air. Reduced distance to fall and a lower angle mean lesser impact, and propellers spend more time immersed with thrust mainly horizontal.

Single-step hulls are similar but the pressure pulse leaps straight from the forward step to the aft surface, so there is likely to be a small increase in pitch movement. Twin steps offer more tolerance of variable LCG position and three (or more) steps can have advantages from the point of view of minimising wetted surface area, depending on the hull proportions and loading.

CONCLUSION

For planing craft requiring high cruising and maximum speeds for the majority of their work envelope, steps are a valid way of reducing power requirement and improving ride. If properly designed and driven, the boat will handle in a perfectly acceptable manner and not 'bite' its driver! Craft that have to spend much time at low and off-plane speeds are possibly not the right candidates for steps, but in the correct performance area their advantages should not be ignored.

A faulty seacock can lead to this.

WAYS TO ENSURE RELIABILITY

The key to enjoyment and success on the water is reliability. A breakdown can ruin your whole day and, more important, it can be dangerous. Things have changed dramatically on this front since I first went to sea and it is becoming rare for a powerboat to break down these days, but there is also a danger in this new-found reliability: because boats and their engines are so reliable, you tend to take them for granted; maybe you have stopped carrying a toolkit, or perhaps you do not do those essential checks before you head out to sea.

The engines and propulsion of a powerboat, as we have already said, play a crucial part in the operation and safety of the boat. Lose propulsion and you will be left virtually dead in the water and need someone to come to your assistance. Believe me, there is nothing quite so daunting as the eerie silence that pervades everything when the engine stops. However, engine and propulsion manufacturers do a great job of developing reliable units and they have come a long way from the sometimes erratic machinery of the early powerboats. I can't remember the last time that the engine itself broke down at sea and this is largely because modern engines are mainly automotive derived and so are tested to destruction before they hit the water. If something does go wrong with the machinery then it is usually the systems supplying the engine that are at fault although, again, most boatbuilders do a good job of installing these. The result is that these days you can expect your engine to start and you can expect it to keep going. However, it will only do this if you play your part, too, and look after the machinery with regular service and inspections. So, what exactly are you looking for when you give your engines and systems a check both during regular servicing and in checks before you go to sea?

A plunge into the unknown
Boatbuilders can rarely spend the time or the money on putting their boats through a long period of testing in adverse conditions prior to getting them on the market, so when buying a new boat the design is to a degree going into the unknown. Boats are still virtually hand built, so much relies on the people doing the work and the levels of inspection and checking. This means that we still have some way to go to ensure the reliability of modern boats, but in their favour is the fact that most owners do not take them to sea in adverse conditions so they are not put through any severe testing that might expose weaknesses.

ENGINE CHECKS

With outboards, many of these systems, or at least parts of them, are incorporated into the engine. The outboard is supplied as a complete tried-and-tested unit and this is its strength, although it does still rely on the outside fuel supply and the electrics to keep it going. For commercial and military operators, one of the benefits of the outboard is that you can have a spare available so that in the event of an engine problem you can simply change the whole engine. Outboards are remarkably water-resistant; in most cases, you can even play a hose over the engine, with the hood off, and the engine will keep running provided that you don't stick the hose up the air intake. This is a measure of how far the outboard has come, and this reliability and resilience means that if the outboard does stop for any reason then the first thing you should suspect is the external connections rather than the engine itself. In addition, you should check the mounting occasionally to ensure it remains tight on the transom.

With built-in fuel tanks, the weak point in the system is likely to be the flexible pipe that connects to the engines. Any pipe that has to move – and you get these on inboard engines with flexible mountings as well – may be prone to deterioration, so check for leaks in the pipe itself and particularly in the connecting joints. This can be where smell comes into the checklist because any fuel leak is likely to smell. So, if you open up the hatch to check the engine and smell fuel, you know it's time for a detailed check, although a mere wipe along the fuel line might show up the leak. The fuel filter also needs checking, first for leaks and then for contamination. There are usually two filters, one in the fuel line and one integral to the engine itself. Modern fuel-injection systems demand very clean fuel so fuel filters now have a very fine mesh and need to be replaced at regular intervals.

Engine checklist
» *Engine oil level*
» *Cooling water*
» *Spare oil on board*
» *Fuel filter*
» *Loose equipment in the engine room and steering compartment stowed and secured*
» *Battery and electrical switches in correct positions*
» *Belt drive for the water pumps and the alternator*

A low set radar antenna can mean the radar is obscured by people on the flybridge.

ELECTRICAL SYSTEM CHECKS

Probably the biggest potential weak point in any machinery installation is the electrical system. On modern boats, everything depends on the electrics and yet when I look around boats I can often see vulnerabilities in the installation. Batteries may be stowed low down in the boat to keep the centre of gravity low, but here they are vulnerable if water gets into the compartment; the batteries will be the first to go under just when you need electrical power to send out a call for help. Batteries are heavy and need to be well secured, so in your checks make sure everything is tight. The batteries should also be covered; I have seen a couple of cases in which the exposed terminals have caused a fire when something, usually a tool, has dropped across them. Another thing to look out for is batteries or electrical panels that have been installed close to the access hatch to the engine compartment, where they can be exposed to seawater when the hatch is open.

These are the things that are easy to spot, but possibly the most vulnerable parts of any boat's electrical system are those that are hidden out of sight: electric terminals corrode in the salt-laden atmosphere and the wires chafe, seemingly always in the areas that are hard to see. This means that you need to rely on the quality of the installer's work to get a reliable system, although you should still look out as best you can for signs of corrosion or chafe. I do feel concerned about this total reliance on the electrical system and think that it would be sensible if there were back-up circuits for the vital parts of the system, but I have yet to see one.

Electrical system checklist
» *Battery location*
» *Battery securely fastened in place*
» *Loose equipment stowed and secured away from the battery*
» *Signs of chafe or corrosion in the wiring*
» *Battery terminals clean and tight*

The batteries need to be secured very firmly for reliability and security.

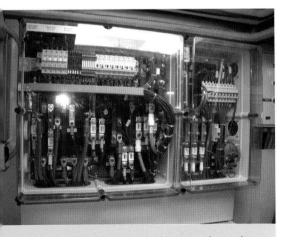

The electrical systems on powerboats are becoming increasingly complex and this one close under a hatch is vulnerable.

PLUMBING CHECKS

Now we come to the plumbing. On modern boats, there can be a complex web of pipework, most of it quite harmless and involved merely in the domestic supplies, though some are exposed to the sea outside, so can be vulnerable if there is a leak. On the engine-cooling system, leaks in the seawater pipes are usually manifested by traces of white salt crystals, but also look for any corrosion on the worm screw clamps (although modern stainless-steel clamps should not corrode). Also check for any signs of swelling in the flexible sections, which could be the first sign that the pipe is reaching the end of its useful life. On the engine, the seawater-cooling system does quite a few jobs on its way around the engine apart from the direct cooling of the engine itself through the heat exchanger. For instance, there may be a heat exchanger to cool both the engine and gearbox oil. Once the seawater has done its main cooling jobs, it is injected into the exhaust pipe to cool down the hot exhaust gases and prevent them melting the flexible rubber sections.

A water flow sensor fitted to an engine inlet pipe can prevent fire and flooding.

Think about what might happen if there were a leak or burst pipe in the seawater. Not only would water be entering the engine compartment and potentially sinking the boat, but the exhaust pipe without its vital water cooling could also melt and start a fire. The engine overheating will be a small part of the overall problem and will not show immediately, so always remember just how vital that seawater cooling system is to the safety of the boat and don't take chances with it. Even a clogged-up intake pipe could be a big concern.

As for the other plumbing systems that might be connected to the sea outside, it is safest to isolate these by closing the seacocks before you go to sea. With a fast boat, there can be considerable pressure on any pipe or system that is exposed to the sea outside as the boat lifts and falls in waves, in addition to the pressure that can be generated by the forward motion of the boat.

Plumbing checklist
» *Traces of white salt crystals on seawater pipes*
» *Corrosion in worm screw clamps*
» *Swelling in the flexible sections of pipe*
» *Obstructions in the intake pipe*
» *Close auxilary (not engine) seacocks before setting off*
» *Check that the belt drive for the seawater pump is not slack*

Seacocks and their piping are open to the sea outside.

PROPULSION SYSTEMS

As far as outboards are concerned, propulsion is almost entirely through a propeller, but with inboard engines, the main choices are a propeller drive and a water jet. With outboards and sterndrives, the oil levels in the lower gearbox need regular checking. Over a season of use, particularly if the boat is beached or operates in shallow water, the propeller can get worn or damaged. If you sense vibration in a drive unit then propeller damage should be the first thing to look for. With a painted propeller, the wear is easy to see as the paint wears off, and this is not normally a problem; what you should look for is nicks in the edges of the propeller blades or the blades being bent, both of which can be caused by striking debris or stones and can gradually reduce the efficiency of the propeller. Unless the nicks are deep, the edge of the propeller can normally be filed down to a smooth edge again without too much loss of efficiency. If the blades are bent, however, you will need to either replace the propeller or take it to a workshop where it can be straightened.

With water-jet propulsion there should be no maintenance required except perhaps to check the gearbox oil levels if this is integral to the jet unit. The jet itself may have oil circulation, but often the water-jet bearings are water lubricated. If your boat lies afloat for any length of time then you could face the problem of marine growth inside the jet tunnel, which will cause a loss of efficiency and should be cleaned off as soon as possible. This could entail dismantling the water jet because access can be very restricted, particularly on smaller jets. This is a case in which prevention is better than cure, so the jet should be run at regular intervals, perhaps every couple of weeks, to reduce this build-up. Alternatively, take it out of the water altogether.

The drop in performance can be quite dramatic when the water jet is not run for a while. This probably explains why they are not commonly used in liesure craft but widely used in commercial craft. Water jet propulsion is popular in RIBs though, but here the boats are often taken out of the water on trailers when not in use.

Propulsion checklist
» Oil levels in the lower gearbox of outboards and stern drives
» Drain a little oil from the lower gearbox to check for any water – if found, oil seals need replacing
» Nicks or damage to the propeller, especially if you sense vibration in a drive unit
» Oil levels in gearboxes that are integral to water jet units
» Clear marine growth and obstructions in the water-jet tunnel

Checks around the boat should not take long but they should take more than a casual glance. Before something goes seriously wrong on a boat there are usually small clues that can show trouble is starting. It can take a trained eye to spot the first signs of trouble such as small water, oil or fuel leaks and in addition to the sense of touch you should use your eyes and nose to sniff out possible problems. Much better to discover them in harbour than out at sea.

MORPH MARINE

Morph Marine experiments with and develops variable geometry hulls – also referred to as morphing or adjustable hulls. Work to date has included the building and testing of a morphing hull sailboat and stand up paddleboard with concept designs for a morphing RIB. The rationale for a variable geometry hull offers potential benefits for powerboat operation, which include improved performance, seakeeping and fuel consumption. A preliminary conceptual design for a variable geometry powerboat based on a RIB hull form has been developed.

The geometric features of a boat hull have a major influence on propulsion resistance and seakeeping properties for different speeds, manoeuvring conditions, payloads and sea states. For example, a shape that performs well at low speeds is not necessarily ideal for higher speeds or vice versa. Boats that are very fast and stable in calm water are unable to be operated at speed in rough water because of dynamic instability. Specific hull geometry is often therefore optimised for a limited set of operational conditions and, as a consequence, does not have the desired shape and features for efficient propulsion and seakeeping across a larger operational envelope.

To address the shortfalls of hulls with fixed shapes, a unique design for an adjustable deadrise powerboat hull has been analysed and is in development. The study has shown improvement in the overall performance and seakeeping for a boat required to operate at non-planing, semi-planing and planing speeds in various sea states when compared to a conventional boat with fixed deadrise.

The Adjustable Deadrise (ADR) RIB design permits the hull shape to be adjusted dynamically while underway. The design described within is for a centre console, 8m (26ft) RIB powered by twin 300hp outboard engines. Displacement is 2,900kg (1.87 tons) and the forward deadrise is nominally 45 degrees with after sections being adjustable from 5 to 35 degrees.

OPERATION OF AN ADR RIB

The operation of an ADR RIB will allow the driver to select a hull shape best suited for the mission and sea conditions. 'Sweet spots' of operation can be obtained across a greater range of speeds, direction of travel and conditions when compared to a fixed hull shape. Specific performance and operational benefits are:

» Roll stability: When not moving or moving slowly, roll angles can be minimised by the selection of shallow deadrise angle, which can be beneficial for loading/unloading, boarding or rescue activities. The study showed that across the range of 5–35 degrees for the deadrise, the righting arm changes by a factor of 4. This means that the 5-degree boat will be very stiff in roll with respect to a deep-vee boat.

» Draft: For the same displacement, the draft changes with deadrise change, ie a flat-bottom boat will draw less water than the deep-vee hull configuration, which can be advantageous for travel through or operating in shallow estuary waters or beaching. Draft changes with deadrise for the ADR RIB are significant.

» Maximum speed: Theoretical maximum speeds were calculated in the study as shown. The 5-degree DRA showed a top speed of 47.2 knots whereas at 35 degrees it was 44.6 knots. While significant, this requires further analysis and is anticipated to show an even greater difference.

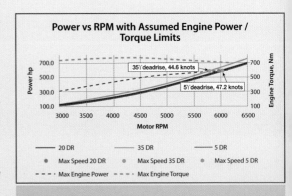

Theoretical maximum speed study.

» *Acceleration: Reaching planing speeds and accelerating to a desired speed is an important performance factor and the study clearly showed a difference in drag based on deadrise in the planing regime. Therefore, with the same engine and propeller thrust capabilities, the lowest deadrise configuration will have a greater acceleration.*

» *Dynamic instability: An important performance characteristic is the potential for dynamic instability, particularly while planing, and is therefore a consideration for an ADR vessel. The analysis accounted for porpoising instability by controlling trim angles through propeller tilt and the addition of trim tabs for the 35-degree deadrise boat. Although none of the configurations analysed were unstable, further analysis is required to examine for example the magnitude of the rolling moment induced while turning.*

» *Ride comfort/vertical acceleration: The ability to adjust deadrise can be used to advantage in managing shock loading on crew and equipment. This is illustrated from the results obtained in the analysis as shown in the table. The reduction in G-loading and improvement in dynamic stability is expected to be significant for high versus low deadrise, offering safer operation, comfort, reduced fatigue and bodily injury.*

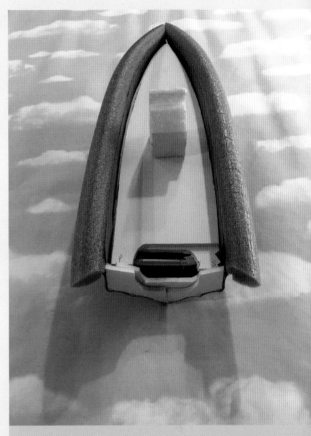

The Morph RIB showing how the transom arrangement works.

Vertical acceleration 'G' at 30 knots' boat speed					
Deadrise angle	5º	10º	20º	30º	35º
Average acceleration, 0.5m (1.6ft) waves	1.58	1.58	1.48	1.17	0.9
Peak acceleration, 0.5m (1.6ft) waves	2.25	2.36	2.4	2.14	1.76

» *Fuel consumption: An ADR boat offers the potential for significant fuel savings with an associated reduction in emissions and drive train wear. The analysis shows a potential 22–24 per cent fuel saving when comparing a 35-degree hull with one that has a deadrise of 5 degrees travelling at 34 knots.*

» *Weight: The equipment and changes necessary to produce an ADR boat will result in a manageable overall weight increase. Major additions are the keel joint, transom, chine actuator and floor assemblies with their associated controllers and sensors. For the specific case of an 8m (26ft) outboard-powered ADR RIB, the increase has been estimated to be approximately 5 per cent, roughly equivalent to the addition of two average persons. Although this increase is not expected to significantly affect performance, it will be a critical element in the design.*

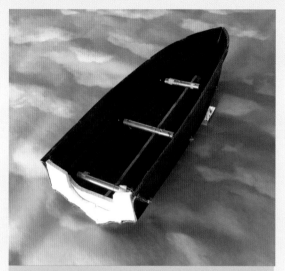

The hydraulic cylinders that are used to change the hull shape.

DESIGN DESCRIPTION

The proposed ADR RIB will be similar in form to production RIBs with the major change being a hull constructed of individual symmetric port and starboard halves joined along the keel line by a flexible joint. A rigid spine connected to the flexible joint provides longitudinal stiffness and is integral with the outboard motor mount supporting the engines, weight and reacting propeller thrust and moment loads. Deadrise is controlled with synchronised athwartship linear actuators. The deck is made from two full-length composite sections attached at the hull side walls, which move laterally as the beam width changes. Slots in the lower section with through-fasteners from the upper section allow lateral motion. The

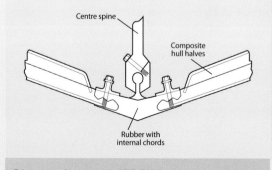

Centre spine

Composite hull halves

Rubber with internal chords

Diagram of proposed ADR RIB hull.

steering station is connected to the upper deck section and is slightly offset to port when beam is narrow, on centre at the nominal 20-degree deadrise and slightly starboard at maximum deadrise.

It is anticipated that the hull halves will be joined together along the keel line by bonding and clamping to a 'living hinge' constructed in a similar way to automotive tyres, ie plies of elastomers with embedded cords. The hull will be constructed of a thick, rigid foam core with hybrid skin fabrics of E-glass, Kevlar and carbon fibre resin infused with a high-modulus/high-strain epoxy. Finally, inflated Hypalon tubes are attached at the gunwales.

Deadrise is controlled with synchronised athwartship linear actuators with a total stroke of approximately 0.5m (1.6ft). Three are located within the floor system attached along the chine. Two additional linear drives are connected to the transom upper outboard corners and hull halves, providing lateral support for the engine(s). When they are all actuated, the waterline beam changes, causing the deadrise angle to change.

The Morph RIB showing the varying propeller heights.

The floor is made from two composite sections and full-length port and starboard overlapping decks are attached at the hull side walls. They move laterally as the beam width changes. Slots in the lower section with through-fasteners from the upper section allow this lateral motion. The steering station is connected to the upper floor section and is slightly offset to port when

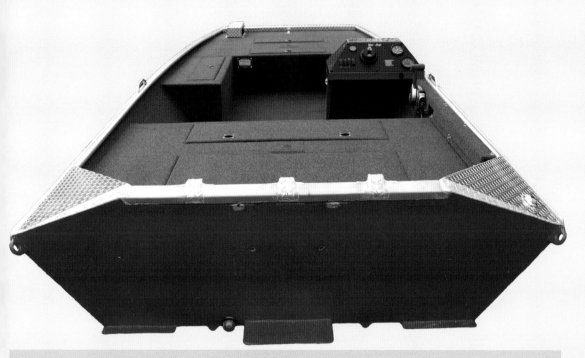

Taken to the extremes, a Morph hull could have an efficient flat planing bottom.

beam is narrow, on centre at 20-degree DRA and slightly starboard at maximum DRA. Mounting of the floors to the hull will be accomplished with elastomeric mounts. Hypalon-inflated tubes are attached along the gunwales using a technique that is similar to the one used on conventional RIBs. The changing shape of the geometry of the hull is easily accommodated by the tubes.

The transom seal and structural integrity is accomplished with a full-width accordion seal. The seal leafs are Hypalon fabric with internal composite battens. Each hull section has an integral transom that articulates with the hull as DRA changes. The seal is attached to flanges on the T-structure and the inner surface of the hull halves. Protection from physical contact and backwash pressure is provided by the hull transom sections.

DESIGN CONSIDERATIONS

There are numerous challenges associated with any new design and this is certainly true for an ADR RIB. These include the integrity of the structure, detailed elements of the design, weight management, optimising and managing longitudinal centre of gravity, control systems

for deadrise, tilt/trim and propeller immersion, etc, in addition to a cost-versus-benefit analysis. Nevertheless, it is the author's opinion based on his experience with the design, manufacture and testing of several variable geometry watercraft, design studies for an ADR RIB and his knowledge of existing subsystems that development of a variable geometry powerboat is both justified and practicable. This work represents a further step in the development of the basic premise that a variable geometry hull will improve the performance and expand the operational capabilities of powerboats. Work to date has demonstrated that it is possible to produce a variable geometry (morphing) hull and that such a hull has the anticipated benefits. Further, that the concept is applicable to powerboats and that there is a potential for fuel savings and seakeeping benefits.

CONTROLLING THE BOAT

One of the joys of driving a powerboat is the way that it responds to your every command. This is especially true of fast powerboats, which are very responsive to the controls, so understanding what they do and how they do it is the key to powerboat driving, particularly as the seas get rougher, when the role of the controls becomes more and more critical.

At the helm of a fast powerboat, you should become part of a combination where man and machine are in harmony. To achieve this level of harmony and control there are two requirements: first, the controls of the boat must be designed and located to allow you to get the response that you need for delicate and positive control; and second, you, the driver, need to be firmly located in the boat to allow you to provide that positive control.

A complex dash layout where it could be hard to find the right information and controls quickly when required at sea.

When you watch many boat drivers operating in lively seas, you can see them using the steering wheel, and sometimes the throttle, more as a handhold than as a control. However, you will never get the delicate control that you need if you are gripping the wheel tightly to locate yourself in the boat. From this, it is easy to see how good and secure location of the driver is essential to being able to operate the controls properly, by means of suitable seating (see Chapter 15), as much as the layout and positioning of controls. This applies for all powerboats. Here, we will look at the various controls so that you can understand what they do as well as some of the secondary effects.

STEERING

There are two types of steering on powerboats:

» Passive steering: using a rudder that is usually in the flow of water behind the propeller to give a relatively gentle steering force. Here, the blade of the rudder deflects the water emerging from the propeller to create a force that turns the hull. Displacement hulls almost invariably use passive steering and so you tend to have a much more gentle response, which is reflected in the more gentle movements of the hull.

» Dynamic steering: the thrust from the propeller is used as the steering force. This is the type of steering you get with outboards, sterndrives and water jets and with some types of surface drives. Obviously, dynamic steering is much harsher and more active than passive steering and this can lead to a much harsher movement of the boat in waves when the steering is turned.

Opposite: One hand on the wheel and one on the throttle is the standard control position for a fast boat. This is a waterjet control unit.

Separate throttle and gearbox controls on each side of the wheel, but they look the same so mistakes could be made.

Few boat drivers seem to appreciate how the steering can affect the way the boat behaves in waves. Turn the steering wheel gently and a planing powerboat will heel over in the direction in which the wheel is turned. Turn the wheel with dynamic steering and this heeling over can be quite sudden and lead to a distinct harshness in the ride because the vee of the hull is no longer acting as a cushion. In most cases, a delicate touch on the steering of a fast powerboat is required, rather than the more brutal movements that are often used. Think of it as like riding a horse: you need to coax the animal to do your bidding; any violent movements are likely to produce a more violent reaction.

To understand this you need to realise how the deep-vee hull behaves when the wheel is turned. To get the full cushioning effect of a deep-vee hull it needs to be upright when landing in waves so that each side of the vee of the hull provides the same amount of cushioning when it is cutting through waves or re-entering the water. For instance, on a hull with a 20-degree deadrise, when the hull is heeled over by perhaps 10 degrees you will get an effective deadrise of 30 degrees on one side of the hull and just 10 degrees on the other. That 10-degree deadrise is very shallow for a hull that is operating in waves and it will offer little in the way of cushioning should the boat choose that moment to impact with the next wave. It effectively means that with the hull heeled over, you are presenting an almost flat surface to the water on impact and the result will be a rough ride.

A vertical wheel does not make it easy to control the steering when sitting. Note the engine controls in the seat arm.

In a worst-case scenario in which the operator swings the wheel first one way and then overcorrects and swings it the other way, the boat can end up rocking from side to side in a very unpleasant and seemingly uncontrollable way. Your passengers will not take kindly to this unnecessary treatment. Rather than trying to correct each and every alteration of course that the boat may make as it impacts with waves, it is much better to let the boat have its head; most of the time it will come back on or near the course of its own accord without you having to make any steering corrections. If it does wander more than you would like, bring it back on course using just small movements of the wheel. I think steering with just three or four turns lock to lock is about right.

It is not easy to adapt and use this lighter touch on the steering because the natural reaction is to grip the wheel tightly in lively seas in order to feel in control. To overcome this instinct, you do need to be sitting or standing securely. Sometimes, I find myself having to actually force my hands to relax on the steering wheel, whereupon the benefits quickly become clear.

On most powerboats the steering ratio, ie the number of turns of the wheel from lock to lock, has to be a compromise. You want a quick steering response at low speeds when you are manoeuvring in harbour and yet out in the open sea you want a much slower response on the wheel so that you can achieve that delicate touch you need to avoid unnecessary heeling. It would be great to be able to switch ratios, but this is rarely possible, so the steering response has to be a compromise. One way to achieve the ideal is to switch from wheel steering at sea to tiller steering in harbour – something that can be done with many modern systems.

The other factor that could make life easier and the control much better would be to have an adjustable steering wheel, so that the angle of the wheel can be altered to make it more comfortable to use.

Steering is a lot easier if the boat has good directional stability, ie it will maintain a set course with only small amounts of correction on the steering wheel. This applies to both displacement and planing hulls. For displacement boats, a hull that has a deeper draft at the stern will probably track better than one with a shallow, level ride. For planing hulls, a hull with a deeper deadrise, which may be more than 20 degrees, will normally have good directional stability. However, if you find the boat tending to wander about and be less sensitive to steering corrections, you may find that trimming the outboard or sterndrive leg out will improve things because this will lift the bow and trim the hull more by the stern. Too much trim could have a negative effect on the steering, though, so it is a matter of trial and error to find just the right amount, something that may not be easy to do when running in waves. Instead, it is best done in calm water when you can gauge the effects of changes much better. You will also find that boats with dynamic steering tend to have reduced directional stability because of the much stronger steering effect of the propeller or jet thrust.

AUTOPILOT

The idea of using an autopilot is commonplace in displacement boats, where they can make life easier and more relaxed since they remove the need to concentrate on the compass all the time. The thought of using the autopilot in a faster planing boat is outside most drivers' experience, however, but I am a great fan. Not only does it relieve you of the tedious

An autopilot control head with a rotary control for course setting.

concentration on the compass heading or on a distant object, but it also does a much better job of steering than you ever can. It also produces a more comfortable ride since the steering is much less dynamic. What's more, there is the benefit of much better course keeping and that can save you quite a bit of fuel or allow you to travel at a higher speed.

A concrete example of this is the record *Virgin Atlantic Challenger* crossing of the Atlantic we did, for which I reckoned that using the autopilot saved us 240km of wandering. Given that we only broke the existing record by two hours, and that extra 240km (150 miles) would have taken us at least three hours to cover, you can see that the outcome would have been very different: no record. We are not alone, either. Fabio Buzzi used the autopilot on his 60-footer when setting a new Round Italy record and he is now a great fan of the system. So, yes, autopilots work in fast boats, and not just for larger boats, either: I have used an autopilot in a 30-footer and it worked very well in lively seas, dare I say it, doing a much better job of controlling the steering than would a human helmsman. I also use the autopilot for steering when entering harbour because you can set the course you want and let it do the job while you concentrate more on the navigation. It does pay to get the right type of autopilot, preferably one with a rotating knob to control the course setting; the larger the knob, the better.

THROTTLES

The throttle lever is the most important control in a powerboat when you are operating in waves. Obviously, you can use the throttle to control the speed of the boat, which in turn controls the speed of encounter with the waves, but one of the important benefits of the throttle in both displacement and planing hulls is that it can also produce quick and short-term changes in the trim of the boat. These can help negotiate the boat through rough seas, and particularly in breaking waves, be used to produce a faster and safer ride in more extreme sea conditions.

Indeed, so important is the throttle control in lively seas that you should drive the boat with one hand on the throttle and one on the steering wheel at all times so that your reactions and responses can be as fast as possible. We will look a lot more into the use of the

throttle in later chapters; here, we will concentrate on getting its angle and location right for easy and comfortable use.

Most throttle controls these days are integrated into a throttle gear control that is supplied by the engine manufacturer. These work well of course and certainly make it easy to operate the boat when at slow speed in harbour, but they are rarely the best solution for use in the open sea. They are also rarely positioned to allow subtle use of the throttle setting. Like the steering wheel, you need a delicate hand on the throttle if you are going to employ it to best advantage: small changes in the setting can give you the level of control you need. This is why race boats and other high-performance boats tend to use a dedicated throttle lever, one that is separated from the gears and that will give the right level of control. For the combined throttle/gear levers, the full operating range may cover perhaps 150 degrees, but of this range of movement perhaps 75 degrees will cover the gears, the ahead, neutral and astern engagement. This leaves another 75 degrees of movement to cover the ahead and astern movements of the throttle.

With standard throttles, if you are lucky, the throttle movement may have just 40 degrees of movement, which is not enough to allow the subtle control you need. This is exacerbated by the fact that on most installations the ahead section of the throttle range is located on the forward side of the control box, which makes it even harder to get the subtle adjustment you

A throttle control unit with the gearbox controlled by protected switches.

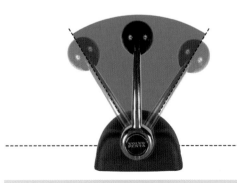

A diagram showing the amount of movement in the control before gears are engaged and the throttle can be opened.

need, as you have to reach over the control box to use it. The result is that you may find that you are exaggerating the movement of the throttle from full ahead to almost idling. If you have to use one of these manufacturer-supplied throttle and gear controls then at least install it at an angle so that the ahead section is upright, has priority and is relatively easy to use.

It is not only location that is important. With the modern fly-by-wire systems, for which the link to the engine is electrical, there is not the same level of resistance to movement, which means that you can make inadvertent shifts of the throttle lever due to the motion of the boat. It used to be possible to vary the resistance to the movement of the lever, but this capability has disappeared with modern systems. It is the same with the steering, which also now uses fly-by-wire systems, which has made the steering light and non-resistant, leading to excessive steering movements because you can't 'feel' them as there is no feedback into the steering wheel.

JOYSTICK CONTROL

Joystick control is now available with many drive systems, such as sterndrives, water jets and pod drives, as well as more tailored systems that use the main engines and bow and stern thrusters. The benefits of the joystick are enormous and the level of manoeuvring control is quite amazing, making it possible to position the boat very precisely and to allow it to be moved in any direction. If you need this level of control and instant response, such as when docking in tight marinas or on some workboat operations, then the joystick solution is a great way to go. At higher speeds when on passage, the joystick control acts mainly as a throttle to set the speed and the steering may switch to a form of tiller steering, which may be separate or else incorporated into the joystick control system.

There are different types of joystick that use alternative logic to achieve precise control. One of these allows the joystick to be pointed in the direction you want to travel and then the computer adjusts the drive controls to achieve this. The speed of travel in the chosen direction is adjusted by the amount that the joystick lever is moved in the desired direction. This is the more or less

Using a joystick control when berthing the boat.

standard format for most joysticks, though extras can be added. For instance, since this type of standard joystick does not alter the heading of the boat, steering can be added, and unless there is a separate tiller or wheel, this steering can be incorporated in the joystick by twisting the handle in the desired direction. The system can also be further enhanced by the installation of a push button in the top of the lever that will engage the autopilot so that the boat will maintain a fixed heading once set.

This joystick control is normally an option for speeds of up to about 10 knots, but above this speed the joystick is normally switched either manually or automatically to a system of separate steering, with the joystick just controlling the throttles, although in some cases there are separate throttles. This separate steering may be a tiller, with no traditional steering wheel – something that I am not a fan of for open-sea operations because it is difficult to get the subtle steering control you need. As I have suggested, only a very light touch on the wheel is required to reduce the chances of the hull heeling over under more aggressive steering and increasing the hull impact in waves, and this light touch is not easy to achieve with a tiller.

Whichever type you use, in rough seas the helmsman does need to be seated and probably strapped in so that he can achieve the best results with the controls and not make inadvertent movements.

For both systems, you have to put a lot of faith in the computer controls because it is the computer that translates your commands into actions. There are usually back-up control systems that can be switched on if the computer does not do its job, but in a tight manoeuvring situation you are heavily reliant on technology. This can of course go wrong: I have seen the joystick control fail at a critical moment when passing through a swing bridge. It is therefore important to balance the possible risk of failure against the huge control benefits that the joystick can offer.

FLAPS AND INTERCEPTORS

Both of these controls are used to adjust the longitudinal and transverse trim of the boat. It is likely that you will only find them on larger boats, say those over 6m (20ft) in length, for which the added complication can be justified.

Flaps are hinged plates installed at the bottom of the transom that can be angled down under electric or hydraulic control to adjust the planing surfaces of the hull in order to generate variable lift at the transom. Angled down, they will cause the bow to go down, and

when raised, the bow will lift and the boat will run on its normal bottom planing surfaces.

You use the flaps together to adjust the longitudinal trim in this way, but to adjust the transverse trim you need to use them individually. If you drop the starboard flap, it will cause the starboard side of the boat to lift, and the same will happen with the port flap and the port side. You probably should only use this transverse trim adjustment when running with the wind on the beam, when a planing hull will tend to heel into the wind at speed, though it can also be used to compensate for uneven weight distribution. If you do use the flaps individually in this way, they will also affect the steering because the flap that is lowered creates increased drag on that side, tending to pull the boat round in that direction.

Interceptors do much the same job as flaps and are the modern equivalent. Instead of having angled flaps, the interceptor is a vertical plate attached to the bottom of the transom that can be raised and lowered. When it is raised it is flush with the bottom of the transom and has no effect, but it only has to be lowered a centimetre or two to intercept the water flow coming away from the transom and cause the bow to lower. It is claimed that the interceptor creates less resistance than a flap when in use and, of course, it is a more compact installation on the transom, with virtually no projections. Interceptors can be electrically or hydraulically operated and again they only tend to be found on larger boats of more than about 6m (20ft) in length.

These faster-acting interceptors have also been developed into an auto-trim system, whereby the movement of

A flap control that uses graphic images to aid understanding.

Twin cylinder hydraulic flaps are let into the transom on this fast boat hull.

the boat is determined by sensors linked to the control computer and the interceptors are adjusted accordingly to counter the movement of the hull to help give a level ride. These auto-trim systems are quite magical in the way in which they can reduce both the pitching and rolling motions of the boat. However, bear in mind that the

Alternative control heads for flaps.

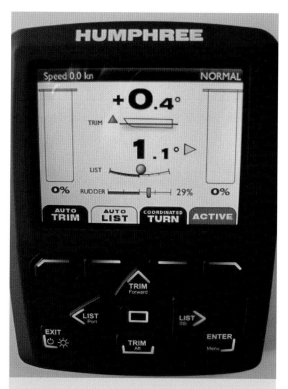

An interceptor control head showing graphically what is happening to the trim.

interceptors can only act in one direction, lowering the bow when it might lift to a wave; they cannot lift the bow, so you might need to open the throttles to get the desired trim for the transient conditions.

Both flaps and interceptors tend to be controlled by a rocker switch, but a form of joystick can also be used. There can be some confusion over these switches, some indicating bow down and bow up, others indicating flap down and flap up, so you need to be clear which type is fitted to your boat and what the movement of the control does. You also need an indicator or dial to show how much flap is down so that you know what is going on at the back of the boat. These indicators come in many forms: a dial with pointers, indicator lights or mechanical indicators. Without an indicator, the only solution is to bring the flaps right up, which provides a datum point for future operation of the flaps.

Interceptors mounted along the bottom edge of the transom on this large hull. Note also the stabilising fins for the steering.

To get a feel for the operation of the flaps and how they work both individually and together, try them out in calm water. From this, you should be able to assess the right settings and adjustments. Because flaps are slow-acting, you will tend to find a setting that works in the prevailing conditions rather than constantly adjusting them, though you may need to reset the adjustment when you alter course.

GYRO STABILISERS

Another automatic system for reducing the rolling is the gyro, which is an enclosed flywheel revolving at high speed that resists the rolling movement of the hull. This is a fixed force and it works very well even on a fast boat, but they can cause the movement of the hull to become quite jerky, particularly on a displacement hull. The gyros cannot be switched on and off at will, so once set in motion you have to live with the results. Despite this, they are effective at mitigating rolling, which of course can help reduce seasickness. They can also be used in combination with other systems. For instance, when an owner wanted a 14m (46ft) yacht tender for his superyacht that would not move in waves, we combined an interceptor auto-trim system with a gyro, and this proved to be a very effective combination even at slow speeds.

A gyro stabiliser unit fitted in this crowded engine room below deck.

POWER TRIM

Power trim is available on most outboards over about 50hp and on most sterndrives. It consists of a hydraulic cylinder connection between the drive leg of the motor and the transom bracket and it allows the angle of the drive leg in relation to the transom to be altered. This might seem an unnecessary complication, but power trim can improve the efficiency of the drive considerably, and it can also be used to trim the boat. These days, control of power trim is usually by means of a switch incorporated into the top of the throttle lever so that

Flaps at the extremity of the transom where they are most effective.

it can be thumb-operated without taking your hand off the throttle lever as the boat accelerates. It is a slow movement, so it tends to be set up for the conditions and then left, rather than being adjusted for each wave as the throttle might.

When running at slow speed and when coming on to the plane, the drive leg is kept trimmed in so that the propeller has a good bite on the water and the thrust is close to horizontal. It is only when the boat is up on to the plane that the leg is then trimmed out – mainly to keep the thrust horizontal as the trim of planing lifts the bow. Initially, with this alteration of the angle of the drive leg, the angle of the thrust from the propeller is changed, making it push slightly downwards in relation

Controls and indicators for flaps and power trim on this fast boat.

to the transom. The change of angle may only be a few degrees but this can be enough to help raise the bow by a similar amount, which in turn focuses the planing surfaces of the hull in contact with the water further aft. In effect, this reduces the area of the hull in contact with the water and thus reduces the frictional resistance. Flaps could do the same job but they add resistance of their own so are not as effective.

When coming on to the plane, the whole boat lifts and this brings the propeller a little closer to the surface of the water, reducing the amount of the drive leg in the water and meaning the propeller can operate slightly in a surface-piercing mode for greater effectiveness. This change may be less noticeable than that created by the change in the hull angle and the amount of power trim applied needs to be carefully judged; the boat can start to 'porpoise', with the bow starting to lift and fall, if you have the leg trimmed too far. This happens because the hull is planing on only a small section of the hull aft and finds it hard to find the right balance, and so the hull hunts up and down trying to find it.

The best way to find the right amount of power trim to apply is to experiment in calm conditions when you will be able to clearly see the effect of adjustments. If you have a GPS or speed log in the boat you will be able to optimise the power trim angle for maximum speed and find a setting that works best.

You can then use this optimum setting when running in waves, but in more extreme conditions you may find it beneficial to trim in a little to help keep the propeller in the water, and to ensure that when you open the throttle you get an immediate response when the propeller bites. You may also need to trim in when executing sharp turns to prevent cavitation, and as you come off the plane the leg should be trimmed right in. With experience, you will be able to look aft to see whether you have the trim set correctly, with a smooth flow of water from the propeller. Any sign of a rooster tail from the wake means that the trim is probably too far out.

As with flaps, it can help to have an indicator to show where the power trim is set, since this will allow you to set the trim at a previously found level. With twin outboards or sterndrives, it is becoming common for the

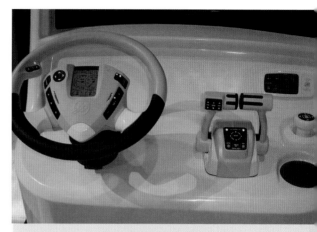

Controls inset on the steering wheel and throttles, but you only have so many hands to use them.

trim of both legs to be adjusted through a single switch, in which case there should be no real need to adjust them individually.

The same hydraulics that adjust the power trim may also double up as the means to lift the drive leg right up when beaching, operating in shallow water or putting the boat on a trailer. This tilt mechanism will almost certainly be on a separate switch to avoid confusion and mistakes. If you do trim the leg up for shallow-water work, make sure you only use low power.

NIGEL IRENS, NIGEL IRENS DESIGN

"

Although my work as a designer has covered everything from offshore racing trimarans to long-range motor cruisers, they could all be boxed up together and simply labelled 'slippery boats'.

When as a young person you've seen and felt the beauty of the ride of a small, narrow boat, the idea of travelling in an overpowered displacement hull that digs a hole in the sea amidships and sucks itself down into it is not what you want. Worse yet is the modern-day motor yacht that is billed as a planing hull and yet can't quite break free into proper planing mode.

Over the years, engine manufacturers have done their best to keep developing ever lighter and more powerful engines to try to coax overburdened planing hulls to reach proper planing speeds, but the ones you see actually under way are often stuck in a half-in, half-out posture, tearing up the sea behind them.

So for me the long, thin boats of my youth are the role model. It is also vital to make sure that the boat is relatively light for her waterline length and, in simple terms, this means stretching out the length of the boat to best advantage and laying out the accommodation in series rather than in parallel, so definitely avoiding building tall superstructures in the hope of creating a bit more room.

From 1977 onwards, I was designing racing sail trimarans. These elegant beasts were usually 60ft (18m) in length and can be thought of as the ultimate indulgence for us 'slippery boat' nerds. With the help of foils they can easily average over 35 knots offshore in suitable conditions.

Their presence on the water was a wonderful showcase for what can be achieved under sail, and paradoxically, the planing motorboats that were provided to allow journalists and photographers to record the events were usually left bouncing around helplessly while these fine sailing yachts disappeared over the horizon in no time.

Reasoning that to follow a trimaran successfully it might be best to use another trimaran, we designed and built the 70ft (21m) trimaran Ilan Voyager, *which still holds the record for a non-stop circumnavigation of mainland Britain; she covered the 2,575km (1,600-mile) route at an average speed of 21.5 knots on a single fill-up of diesel.*

Still following the 'slippery boat' trail, we coined the acronym 'LDL', which stands for 'Low Displacement/Length (ratio)'. As a guideline, these LDL hulls are optimised for a speed/length ratio of some 2 x $\sqrt{LWL}$ (ft) (Froude number 0.6). In reality, a 'natural' long-range cruising speed seems to be around 1.8 x $\sqrt{LWL}$ (ft) (Froude number 0.54).

Nigel Irens favours a long, thin hull for a fuel efficient motor boat.

Cable and Wireless, *the trimaran that broke the Round the World record.*

We recently brought our own 31ft (9.5m) 2-tonne test vessel back from Cowes to Dartmouth. On this occasion, we averaged 10.8 knots over the eight-and-a-half-hour 148km (92-mile) passage. The engine's maximum output is 23hp (17Kw), and the fuel consumption measured at 36 litres (7.9 gallons) for the voyage.

To achieve a satisfying result, we aim to achieve a speed/length ratio of between 65 and 85 on new projects on this theme. We are currently working on a 39ft (12m) production vessel and the finished boat must fall within those speed/length ratio numbers.

Some of the LDL vessels we have designed have been required to achieve up to as much as $3.3 \times \sqrt{LWL}$ (ft). This is quite feasible, but if higher speeds are routinely required then the LDL hull type may well be surpassed in performance by a conventional planing hull, which is likely to be more efficient under these circumstances due to the reduction of wetted surface area available to a planing-hulled boat

In a nutshell, LDL hulls are designed to explore the territory that lies just outside the capability of the displacement hull up to the point at which a planing hull is lengthening its stride and is settled into full planing mode. At the bigger end of the scale, we designed a 63-footer that on a 483km (300-mile) passage averaged 10 knots with fuel consumption almost exactly 1 litre (0.22 gallons) per nautical mile.

Over the 15 years that have passed since the first LDL vessel was launched, we produced seven different designs that have been built – amounting to around 24 individual vessels in all. These range from 22ft (6.7 m) battery-driven launch Elektra to that 63-footer.

It appears that there are two possible types of LDL boats that could potentially be commercialised. The first is a production yacht capable of offering long-range performance. Although it is often said that fuel bills represent only a small percentage of the annual running costs of a motor yacht, it is the case that not many existing planing vessels cover very many miles during a season's use.

It is the very fact that the LDL equivalent burns very little fuel per mile by comparison that makes long-range cruising a real proposition. It is envisaged that owners would have the freedom to carry out passages of several hundred miles if they wish, but, almost more interestingly, owners would enjoy the freedom to cruise in the same way that a sailing boat does – so perhaps hopping from place to place enjoying passages that typically might amount to 800km (500 miles) being covered during a ten-day cruise without the need to plan the cruise around the availability of fuel stops.

The second option is to benefit from the low power consumption of an LDL vessel travelling at modest speeds and to offer a 'battery only' propelled version. A 39ft (12m) version would require some 25kW of power to travel at 10 knots. Using a currently available battery pack with capacity of 50kWh would offer a range of some 32km (20 miles), so for day trips to the beach and back the equation looks good – especially if a range-extending generator is available.

By far the most important favourable aspect of the LDL configuration is the very smooth nature of the powering curve. This allows the vessel to be operated efficiently at any chosen speed according to:

» sea conditions (upwind/downwind/beam wind)
» avoidance of resonant pitch frequencies when motoring upwind
» weather conditions (in particular the ability to avoid heavy weather through strategic navigational speed/heading changes)
» length of voyage (so management of fuel reserves)
» need to limit wash when operating in confined waters
» need to slow down at night to provide relaxed sleeping conditions.

By contrast, any 'planing' hull suffers an acute lack of choice in determining speed since high-speed operation is not possible in anything but calm conditions, and yet little or no fuel saving is possible at sub-planing speeds. The need to achieve the desired LDL requires that superstructure be kept low.

LDL hulls naturally have high length/beam ratios, and waterplanes tend to be quite vee-shaped to allow fine entries forward and yet retain lateral stability by having relatively wide waterlines aft, which is also convenient if a twin-engine installation is envisaged. The result of this seems to be that LDLs have a markedly reduced tendency to suffer from resonant rolling motion, whether at sea or at anchor. This positive phenomenon seems to yield more benefit to smaller LDLs as beam/length ratios are lower on smaller boats.

If the rate of wave encounter is synchronous with the natural pitch frequency of an LDL then pitching can become a real problem. There are three ways to address this problem. The first is that the rate of encounter can be varied to the boat's speed, either up or down. Changing the heading will also change the rate of encounter, although it may be necessary to alter course by up to 30 degrees before the frequency is significantly changed. The second is to add a ride control system, although this is not always feasible on a smaller vessel. The third is to fit a ballast tank well forward in the vessel. It may also be that the use of a hull vane might be a useful refinement in both further improvements of efficiency and in helping to reduce the wave pattern behind the vessel to a minimum. This is currently being investigated.

Ilan Voyager, *Nigel Irens' first attempt at wide trimaran design.*

A particular problem that bothers most designers is that owners of motorboats often mention that they don't mind the idea of cruising at 12 knots but they'd like to be able to achieve 20 knots as a top speed. This request is usually very difficult to respond to because all designs can only be optimised for one particular speed. On an LDL, however, that gentle resistance curve seen on the graph makes this problem go away.

The result is that having installed enough power to meet the 20-knot criterion and fitted the boat with a prop that is also optimised for such a speed, the vessel runs inefficiently all the rest of the time when it is operating at normal cruising speed. This can be solved by using a CP propeller.

On the negative side, the most obvious questions concern the fact that these vessels are very long for the interior volume contained within them and a potential buyer will figure out that it wouldn't be a good move to invest in an LDL if the vessel is unlikely to travel more than a few miles from its home port. One of the great merits of the 'planing' hull configuration is that it is quite 'people shaped', with lots of internal space. It is also quite short, which means that docking charges, which are often levied on a length

basis, are moderate compare to those of an LDL with the same living space.

Developing the LDL concept over the past 14 years has been an exciting adventure. The basic principles are, of course, very simple, but the 'slipperier' the boat, the more pleasing the ride, and the evolutionary process has only heightened the pleasure.

LDL yachts are designed to go offshore, and they offer a great way of facilitating access to the less-populated corners of the world under power – even in vessels in the sub-25 tonne displacement size. The ride quality together with effective noise suppression and frugal fuel consumption should mean that, once out there, owners can really take great pleasure and satisfaction in the voyaging experience itself.

DRIVING TECHNIQUES: DISPLACEMENT HULLS

The slow speeds at which displacement hulls operate and the reduced trim controls available means that driving a displacement hull tends to be focused on adjusting the throttle setting to match the conditions and possibly finding an economical speed at which to operate to reduce emissions and fuel consumption. The inference associated with owning or operating a displacement boat is that you are looking for comfort rather than performance, although of course there are a number of commercial operators who have a higher focus on performance. When considering how to handle displacement boats, it is useful to divide up the sections depending on which way the boat is heading in relation to the waves, because at the end of the day this is what dictates the boat handling.

HEAD SEAS

When operating in a head sea, the main thing to do with a displacement hull is find a speed at which the boat proceeds comfortably. A lot will depend on the height of the waves and their wavelength, but provided that the boat is strongly built, even in quite rough seas it is possible to find a speed at which the boat will lift over the wave and drop down the other side without causing too much discomfort to the craft or the crew. Matching the speed to the conditions is the secret, if the waves have a normal gradient and a wavelength that allows the boat to do so without any undue change in attitude. Obviously, the size of the boat has a considerable influence on the way a displacement hull behaves, with a larger hull happily spanning the wave crests while a small boat will start contouring them much sooner.

When a displacement boat is driven hard into a head sea, the bow will lift to the wave and then become unsupported as the wave crest passes aft. In this situation, the bow will drop to restore equilibrium before lifting once more to the next wave. The problems start in a short, steep sea when the bow may not have time to lift to the next wave, particularly as the stern will still be raised under the influence of the wave that has just passed. Reducing speed will give the boat more time to adjust to the changing wave profile and will thus help to make the motion easier.

If the vessel is driven too hard in a head sea, there is a real danger of a wave breaking on board as the bow is forced through, rather than over, a wave. Water has surprising weight and solid water breaking on board can pose a risk of structural damage. In this situation, the most vulnerable parts of the boat are the wheelhouse windows, although having said this I have never experienced them breaking, despite seeing tons of water crashing down on many occasions when operating the old displacement-type lifeboats. In a boat with a fine bow there is a greater risk of the bow burying into a head sea because it has less buoyancy. This is perhaps alarmist talk, though, because in the interests of seamanship and comfort you should have slowed down long before you get to this point.

Opposite: There will barely be time to recover from one wave encounter before the next in these very rough conditions.

Driving a displacement lifeboat to the limits of performance.

A Dutch lifeboat powers its way through a wave crest in breaking waves.

That said, when trying to find a comfortable speed for operating in particular conditions, it is important to ensure that sufficient speed is maintained to give steerage way. In rough seas, I have seen the speed reduced and reduced in the interests of limiting the pitching until the boat is barely making headway, at which point you can start to lose control. This is because at a slow speed, the response of the helm will be reduced with rudder steering – as is fitted to most displacement hulls – and the bow could fall quite a way off course before the corrective action on the rudder starts to take effect. If, at this time, a wave should rise and strike against the weather bow, the slow rudder

response could mean that the boat will be knocked round, beam-on to the sea, before the corrective action is effective. In this situation, opening the throttles is one way to get a fairly immediate improvement in control, bringing the boat back on course quickly without any rapid increase in momentum. The safe minimum speed to maintain steerage way will vary from boat to boat and with wave length, height and steepness but it is unlikely to be less than 3 knots, or more for craft that have small rudders. The risk of being knocked off course is greatest with a breaking wave where the water is actually travelling towards the boat, as this exerts a considerable force on the bow.

A planing hull running at displacement speeds will have very different characteristics.

If the boat has to be forced hard in order to maintain steerageway in deteriorating conditions, it is time to start nursing the boat over the waves. This is when the throttle can be used to good effect. By opening the throttle as the wave approaches, the bow of the boat will lift. A burst of engine power will also improve the steering effect. As the bow lifts to the wave, ease off the throttle before the bow punches through the crest. This will cause the bow to drop slightly, thus reducing the tendency for it to fall heavily into the trough. As the next wave approaches, be ready to open the throttles again. The effectiveness of this technique will depend on the speed of the throttle response, which on a heavy boat could be quite slow.

By using this throttling technique, reasonably comfortable progress can be made to windward. There will be better control of the boat and if a larger-than-normal wave comes along, the person at the helm will

There is no escape but it is important to maintain steerage way in this situation.

be better prepared. However, because there is always the risk of being caught out of step by the irregularity of the waves and the larger-than-normal wave, this type of operation does require considerable concentration. This can be very tiring and can only be maintained for around an hour or so. However, experiencing such challenging conditions should be a rare event if you have planned your passage carefully with regard to the weather forecast, and certainly for leisure versions, such as trawler yachts, you should have taken steps to change the situation long before you get to this point.

A displacement fishing boat going too fast for the harsh conditions.

In head seas in which the conditions have become challenging, another option is to alter course by perhaps 20 degrees one way or the other, effectively adopting the sailboat technique of tacking. This has the effect of stretching out the wavelength and reducing the speed of encounter with the waves, which should allow better and more comfortable progress and, equally importantly, not have a major effect on the time taken on passage because although you may not be heading in quite the right direction, you will be travelling faster and in more comfort.

BEAM SEAS

Travelling with the wind and sea on the beam in moderate seas has the disadvantage of discomfort, due to the heavy rolling that is likely to occur, although with modern stabiliser systems this can be reduced. In these conditions, full speed can generally be used on a displacement boat without any real problems arising, because the boat is lifting bodily on the waves and the bow and stern have little movement in relation to each other. However, occasionally the boat may drop off the edge of a fairly steep wave front, which can be both uncomfortable and a little frightening so, as the beam seas start to increase in size, more care has to be taken.

Again, a small alteration in course can possibly lead to a significant improvement in the ride. This raises the question of whether you alter the course up into the wind or turn slightly downwind. The temptation will be to turn downwind as this will almost certainly offer a more comfortable ride, but by doing this you can end up quite a long way off course as the leeway from the wind on the side of the boat will also be taking you downwind. What action you take will largely be dictated by the navigation situation, but heading slightly upwind could be the preferred course of action, in which case take the opportunity to cross an approaching wave at a low point if possible.

There are two main problems with beam seas. First, as the waves become steeper, the boat will try to adjust to the tilted surface of the sea and, consequently, will heel to quite a large angle. This in itself is not too serious, provided that the range of stability of the boat is adequate, but it has to be remembered that the wind will also be pressing on the windward side of the boat, tending to increase this angle of the heel. The second problem is more serious and occurs when breaking waves are encountered. This means that the surface of the water is moving bodily to leeward and can exert very great pressures on the windward side of the boat. The pressures are resisted by the still water on the lee side of the hull, which produces a heeling moment, which could develop to the point at which the boat has the potential to capsize. However, you will almost certainly have found a more comfortable course to follow long before you get to this stage.

Fortunately, a wave rarely breaks along a long front except in shallow water, in which you shouldn't anyway be navigating, but tends to do so in patches so that, with anticipation, it is possible to avoid breaking waves in beam seas. This means watching the sea ahead carefully and anticipating which part of the wave crest is going to break. It is then necessary to reduce speed to let the wave break in front of the boat, or turn into or away from the wind so that the boat passes either behind or in front of the breaking crest. Even in moderate breaking seas, life can be made a lot more comfortable on board by using this method of avoiding the largest of the waves and steering round the less-friendly-looking crests. In

moderate seas, there is not too much to worry about if you get it wrong and find a larger-than-normal wave rearing up alongside you, but once the waves start to break then the stakes become higher and it is necessary to be much more cautious.

If, in a beam sea, a situation occurs in which a wave that is about to break is bearing down on the boat and it is too late to reduce speed, then there are three options:

» the course can be maintained, in the hope that the boat will cope

» the boat can be turned towards the wave

» the boat can be steered away from the wave.

A lot will depend on the type and capabilities of the boat, but the best action is normally to turn away from the wave, because this has the advantage of not only buying time, but also reducing the impact of the wave on the boat, which is then moving in harmony with the wave direction. The breaking crest often rolls only a limited way to leeward and it can be possible to escape the breaking water altogether by this action. If you turn away from a breaking wave in this fashion, the throttles should be opened wide, both to get the maximum steering effect and also to keep the distance from the breaking crest as large as possible. If the opposite course of action is chosen and the boat is headed into the wave, a reduction in speed will probably be necessary to lessen the impact of the wave.

As always with displacement hulls, you may find that a small alteration of course can improve the ride comfort quite dramatically in moderate conditions and you should remember that you have two controls to help you cope, the throttle and the steering. Both can be used to find the most comfortable course of action in adverse conditions.

A point to notice when in a beam sea is that a wave will often be seen on the quarter starting to break. It may seem lucky to be always in front of these breaking crests, but they are, in fact, caused by the wash of the boat combining with the approaching wave to create an unstable wave that consequently breaks, when it would not otherwise have done so. Such seas seem to have little force in them and because you are moving away from them they have little consequence to your course of action.

FOLLOWING SEAS

Running before a following sea should give you a comfortable ride when the waves are no more than moderate in height. The speed of encounter with the waves will be much reduced so there should be none of the heavy pitching movements that you might encounter in head seas. Indeed, you can consider following sea operations as head seas with a much longer wavelength. The only problem that you might encounter is that when the stern lifts to a wave coming up behind and the boat starts what might be a downhill run down the face of the wave you might lose some of the steering effect. This is only likely to occur when the wave height is somewhere around a quarter of the length of the boat, which is rare in normal cruising. You can get excessive rolling in larger following seas because the boat can position on the crest of a wave for some time as the wave passes under the boat, and with bow and stern relatively unsupported, the stability of the boat can be reduced. We will look at this in more detail in the appendix.

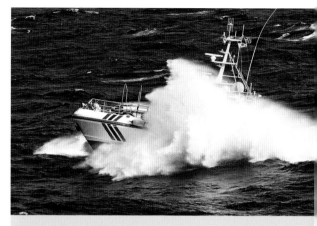

The explosive nature of water can be seen in this photo as a displacement hull powers its way through.

Allaying following sea fears

Following seas have the reputation of being the seaman's nightmare, conjuring up visions of broaching, capsizing or being swamped. Much of this fear stems from sailing boats, where running before a sea may be the only action left under extreme conditions. There is no doubt that running before a following sea in a gale of wind has its dangers, but provided that they are recognised, they can be compensated for and minimised. For example, I took a 14.6m (48ft) prototype lifeboat down the Irish Sea to Land's End in a force 11 from the north-west in a following sea and she behaved superbly, running straight and true in those enormous following waves. Trying to analyse the performance afterwards, I think that the lack of inclination to broach in those big waves was due to the sheer size of them; we just accelerated down the face of the waves and then slowed right down after the crest had passed when we seemed to be climbing uphill!

At first glance, it would appear that running before a sea and travelling in the same direction as the wind and sea would be a far safer course to take than battling against the waves. However, the rudder of a boat needs a good flow of water past it to be effective. If the water flow is reduced or even reversed because of an overtaking breaking wave crest, there will be much less control of the craft, or control could be lost altogether, and it is this factor that presents the major hazard in a following sea. It is very unlikely that you will find yourself in this situation during normal cruising, however; it is more commonly experienced by commercial craft and fishing boats that might have a stronger motive for staying out at sea in deteriorating conditions. For leisure displacement boats, the only time you might encounter this situation is when running an inlet or harbour entrance when the incoming wind and waves meet an outgoing tide and you have a series of breaking waves across the entrance. We will look at the techniques for running an inlet and the problems with broaching in Chapter 14.

When operating in a following sea, it helps if you understand the size and speed of the waves. The larger the wave, the faster it will travel. You can get some idea of the height of waves generated by various wind speeds by referring to the Beaufort Scale. An average open sea wave is likely to be travelling at somewhere between two and three times the speed of the average displacement boat, so the wave will take some time to pass the boat.

Smaller waves will be travelling only marginally faster, but you can assume that any wave that is likely to cause the boat to pitch will be overtaking the boat. A wave that starts breaking and having a crest that is running forwards faster than the wave itself will have a gradient of more than about 18 degrees, which is when waves start to become unstable. If you start to see breaking wave crests astern then this is perhaps the time to consider your position and decide whether you should alter course or even your destination.

Rogue waves

Another point to remember when operating in following seas, and indeed seas from any direction, is that waves come in all shapes and sizes. So, while you may look astern and see waves that appear quite comfortable to deal with, there may be much larger waves lurking among those average waves. So-called rogue waves tend to be found only when the wind is gale force or above, but a wave that is double the size of the average could easily be found when the winds are only force 4 or 5.

As we saw in beam sea operations, the wash of the boat can affect the wave crests behind it. This can particularly be the case in following seas, where it is likely that you will be running at speeds close to the maximum. This

The very irregular nature of rough seas is seen in this photo but a good helmsman can negotiate the way through them.

can cause a considerable wash behind and when this combines with the crest of the wave coming up behind, it will tend to encourage it to break. This means that, looking behind, it will seem as if you have drawn the short straw and the wave crests are intent on attacking you rather than being spread across the rest of the sea. There is not a lot you can do about this apart from reducing speed to reduce the wash, but as always when operating a displacement boat, understanding the waves and the boat can go a long way towards coping with the conditions you face.

SEMI-DISPLACEMENT BOATS

Semi-displacement hulls fall between two stools when it comes to handling. The theory is that they will behave and perform much like displacement hulls when operated at lower speeds and more like a planing boat at higher speeds. I am never quite sure about this philosophy as quite a few of the semi-displacement boats that I have driven have had their own characteristics, which do not necessarily relate to either of the main types. This is largely because the hull shape for semi-displacement boats tends to be much finer than that of a displacement boat, and it does not lift on to the plane like a planing boat, so you lack the trim and speed controls that dictate the performance of those.

The relatively fine bow of a semi-displacement boat does not respond to waves in the same way as the fuller bows of a displacement boat. When you are able to operate a semi-displacement hull at its faster cruising speed it can be a fine sea boat, with the trim automatically adjusting and the bow lifting to provide a comfortable encounter with the waves. This raised-bow attitude can also work well in following seas and help to keep things under control, since the boat tends to overtake the waves rather than vice versa. However, once the waves get larger and start to travel faster than the boat, the fine bow shape with its reduced lift can start to bury. It is at this point that you should reduce speed, whereupon the boat will act like a displacement hull but without the bow buoyancy needed for comfortable following sea operation. This is something I know from experience, since during a sea trial, I took a semi-displacement 40-footer into the wild Portland Race to see how it would behave in those

This planing hull is not comfortable running at slower, more leisurely speeds.

speed. Heading directly into a head sea, this spray is displaced each side of the hull, but with the wind on either bow, the spray can be directed back on board and it can be almost continuous, which can affect the visibility from the helm. I have found myself having to slow down to see where I was going on a couple of semi-displacement hulls, and from watching other boats it seems that this is a fairly widespread problem. This spray can be controlled to a certain extent with pronounced spray rails and chines, but these do make the ride harsher.

unpredictable seas. It was reassuring to see it operating just like a displacement boat at slower speeds, but with the ability to have better acceleration when I wanted to lift the bows to an oncoming breaking wave.

It is much the same in head seas: when speed can be maintained, all is well and the boat behaves effectively as if it were a planing hull. Reduce speed, however, and again that lack of buoyancy in the bow does not give the good lift required to negotiate over the approaching waves.

As always with boat design, there are a variety of hull shapes available for semi-displacement designs, some of which have a fuller bow shape that should perform better in larger waves. However, one characteristic of many of the semi-displacement boats that I have driven is the amount of spray that is generated by the hull at

Flaps: displacement and semi-displacement hulls

I have yet to find a modern semi-displacement hull that is fitted with flaps or interceptors and I have often wondered why this is so. Years ago, I had the opportunity to do a sea trial on an older semi-displacement boat with flaps and thought they were a very useful addition to the driver's repertoire of handling options, even though they were only effective at speeds of over 12 knots or so and the main benefit was the way that adjusting the trim of the boat could improve the fuel consumption. However, there was a penalty to pay when out in lively seas because bringing the bow down by using the flaps increased the spray that was generated. Perhaps this explains their lack of use on semi-displacement boats, although the spray issue is hardly unique to this application.

A semi-displacement hull pushing a lot of water in front of it even in calm seas when going faster.

Speed is critical in rough seas and this displacement hull is about to encounter a bigger than normal wave.

DRIVING TECHNIQUES: PLANING HULLS

Once you start driving boats that are operating at planing speeds, you enter a whole new world in which things start to happen more quickly at higher speeds. Whereas displacement boats tend to take a relatively leisurely approach to wave encounters, in a planing boat travelling at 30–40 knots you could be encountering a wave every couple of seconds. As we have already said, virtually every wave is different and in many cases, you can just set the throttle at a suitable speed and go. Many of the sea conditions that you will encounter during normal powerboat driving will be such that the boat can handle them and have enough in reserve so that you don't have to pay constant attention to the way the boat is performing. This is not to say that you do not need to concentrate at all, however, because you still have to concern yourself with other boats around you and general navigation in busy waters, as well as the possibility of meeting an extra large wave. Also, you need to be aware of the wash from other vessels, particularly that from the new generation of large, fast ferries; meet the significant wash from one of those and it can spoil your whole day if you do not slow down to negotiate the larger waves.

UNDERSTANDING WAVES

When driving any fast boat you do need to be aware of and have an understanding of the sea conditions because these can have a significant impact on the performance of the boat. The surface of the sea is a complex area that is constantly changing and if you are going to drive a planing boat intelligently then you need to understand the environment in which you are operating. Waves are mainly generated by the wind, but they can be influenced by other factors. The wave will start life as a ripple when the wind is just a zephyr, then as the wind freshens, the waves grow in size. The Beaufort Scale gives a very good idea of the sort of sea conditions that are associated with different wind strength, but remember that these conditions relate to the open sea with a developed wind, and could be different in inshore waters. What's more, the wave conditions can also be affected by the topography of the land and by tides and currents.

If you sit on the shore and study the waves you will see that the waves are by no means regular. In any wave train there will be high and low points to a wave crest. These may be created by local wind effects, but more likely are developed by smaller crossing wave trains. It is rare to find just one wave train in any sea area; there may be two or three criss-crossing it. When two waves meet, the resulting wave will be the total of the two wave heights, which is why you get this variation in wave height along a wave crest. You may find yourself going at a speed at which the boat is happy in the average of the wave heights, but if a wave that is considerably higher comes along then you have to be ready for this.

We tend to think of waves in terms of height, but remember that there are troughs between the waves and these can be just as much of a problem to a planing boat. The boat may drop

Opposite: Upright and in good shape to cope with on-coming waves.

159

The high speed of this fast lifeboat forces the water away as it powers through a wave.

into one of these 'holes' and then it can be a struggle to exit, although this mostly applies to extreme conditions, in which you are not likely to be out if you are boating for pleasure. So, be prepared for the irregular nature of waves, an inevitability that will demand your close attention in any winds over about force 4.

The wake of a boat or ship can be quite dynamic and different for normal waves.

Other areas that require concentration are possible tide races around headlands. This occurs when the wind is against the tide and the wavelength gets significantly shortened, creating challenging sea conditions with possible breaking crests. Something similar can occur in shallow waters, and reflected waves off breakwater walls are also possible.

In light of all these potential conditions, it is worth spending a bit of time trying to identify potential difficult sea areas both before you set out and while underway. This involves making a brief analysis of some of the sea conditions that you might experience, bearing in mind the changeability of the waves. The more you study the sea, the more you will understand its varying nature, so I encourage you to spend time just watching waves.

OPERATING IN CALM OR MODERATE CONDITIONS

When conditions are calm or moderate, boat driving is often at its best, since the motions of the boat are minimal and you can take full advantage of the exhilarating performance. In these scenarios it is largely a matter of opening the throttle and going as fast as you think fit. You will, however, need to set the power trim for optimum performance once up on the plane, but there should be no need to adjust the flaps unless there is a wind on the beam, in which case you might find the boat heeling into the wind and a correction is needed.

It should be possible to find a speed at which you are comfortable and leave the throttle on that setting. This is not an excuse to wander away from the helm and leave the autopilot in control, however: the recommended position is to keep one hand on the throttle and one on the wheel so that you can respond quickly to any changes in the sea conditions, such as the wash of a passing ship. This is part of the business of concentrating on the driving and the surroundings. When the sun is shining and the seas are calm it is so easy to let your mind drift and lose that focus, but that can be dangerous. Remember that you are possibly travelling at 1/2 mile per minute or more, and things can change quickly at that speed. What's more, there's always the risk of debris in the water and other potential collision risks. Keeping a good lookout is an essential part of fast-boat cruising, and that means astern as well; even though you might think you are the fastest boat out there on the water, there may be someone faster coming up astern.

This boat is going to have a heavy landing on the flat of the vee – the result of over-enthusiastic driving.

The kill cord

In an open RIB, the 'kill cord' should be worn by the driver, although there can be exceptions to this. The kill cord is there to stop the engine(s) if the driver moves away from the wheel either on purpose or involuntarily, so that if he does go overboard the boat will not continue with the engine running and turn round and run over people in the water. This has happened, and it is not a pretty sight, so consider the kill cord essential and have a spare on board readily available so that those left on board can restart the engine if the driver has gone overboard and taken the kill cord with him. The exception to the wearing of a kill cord is on rescue boats. Here, it can be an option of course, but in general, rescue boat crew sometimes have to move quickly about the boat and they do not want the engine to cut out at sensitive moments in a rescue. The same may be true of military operators.

OPERATING IN HEAD SEAS

Head seas probably present the most challenging conditions for fast-boat operations because, with the waves moving towards the boat, the speed of encounter with the waves is at its highest. The situation is compounded because the boat is encountering the steepest side of the wave first, which lies on the lee side of the wave. That steeper lee side of the wave means that the boat has to adjust its attitude in relation to the wave faster as the boat tries to adapt to the lift of the wave. Also, because the wave is travelling towards the boat, the time factor is compressed, so head seas give the driver less time to match the attitude of the boat to the approaching waves. This means that both reactions and responses have to be faster.

Because head seas represent such a challenge to fast-boat operations, most of the controls available to the driver are geared to coping with them. For instance, tabs and power trim are available to help keep the bow down and to prevent the boat flying off the crest of the wave as it climbs over. These controls, along with the throttle, can be used to help improve the balance and attitude of the boat in head seas.

With all planing boats, both large and small, there comes a point in the sea conditions when the boat cannot span the distance between wave crests and it starts to contour the waves, the bow dropping into the trough before it has to rise again to negotiate the next

Calm and collected. This planing power cruiser is well under control in these slight seas.

wave crest. You can delay this point by careful trimming of the boat; I have often found that there is a sweet point at which the boat may be contouring the waves at slower speeds and then that you can open the throttle, rather than close it, which provides the boat with the momentum to span the wave crests and adopt a fairly level ride. It can take some courage to open the throttle to get to this stage when your instincts tell you that you should be slowing down, and that sweet spot may not always be found. In general, it's something you might do when racing or when otherwise in a hurry.

Hitting the sweet spot

The first time I experienced the sweet spot was in the Cowes-Torquay-Cowes powerboat race when heading across Lyme Bay in Cesa*. Buzzi had the boat running level and true at over 160km/h (100mph) in a force 4 wind and sea, and the trim hardly changed over all those 64km (40 miles). It was like a magic carpet ride achieved through careful trim. Another time was in a 21m (70ft) patrol boat built for the Greek Navy that I was delivering to Greece. Majorca was our next stop, but we encountered the Mistral on the way from Spain and conditions were deteriorating. With 80km (50 miles) to go, we were constantly slowing down as the sea built. The boat was the world's first large deep-vee and having seen small deep-vees get up and ride on the wave crests I was wondering if it would work on this larger boat. Having opened the throttles, there were three heavy bangs as the speed rose and then we were up and riding the crests. Two hours later, we made Palma. It was another wild ride, but it worked.*

Whether or not you try this tactic has to be your choice and it may require careful trimming – flaps down and power trim in a bit – but it can certainly open up a window of opportunity. You can adopt the same approach when you see the wash of a large boat or ship coming towards you. Instinct will tell you to slow down and negotiate the waves at slow speed, but opening the throttle can get you through those wave crests with impunity. It can thus be a fine judgement, depending on the height of the approaching waves.

As always with head seas, once the waves start to increase in size, matching the speed of the boat to the waves is the key to high-speed head sea operations. For every particular set of wave patterns and every particular design of fast boat there will be an optimum speed of operation. There are no hard-and-fast rules or tables that can demonstrate what this speed is, but the optimum one will become obvious. Due consideration must always also be taken of the type of boat being driven and the passengers/crew on board.

That said, there are some general guidelines:

» Full speed can be comfortable in slight or even moderate sea conditions, depending on the size of the boat.

» Small, fast boats are obviously going to feel the impact of waves much sooner than larger ones. The warning signs that you are going too fast for the conditions will be felt when the boat starts to pitch and you start to feel serious wave impact, or the boat starts flying off the top of the waves.

For full-speed operations, the wavelength needs to be short enough to allow the hull of the boat to span the distance between the wave crests so that both bow and stern are supported at the same time. The momentum of the boat will help it to travel between crests with little or no change in attitude and progress can be rapid.

For larger waves, there is a greater distance between wave crests, ie they have a longer wavelength and they will also travel faster. This means that while the larger wave may be travelling faster towards the boat in a head sea there is also a greater distance between the wave crests so that the actual speed of encounter may not differ greatly. Where the difference does become apparent is when the wavelength becomes longer than the length of the boat. In these instances there is a chance that the stern of the boat may still be supported by a passing wave before the bow encounters the next wave. This can cause the bow of the boat to drop and pitching to begin. When this happens, the attitude of the boat is not correct for negotiating the wave ahead and it is time to start doing something about it.

The boat will start to contour the wave, ie it will want to follow the surface shape of the wave rather than span the crests. Once this starts to happen, the natural reaction is to want to slow down to give the boat more time to recover between each wave. However, this is not always the best solution. At slower speeds, the bow will tend to drop even further between waves as it tries to contour them, increasing the pitching motion. Often, a comfortable ride will only be found once the boat is fully contouring the waves, which will mean that the boat is then operating relatively slowly.

A higher speed will keep the bow up, and the inertia of the higher speed will also mean that as the boat comes off the wave passing behind it, it will hopefully be in a better attitude to meet the next wave in front. The aim should be to meet the next wave with the bow slightly up so that the boat will ride over the wave in front rather than trying to plough through it, but not so fast that the boat accelerates up the face of the wave and 'flies' off the top. A quick burst of power is all that's required –

Time to open the throttle to maintain steering way when facing the heavy breaking wave.

Planing boats often have to come down to displacement speeds in these rough conditions.

just enough to lift the bow. Then, by easing the throttle, the boat can be persuaded to cut through the crest rather than rise over it, with sufficient momentum to stop it from dropping too much into the next trough. The throttle can then be opened up again for the next encounter. When you get it right, there should be a more or less level track for the boat through the waves.

To achieve this sort of sensitive throttle control, you ideally need a wide range of throttle lever operation as well as comfortable access to the lever. Even with these, this throttling technique requires constant adjustment and assessment, and is therefore tiring, requiring high levels of concentration that cannot be kept up indefinitely.

With the props out of the water, this racing boat has lost control whilst airborne.

For this reason, in order to try to make rapid progress a driver may sometimes choose to make quick changes to the trim of the boat as a sort of reserve for use when he sees a larger-than-normal wave approaching. By using the flaps and the power trim it should be possible to find a comfortable balance for the boat to match the prevailing conditions. The flaps will be the main weapon in counteracting the upward lift of the bow in head seas. Interceptors, with their rapid response, can be used effectively to help give a level ride and in automatic mode they proved very effective in the trials I have done. The automatic system takes a lot of pressure off the driver and helps to promote a much more level ride, which can be adequate in many circumstances.

If you find there is a need to slow down when approaching a wave, the boat is probably going too fast for the prevailing conditions. Even so, the reduction in speed should only be small and the throttle should still be opened with a quick burst to lift the bow for oncoming waves. Of course, you can only use this technique if you have a light and responsive boat and it may not work on the average cruising motor yacht.

Over-enthusiastic use of the throttle causes the bow to lift as a boat comes onto the plane.

In head sea operations, the design of the boat also has to be taken into account. A boat with a fine, or narrow, bow section will generate much less lift when it encounters a wave in head seas and therefore should be able to achieve a more level ride because the hull will be less sensitive to the passing waves. This is one reason why high-performance boats are typically long and narrow. A boat with full bow sections, such as you find on most cruising powerboats these days, will be much more sensitive to the shape of passing waves. You cannot change the hull shape once you are out there on the ocean, but anticipating the reaction of a particular boat design can help with finding the best operating solution. Putting the flaps down should improve the ride on boats with a full bow shape and allow you to keep speed up for a bit longer.

This boat is trimmed bow up as it comes onto the plane.

OPERATING IN BEAM SEAS

With the wind and waves on the beam, the ride on a planing boat will be a lot easier than it is when trying to cope with head seas. This is because in beam seas there are fewer sudden changes in wave gradient, although the driver still has to be aware of the sudden changes in wave conditions that can occur in any wave train. For example, breaking wave crests can be a danger in beam seas and these can rear up suddenly alongside the boat. Also, with the wind on the beam, there is the increased risk that the boat will land on the flat of one side of the hull rather than centrally on the vee – a scenario covered in Chapter 14. In these conditions, there is a need for certain driving techniques to be adopted to minimise this risk of impact.

The deeper the vee, the more likely a fast boat will heel over when turning.

In slight and moderate sea conditions, there should be no problem with operating at full throttle in beam seas and the size of the boat will be less critical because the ride comfort will not be dependent on the wavelength, as it is with head seas. In beam seas, though, you will become more aware of the irregular nature of waves and just when you're thinking you're running comfortably along in a trough, you will find a wave crest coming right at you. It is easy to forget that the waves themselves are moving downwind. This means that if you maintain a course that is parallel to the waves, the crests will go past you, which makes it feels like you are going slightly upwind all the time.

In beam seas, there is reduced requirement for matching the speed of the boat to the waves, but you'll still need to find a comfortable speed at which the boat can operate without risk of serious wave impact or dangerous changes in the attitude of the boat in relation to the waves. The risk here mainly comes from the possibility of there being an underlying wave train coming from a different direction from that of the main pattern of the waves. You are less likely to notice this in head seas but in beam seas these secondary waves become more apparent.

A planing deep-vee almost leaves the water in these moderate seas.

These secondary wave trains can generate pyramid waves, which can rear up without warning. In moderate seas, these may not be especially large but they can still be a disconcerting change in what is an otherwise regular pattern of waves. There is also the possibility that the boat may have to cross over one dominant wave train and into the trough between the next two waves in order to maintain the approximate required course. To do this, you can experience conditions that may at times appear very similar to those found when operating in head seas or nearly head seas.

Unless you are in a great hurry, it is best to operate in beam seas with a degree of speed reserve in hand. Keeping this reserve not only gives the boat a chance to cope with some of the more difficult conditions, but it also gives the driver the possibility of accelerating his way out of a problem. This could be avoiding the breaking crest of an oncoming wave up to windward that is bearing down on the boat, or simply dodging a pyramid wave that has appeared close by. In beam seas, you will find yourself using the steering much more than you would in head seas as you try to steer your way out of trouble, but

of course you can also accelerate or slow down to avoid breaking wave crests or steer away from them.

Ideally the speed in beam seas should therefore be in the mid-section of the planing range, ie if the boat has a top speed of 40 knots, then a 35-knot speed would be appropriate. This allows the driver the flexibility to drop the speed down to around 25 knots if a difficult wave is approaching and wait for it to pass, or to accelerate up to top speed in order to go around it, the latter often being the preferred course of action.

Beam seas will not normally call for the constant operation of the throttle in order to adjust the trim of the boat. In most cases, the boat can be allowed to operate at a constant speed, although you should still keep your hand on the throttle lever. If a challenging wave appears up to windward you have two options to avoid it. The first is to steer upwind across a lower section of the crest before the steep section arrives. The second, and probably better, option is to steer away from the problem wave section by heading away downwind. Steering away and opening the throttle at the same time will take the boat safely out of the potential danger area, and once past the crest, the boat can be brought back on course and normal speed resumed.

This RIB is being pushed hard when out on a rescue where time can be critical.

In rougher seas, in which the controls have to be used to make safe progress, good concentration is needed, as always. This is particularly the case in beam seas, as a higher degree of anticipation is required in order to take avoiding action at an earlier stage than you would in head seas. Most attention will be focused on the waves coming from the weather side, but you also need to keep an eye on what is going on ahead. There may not be a demand for the immediate response to the controls that there is in head sea operations, but the ability to power away from trouble is still important.

OPERATING IN FOLLOWING SEAS

Operating in following seas appears to be an easy route for fast boats because the boat is running with the waves rather than fighting against them. In slight or even moderate sea conditions, this route is easier because you will have less wind effect and the rate of encounter with the waves will be much slower than with head seas. In most conditions, you should be able to choose the speed at which you want to run. Only when the bow starts to drop between waves do you need to start taking control and work the throttle.

Once the waves start to build, however, following seas can provide a real challenge for fast boats. This is because they make it much more difficult to control the attitude of the boat. It is important to remember that the design of most boats is usually optimised for head sea operations, which means that the controls, such as flaps and power trim, do not help a lot in following seas. Your main weapon in these conditions will be the throttle and even this needs to be used with skill and care when the waves grow in size. Boats with a fine bow shape can be especially challenging to handle since the bow is likely to bury as it drops into a trough. For this reason, some fast-boat designs use anti-stuff fins or shapes near deck level to provide additional lift in this situation. The full bow shape of most motor cruisers should work

A large planing powerboat can keep good control in quite rough conditions.

effectively in following seas although there can be a fairly abrupt change in attitude as the lift comes into effect, leading to uncomfortable boat motions.

The way that a planing boat behaves in following seas will depend on several factors. The speed of the boat is one, and when a boat has a speed that is around more than twice the speed of the waves, there is a chance that the boat will react in much the same way as it would in

The squared off bow of this planing hull is an anti-stuff device for following sea operations.

a head sea. With these higher speeds it is possible to maintain the attitude of the boat as it leaps from wave crest to wave crest, and rapid progress can be made. Around 40 knots is probably the minimum speed at which this approach can be taken, but it is only really effective at speeds in the 50–60 knot range and above. As always, much depends on the relative size of the boat and the size of the waves, and the relative speed between the waves and the boat. The higher the boat speed, the more chance there is that this tactic can be viable as long as the wavelength is relatively short, but it can result in a rough ride because of wave impacts.

The various types of following seas will also have a significant influence on the way a boat behaves in them. Long, low waves are relatively easy to cope with and their effect will not have a significant influence until they reach a certain height, probably around the 1–1.5m (3.3–4.9ft) mark in relation to, say, a 10m (33ft) boat. At this wave size, the boat should be able to come cleanly through the waves at their crests and maintain full speed because the wave crests are relatively close together and the ends of the boat are not left unsupported, which would cause the bow to drop into the trough.

As for head seas, a lower speed could allow the bow to drop as it comes over the crest of one wave before it encounters the next one, particularly as the lee side of the wave is steeper than the weather side. Once a boat starts this contouring between wave crests, the attitude of the boat is more difficult to control and it is likely to plough into the wave in front rather than ride over it.

It looks worrying to see a boat like this, but this is mainly spray which is relatively harmless.

As conditions deteriorate and the waves become higher, the boat operator is faced with two alternatives. The first is to maintain a speed considerably faster than that of the waves and attempt to lift the bow up over the waves with only a minimum amount of contouring. In this situation, keeping the flaps up and the power trim out will help to keep the bow up. If there is a chance to move weights in the boat then this should be as far aft as possible to maintain bow buoyancy. In this way, it should be possible to maintain speed as conditions deteriorate, although eventually you will be forced to reduce speed as the bow starts to bury into the wave in front. At this stage, the second option becomes viable.

This second option is for the boat to travel at or just above the speed of the waves. In this way it is possible to hold the boat on the back of a wave and drive it over the wave in front only when you find this wave having a lower crest. This will allow the boat to cross over the lowered crest without fear of encountering a deep trough on the other side because the lowered crest will often mean that the wave has just broken, with the water from the crest running forwards to fill up the trough in front. This type of driving requires considerable

concentration because it is very easy to go too slowly and allow the wave behind to catch up. If this happens and the wave crest behind is breaking, the boat could get into a broaching situation. If there are any doubts about what is happening behind, the solution is always to open the throttle and drive out of trouble. Wave crests have a nasty habit of appearing and disappearing without warning and one challenge in following seas is monitoring the waves both ahead and astern.

A boat will accelerate naturally when it is on the lee side of a wave in a following sea because the downward slope of the wave causes the boat to speed up under the force of gravity, so opening the throttle to lift the bow in this situation will only have a limited effect. A short burst of throttle might work to lift the bow but there is a risk of driving the boat into the back of the wave in front without enough lift to rise over it. What's more, coming over the crest of a wave in a following sea could easily mean that the propeller is not operating in solid water, and so the response to opening the throttle may not always produce the desired results. All of these points are covered in more detail in Chapter 14.

Finding a speed at which to operate in following seas therefore requires careful judgment and becomes more and more difficult as the conditions deteriorate. At this point, it may be time to revise the tactics and look at alternatives, such as varying the heading to effectively produce a longer wavelength. Steering can be used to drive around larger wave crests, but here both throttle and steering need to be used in conjunction to give full effective control.

A change of tack

Always remember that headings are not cast in stone and sometimes even small variations can make a significant difference to the way the boat behaves. It is therefore always worth trying to change course by 10 or 20 degrees every so often when things get difficult just to see what happens; this can work in all sea conditions.

A well-controlled turn
without too much
heeling.

REFINING THE PERFORMANCE

We have covered the broad spectrum of boat handling for both displacement and planing boats, but there are a lot more detailed techniques that are relevant in particular circumstances. These can be used in particular challenging situations that an operator might be faced with as well as for coping with difficulties that are inherent in the design of some boats. Here, we will look at a wide variety of detailed aspects of handling boats that should give you an insight into the value of experience and seamanship in boat driving.

HEELING INTO THE WIND

When a boat with a deep-vee hull is running with the wind on the beam, or indeed with the relative wind direction anywhere between 45 degrees on the bow to about 45 degrees astern, you will notice that the hull tends to heel into the wind when there is a fresh breeze. This is probably more of an irritation than a major concern, but because the boat is heeling it does mean that it will tend to land more on the flat of the vee that is to windward than it would if the boat were upright and so there can be a harsher ride.

This heeling is common to most deep-vee hulls and the deeper the vee, the greater the angle of heel. The reason for this is that you are probably instinctively applying a helm correction to counteract the fact that the wind is trying to blow the bow away downwind. You need to picture the way that the boat is in the water at planing speeds, with the stern well immersed and the bow probably riding high out of the water. This means that the bow will want to veer away from the wind, with the stern providing the pivot for this to happen. You correct this tendency by applying a helm correction to keep the boat on the desired course, but as we have seen, if you apply helm on a deep-vee hull the boat heels over, which results in the boat heeling into the wind.

This can be corrected by lowering the flap or interceptor on the windward side, which will help to bring the boat upright. However, bear in mind that by lowering the flap you will create additional drag on the windward side and you will need to correct this by applying a steering correction the other way, which hopefully will bring the hull upright and give you a better ride through the waves. With auto-trim systems, the correction should be made automatically because they are designed to keep the boat upright at all times.

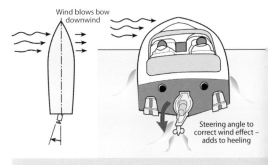

Wind blows bow downwind

Steering angle to correct wind effect – adds to heeling

Moving a propeller shaft from side to side for steering – known as dynamic steering – also contributes to the heel of a fast powerboat when the wind is on the beam. In this situation, the bow tends to blow off course, and the helmsman's instinctive correction with the steerable propeller increases the heel.

UNDERWAY HIGH SPEED

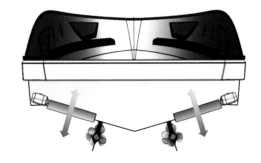

Magnus Effect stabilisers folded into the transom for high speed operations.

ADJUSTING THE TRIM FIN

On older outboards and sterndrives you will find a small fin attached to the lower side of the anti-cavitation plate that sits above the propeller. This fin is there to counteract the tendency of a single outboard or sterndrive installation to exert a steering pull to one side or the other, which can be both tiring when driving and potentially dangerous if you fall overboard and the boat turns round still under power. This steering pull is generated by the turning of the propeller with the lower blades of the prop potentially in denser water than the top blades, which are close to the surface. This means that in effect the propeller is 'walking' sideways, creating the pull on the steering. Adjusting the trim fin, usually by 5–10 degrees, exerts a steering correction and makes it possible to balance the steering with minimal pull on the steering wheel. (Incidentally, this 'walking' of a single propeller can be used to advantage when manoeuvring the boat in harbour as the boat will tend to turn more readily to starboard, and this can be exploited.)

It sounds like a small point in making the driving of the boat more comfortable, but this steering pull can have disastrous consequences if it is not minimised. For instance, I once had to do trials for an insurance company to investigate a scenario in which the driver of a small, fast boat that was towing a waterskier lost control and was thrown away from the wheel when the

The small, silver, trim tab can be clearly seen on this stern drive leg above the propeller.

boat hit the wash of another boat. She did not have the kill cord attached and so the boat turned sharply under full power and ran over the husband who was waterskiing behind, almost taking his arm off. During the trials with the boat, I measured a pull at the rim of the steering wheel of 9.5kg (21lb), which would take some holding even under the best conditions.

Had the trim fin been adjusted, it would have been possible to eliminate most of that steering pull, although the pull on the steering can vary with speed so it is not possible to eliminate it altogether. Of course, the driver should also have been wearing a kill cord.

On modern outboards that use fly-by-wire steering, although the steering pull is there at the transom, there is no feedback to the steering wheel, which means that the trim fin is eliminated. However, if your outboard has one then make sure the trim fin is adjusted correctly. With twin outboards or sterndrives, the propellers rotate in opposite directions and so this steering pull is also eliminated.

SPIN-OUTS

A spin-out on a powerboat is only likely to occur when the boat is racing or being driven as hard as possible. When racing, it can occur at a turning mark when the boat has to be turned through a considerable angle, hence the mantra: 'wide in and close out, or close in and wide out'. In other words, do not attempt to make the turn too sharply. One type of spin-out can occur when you start the turn and then, finding you are going faster than you want to be, you close the throttle as the boat enters the turn. As we have seen, closing the throttle will make the bow drop, which has the effect of moving the steering pivot point of the hull forwards. With the engine weight concentrated at the stern, the momentum of this weight will cause the stern to want to catch up with the bow, resulting in a spin-out with the boat turning end for end. There should be no harm done except to your pride and the boat should stay upright at the end of the spin, but if there are other boats in your vicinity there is the potential for a collision.

The risk of a spin-out will be increased on a boat with a stepped hull, whereby the boat will be riding on two or more points under the hull. This means that the forward step could act as a pivot point for a spin, particularly when more weight is transferred when the engine thrust is cut and the bow drops.

Another type of spin-out can occur when the boat has dynamic steering, ie when the propeller thrust is used for steering, as with outboards, sterndrives, water jets and some surface drives. When the boat leaves the water, as often happens at high speed, and then 'flies' off the top of a wave and the propeller comes out of the water, the steering effect is temporarily lost. When the boat hits the water, the first part of the boat to re-enter will be the propeller and if the propeller thrust is angled to one side or the other from amidships, there could be a short period when it has nothing to act against because the hull is still out of the water. This could put the boat into a dangerous situation of instability, something that is thought to be one of the primary causes of a spin-out in rough seas.

In theory, the same situation could occur with rudder steering, but because the steering effect is considerably less with a rudder, the chances of this happening are much reduced. The solution here is quite simple: first, drive the boat within its capabilities so that it does not leave the water; and second, do not attempt to turn the wheel when the boat is airborne. Basically, a spin-out is due to bad or over-enthusiastic driving, so the remedy is in your hands.

BROACHING AND CAPSIZE

Broaching occurs when a breaking wave overtakes the boat, lifting the stern. This puts the hull in a downward angle with the bow potentially digging into the wave in front and acting as a fulcrum. The moving water of the breaking wave coming up behind the boat then forces the stern to go to one side or the other and, unless corrective action can be quickly taken, the boat will turn broadside to the wave with the risk of it being rolled over by the breaking wave crest. It is a scenario that can happen very quickly and once put into motion there is very little that the driver can do, except become intent on survival.

Broaching is a problem that normally would only affect a displacement boat that is travelling at a slower speed than the waves, and it is more likely to occur with modern designs that have a transom stern, which gives the stern a lot of buoyancy and is exposed to the breaking wave. Traditional designs had a pointed canoe stern, which would tend to divide the wave and hopefully allow the breaking water to pass either side of the hull and let the boat continue in a straight line.

Burying the bow in following sea conditions whilst entering harbour.

On a slower displacement hull, one problem that can make broaching more likely is that the water from a breaking wave crest is moving faster than the boat, so overtaking it. This means that the rudder becomes ineffective because it has no water flowing past it to give a steering effect. In fact it is possible that the water is flowing past the rudder in the opposite direction from normal, from aft to forward. I theorise that you should be able to get a steering effect by reversing the way you use the rudder but I have never had the courage to try this. When considering operating in big following seas, you should bear in mind that when a wave breaks and can become a threat, the water from the crest that is moving forwards is at most only 1m (3.3ft) or so deep. This means that with a deeper-draft boat, hopefully the rudder and the propeller will remain in deeper water and you will still have control; I have found this works well when running an inlet.

The seamanship solution to reducing the chance of broaching is to tow a drogue astern. This exerts a pull on the stern that should be sufficient to keep the stern into the waves and prevent it from going sideways under the influence of the breaking wave crest. I did a lot of trials with towing a drogue in a tide race off Strumble Head on the coast of Wales and we found that there are several factors that can be quite critical to make the drogue effective:

» You need to use full power so that the pull on the drogue is maximised. This also means that the drogue has to be strong, because we measured pulls on the drogue line of more than 3 tonnes.

» The length of the drogue line put out should be one-and-a-half or two-and-a-half times that of the wavelength so that the drogue stays in the solid water behind a wave rather than pulling out of the water and losing its effect if it is somewhere near the crest.

» You need to have somewhere strong to make the drogue line fast and a stern without a transom.

Given the above, you can see why the use of drogues on anything other than a displacement lifeboat is unlikely to be a viable proposition.

When drogues come into their own

One of the most challenging boating situations in my life occurred when I had to come in over the dreaded Doom Bar at Padstow in an onshore gale at night. We were in a lifeboat and had been delayed because we had been called out on a search when on passage, so our planned daylight arrival did not happen and fuel was getting low. The following sea was making control difficult and this was the one time in my life when I have used a drogue in earnest. Instead of struggling with wild, sometimes uncontrollable steering, having the drogue out was like having the hand of God on the steering wheel and we could run straight and true, find the channel marks and negotiate the shallows. Never has the calm water of harbour been so appealing and never has a drogue been more appreciated.

Streaming a drogue. The drogue must be well in the water when the maximum pull is required on the drogue line. There must be adequate slack in the tripping line to prevent accidental tripping.

With planing boats that can travel faster than the waves there is quite a lot a driver can do to avoid getting into a situation in which broaching can occur. The best course of action is to always be running at a speed at or above that of the waves. At these speeds, there is no chance of a wave behind catching up with the boat and causing a broaching situation. However, maintaining this is not always simple in a following sea because even individual waves in a wave train can move at different speeds because they have different heights. Just when it appears that the boat is safely on the back of a wave with the crest running just ahead of it, this wave in front can disappear and suddenly you look astern and there can be a breaking wave curling up ready to pounce. Even in this position, escape is still possible simply by opening the throttles and driving the boat forwards away from that breaking crest. In order to do this it is first necessary to be aware of the breaking crest behind and in these sorts of conditions it can be a wise precaution to have one crew member watching the seas astern.

A broaching situation only becomes really dangerous when the stern is lifted and the bow is down, probably immersed to the stage where opening the throttles will only drive the boat deeper into the wave in front rather than away from the breaking crest. Up to this point, there is still a chance to power the boat away from the breaking crest. Fast boats operating at slower speeds are more prone to broaching because they have relatively little grip on the water to give them directional stability and the weight of the engines concentrated at the stern will encourage the stern to swing if the bow becomes a pivot point.

The golden rule when operating in following seas where there are breaking wave crests is always to travel faster than the waves. However, this is where difficulties can occur because the lee face of a wave is steeper than the weather side so as the boat comes over the crest of a wave the bow can be quite suddenly unsupported and start to drop into the trough. You can't see into this trough until you come over the crest so the time to take action can be very limited. The resulting downward angle of the boat will cause it to accelerate down the wave front. In coming through the crest, the boat can also have the effect of making the wave crest unstable, with the wash of the boat dragging the crest of the wave forwards and encouraging it to break.

When looking at fast boats, mainly RIBs, that have capsized at sea, it seems that the event usually occurs when the boat is going slowly in following seas. For instance, capsizes have occurred when a boat is coming alongside a mother ship and has slowed and then got caught in the wash from the mother ship. Another high-risk area for capsize is in surf or tide races and again, the capsize will usually occur if the boat is going too slowly, perhaps even off the plane. Rescue boats in particular

are vulnerable, since they may have to go slowly when recovering a casualty. If this is the case, it is best to undertake recovery heading into waves.

If you have a long run in following seas and you have found a speed at which the boat is operating relatively comfortably then it can be good practice to occasionally turn the boat round to see just what the wave conditions are like. Bear in mind that waves will generally appear much more moderate than they really are because they are breaking away from you. By turning around, you will be exposed to the reality of the situation. This can be a help in deciding whether it is in fact safe to continue operating in the prevailing following sea conditions, or whether it would be better to consider an alternative course or to run for shelter.

Operating in rough following seas therefore requires considerable skill and judgment, especially since the penalty for getting things wrong can be quite severe. A driver should be just as interested in what the waves are doing behind him as he is in the waves in front of him.

The wake of a ship can produce some dangerous waves that require careful negotiation.

RUNNING AN INLET

The one time when you are likely to be faced with operating in challenging following seas is when coming in from seaward into some harbours or river entrances when the wind is blowing onshore and the tide or current is running out; running an inlet can be one of the more exciting times when driving a powerboat. There should be no problem when the wind is off the land because you will be entering sheltered waters as you approach the land, but even then the flow of water coming out of the entrance on an ebb tide or outgoing current can produce areas of breaking waves generated by the shoals or narrow channels in the entrance. The real challenge when entering this type of harbour comes, however, when the wind is blowing in from seaward because not only can there be a wind-against-current situation, but there is also the added complication of narrow channels and shoals. At night, the situation is much worse because you may not be able to see clearly what is going on.

You may want to run the inlet to get back safely into harbour, but rather than rushing straight in, take time to stop and think things through. One of the problems with coming in from seaward is that you cannot always clearly see what the conditions are like because the waves are breaking away from you. You cannot judge the wavelength of the breaking seas and it may not be fully clear just where the channel lies, so time spent thinking about the situation is time well spent.

You may not have any option if you are running short on fuel, but if you are not happy with the conditions in the entrance, look to see what alternatives are available. Is it worth trying to raise someone on the VHF in the harbour so that they can offer an opinion about the local conditions? Are conditions likely to improve if you wait a while, perhaps for the tide flow to change or the wind to ease? Are you familiar with the harbour and marks so that navigation will be straightforward? It's worth considering all these aspects before deciding what to do.

Here the bow lifts as the boat is driven over a wave.

You need to keep a careful watch astern when running an inlet in these conditions.

When it comes to the actual run in, you should do this without hesitating. The breaking waves over the shallow water of the entrance or the wind-against-current zone are no place to stop if you are not sure about things. So, plan your navigation before you enter, make sure that everything in the boat is secure and that the engines are all in order – the last thing you want is a breakdown as you run in – and after that it is largely a case of using the driving techniques we have talked about for operating in breaking following seas, riding in on the back of a wave and letting it break before you ride over it. This is one situation in which you really do need to watch out astern because the waves will be unpredictable in the shallow water, with the possibility of large standing waves. It could be a wild ride and you need your wits about you and full concentration on the job in hand. You will have better control in a planing boat because there will be a much wider range of speeds at which you can operate. In a slower displacement boat you might want to pause until conditions improve. This is a judgement call that only you can make at the time.

A wild ride

Running an inlet is always a challenge, and this proved especially true when I and my crew had to enter St Augustine Inlet in Florida in a planing boat. We had made passage down the coast and this was our planned stop to refuel, but we had not bargained for the big swell coming in from the Atlantic combined with fog. This was in the days before GPS, and although the LORAN (long-range navigation) plot was pretty accurate, it was still a challenge to find the channel – which in those days before dredging, had a dogleg in it – where it was essential that we picked up the buoys before we hit the shoals. It was a tense time and we split duties, one crew to look out for the buoys in the fog, one to watch astern for threatening waves. I was on the helm. There was considerable relief when we picked up the first channel marker but I was concentrating on coping with the speed to match the waves, which were constantly changing. It was a wild ride, particularly when we had to turn beam-on to the breaking swell to follow that channel, but we made it safely thanks to the quick throttle response from the engines.

Running an inlet off the Florida coast using full speed to travel faster than the waves.

NIGHT OPERATION

Operating a boat in darkness adds a whole new dimension to navigation. The biggest challenge here is that you cannot see and read the waves and so quite naturally you adopt a more cautious approach. In reality, the best you can do at night is to find a speed and course at which the boat is operating relatively comfortably, which will allow a margin of safety for when a larger-than-normal wave comes along.

However, although this approach works if you are just on passage and can indulge in a more cautious approach, for rescue work and for some military operations speed at night may be essential. This is when you have to push the margins harder than you might like and risk the consequences of encountering larger breaking waves. Most modern boats will take the punishment in these more extreme conditions; it tends to be the crew who are the weak point. If the ride does get tough and there is a reluctance to slow down because of the urgency of the situation, then one tactic that might work is to try heading off the desired course by a few degrees,

which may ease the ride without impacting much on the distance being travelled.

At night, the whole navigation scenario changes and instead of being able to see directly what is going on, everything is now in code. Navigation lights flash with a wide variety of timings and you have to refer to the chart to understand which is which, while the heading of ships and boats has to be deciphered from the lights that they display. This can make running at speed quite a challenge and it pays to have the autopilot steering the boat. You will then be able to concentrate on collision avoidance. There can also be considerable benefit in having a steady course so that lights do not swing about the horizon.

FOG OPERATION

In fog, the situation is very different and much will depend on the type of fog. If it is a radiation fog – the fog that is usually found early in the morning in still air – then you can be reasonably confident that it will clear as the sun starts to warm things up, and also when you get away from the land. The challenge comes with advection fog, which is formed when warm moist air meets colder water. This can last for days and it can also occur in a fresh breeze, so there may also be the challenge of rougher seas. Visibility in this sort of fog should be sufficient to enable you to read the waves and to make rapid progress; the challenge is in safe navigation. The electronic chart will give you the position and course quite adequately in fog but collision avoidance is a different story: intense concentration on the radar display, if you have one, is required to 'see' other vessels when the boat is bouncing in waves, and focus is also required if you are to take avoiding action. Small targets may not show up clearly, so you need both a good lookout to visually spot other vessels in time to take avoiding action and you simultaneously need to be reading the waves. This means you have to have a combination of short- and longer-range vision, ie more than one crew at the helm.

Fog is a challenging environment particularly for faster-boat operations and the logical solution is to slow down so that you have more time to make decisions. The Colregs demand that you operate at a 'safe speed', which of course means one at which you don't go aground or have a collision. However, you don't know what a 'safe speed' is until you don't hit something! For those who have to maintain speed in fog, such as rescue boats, the level of concentration needs to be very high, and navigating and driving the boat should be very much a two-man job.

TACTICS TO IMPROVE THE RIDE

In most regular sea conditions it is possible to find a speed at which reasonable progress can be made in head seas, and this can often be improved by optimising the settings of tabs and power trim, and fine-tuning the ride by throttle control. However, there will be conditions, such as when the wind is running against the tide or current, when the waves can become very short and steep, so that the boat cannot ride over them in a reasonably true and level attitude. You can also find that in certain sea conditions the boat finds it hard to keep in step with the waves.

Short, steep waves require careful negotiation and speed control.

These conditions may be local in extent and it may be possible to navigate around them. Even if it is necessary to pass through them, quite a small change in course can often bring about a dramatic improvement in the ride conditions. It may also be possible to make much better progress going upwind by 'tacking', like a sailboat, so that the waves are approaching from 45 degrees on the bow rather than directly ahead. This 'tacking' effectively increases the wavelength because the speed of encounter with the waves is reduced, and the boat and the driver have more time to adapt to each wave as it comes along. This change in course will certainly produce a more comfortable ride and reduce the stresses on both boat and crew, even though the rate of progress to windward may not be greatly improved.

Another tactic is to plot an easier course, even if it results in a longer route. When racing offshore, for instance, we have often found it can pay to follow the coastline around a bay rather than proceeding directly

These are conditions where you might want to consider tacking in order to improve the ride.

A lifeboat operating at full power (image courtesy Arie van Dijk).

across from headland to headland. Not only will you be heading slightly off the wind in the earlier stages of the diversion, but you will also be coming under the lee of the land further round the bay and this can give calmer seas. You still have to negotiate the headland but you would have had to do that anyway, and the conditions will be much improved for most of the inshore route.

DEALING WITH BREAKING WAVE CRESTS

When driving into head seas, breaking wave crests are something to avoid. A breaking wave will have a more vertical face and this will make it very difficult for the boat to lift over unless it has sufficient momentum. Because there is an actual body of moving water in a breaking wave crest, the moving water meeting a moving boat head-on can create a considerable impact and could cause damage to the boat and injury to the crew. Waves rarely break the whole way along a wave front, except when they are in shallow water

on a beach; breaking wave crests tend to be found in irregular, isolated patches. These have a much steeper wave front that a fast boat will find difficult to negotiate. The best solution in these conditions is to try to steer around the breaking wave crests. It should be possible to anticipate a breaking wave approaching one or two wavelengths away and this should give adequate time to turn the wheel to avoid the worst of the breaking wave. The alteration in course should be no more than 45 degrees because you do not want the boat to end up beam, or broadside, to the breaking crest because of the risk of capsize. A smaller angle of alteration should be adequate to avoid the crest in order to let it pass harmlessly down the side of the boat. If the crest cannot be avoided, as stated before, it is better to open the throttle in a quick burst to lift the bow rather than to close the throttle and risk ploughing into the wave wall ahead.

In severe conditions, when breaking wave crests are increasing, it may not be practical to avoid all the breaking wave crests by steering around them. This could be a time when it is necessary to look at the overall situation and decide whether trying to make progress to windward is the right objective. Tactics will depend on what you are trying to achieve by being out at sea in these conditions. When breaking waves start to present a danger to the boat and crew, the tactics should be focused more on survival than on continuing on a particular course. This may be the time to head for shelter if it is available.

In beam seas, we have already covered the idea of heading upwind or downwind to dodge any breaking wave crests that may threaten the boat, but you might want to consider the idea of an alteration in course, a form of 'tacking' to try to improve the ride. We tend to focus on throttle control to give boat and crew a more comfortable ride but in beam seas even a 5–10-degree alteration in course might offer a better ride. It costs nothing to experiment and the results can sometimes be surprising. The same tactic can apply in following seas but here you need to be a bit more careful about how much you alter course to make sure that you do not get caught by waves on the quarter.

ENGINE RESPONSE

Given all this talk about using the throttle both for short-term changes of trim and for driving out of trouble, the engine response to the throttle commands is clearly very important, particularly on faster boats. With outboards and most lightweight petrol engines, the response is good and almost immediate so that you can be confident that your throttle commands will be obeyed more or less instantly. With heavier diesel engines, the response may not be quite so quick, although most modern high-speed diesels have a good throttle response. It is only likely to be in displacement boats, where the boat itself can be heavy and the engines perhaps on the weighty side, that you may find a slow response to the throttle. This will reduce the number of options open to you when driving the boat in rough seas. You may also find that some modern diesels that have electronic controls may not offer the quick response that you want because the engine designers have introduced a slower response through

the engine software in order to reduce the stresses on the engine that can be generated by quick opening of the throttle.

CONCLUSION

There is a lot to discover about powerboat driving and I find that even after 60 years of experience I am still learning. There are courses you can go on and qualifications that you can gain, but remember that these are only the starting point. Experience is the most important part of learning to drive a motor boat and with planing boats operating in waves, it always seems that the more experience you have, the more there is to learn. The sea is never predictable.

I see some boat drivers who look on operating a fast boat in rough seas as a direct challenge; they see the sea as the enemy and want to prove that they can conquer it. This is the brutal way to drive a boat, which is not kind to the boat or its crew and both may arrive at the destination in no fit state to perform any task. Boat drivers should work in harmony with the seas, negotiating and finding a course that minimises the stress of boat and crew while still making good progress. It may not look quite so dramatic but it will get the job done and that is what really matters. It is all a matter of negotiation at the end of the day.

OCKE MANNERFELT, MANNERFELT DESIGN TEAM

"

As a young boy, I built a lot of scale models of all sorts, including my first full-size OK Dinghy at age 14. I then did all sorts of sailing competitions in various classes, such as Snipe, Lasers and Tornado cats etc. My schooling was as a mechanical engineer and I later worked as a technical designer for a modern furniture company, but at the age of 28 I said to myself that I should take a break and test my boat-designing skills; I duly produced the design of a 42ft (12.8m) modern sailing boat. Three years later, 53 boats had been sold and thus my boat-design career started. However, my son Ted did not like sailing so we built many smaller motorboats together instead, and I soon realised he was a good racing driver.

My long-term aim was to develop energy-efficient boats using my know-how from sailing boats. I researched the latest hydrodynamics and aerodynamics, looked at what nature had done in terms of fast fish and fast birds, and started a huge development programme. I realised that the best way to test these ideas was to design and build a racing boat and test it against the others. My first boat to incorporate all the new ideas was the B-22. By that time in 1990 I had the new Macintosh 3D computer so I knew technically what I was doing. The B-22 boat was my first with a stepped hull and an aerodynamic shape that stabilised the boat at speed, just like a dart arrow.

On our first time out with the boat it was 15 knots faster than predicted, so we realised we had done something good here.

Ted raced the boat and in 1995 won the UIM 1.3-litre World Championship race against catamarans, among others. The research programme was upgraded and we developed the B-23 and then the B-28 design, working now in a very professional way. The B-23 was outstanding in its class and won several world titles, and indeed still wins races all over the world. The B-28 was presented together with Volvo Penta at the Miami Boat Show in 1994 and it took the US market by storm. They had never seen a stepped hull bottom before and the B-28 with a standard VP engine and drive was faster than anything they had seen before.

The year after this, the boat was raced in the A Class and was so outstandingly fast that the APBA changed the rules in the middle of the season and the B-28 was banned from racing! This was the best advertisement that we could get. Our introduction of the stepped deep-vee hull prompted all the US boatbuilders to start introducing stepped hulls, of which some were good and some were bad because they are not that easy to get right. That B-28 boat still wins races 25 years later!

One of Ocke Mannerfelt's Bat Boat designs in race form.

An aerial view of a Bat Boat.

We then created the V-24 boat as the first one-design UIM class ever. This is a 24ft (7.3m) boat with a closed safety canopy and a standard small-block V8 petrol engine. This boat was a stunning-looking design and ran like a rocket, and most importantly, it was safe. The V-24 is today an icon of boat-racing designs.

I was approached by the Victory Racing Team from the UAE around 2005 and asked to design a new 6-litre cat that later became the X-Cat class. This design was very successful and I drew upon my know-how from stepped hulls and good aerodynamics. This Victory-built boat has been almost a one-design in its class due to its winning potential and has won all X-Cat world titles since the start.

In 2010, we came up with the Vector-40 design as a racing/pleasure boat and this also became a very successful design, winning the famously tough Cowes–Torquay–Cowes offshore race two years in a row at the

best average speed ever of 154.5km/h (96mph) over the 194NM course along the south coast of Britain.

Altogether, my racing boat designs have won 22 UIM World Championship titles up to now. So what is the secret of so many winning designs? I think I have a good know-how with regards to aero- and hydrodynamics and have always used a 3D computer to do things thoroughly. I have studied and tested the boats very well and always listened to what the drivers tell me. To make a fast boat is easy, but to design a boat that will actually win a race is not so simple. We always design boats that are capable of a high average speed but that are also able to keep the crew fit and happy. We try not to make the boat too thin in the bow because some day you will stuff the boat and you want to be able to recover in good shape.

When I started my design career, my intention was to learn how to design more environmentally friendly boats.

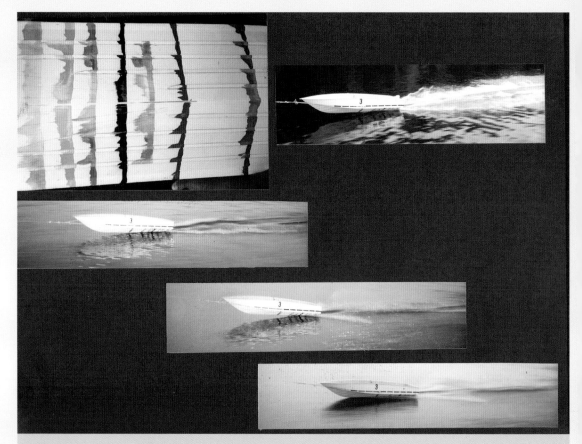

Mannerfelt's novel way of hull testing

In learning what to do, I read everything I could find and decided to match my designs to those of the top racing boats. I came up with some early racing boats that were good from the start but I did not actually know why. We then started a more thorough programme of making model boats of 4.9ft (1.5m) in length that we towed on a better or worse result method. We made copies of boats that we had made previously and all sorts of new

An advanced deep-vee stepped monohull showing the Mannerfelt style.

A stylish large RIB designed by Mannerfelt Design.

developments, altogether about 50 hulls I guess. This was a cheap and easy-to-understand method and from it we learned a lot.

We took the best hulls and tested them with wet colour, applying various colours to the planing surfaces to see what the actual water flow was. We repeated this with stepped hulls to see what the flow was from the trailing edge of steps, and we discovered even more. When we managed to understand the puzzle of water flow under a stepped hull we could arrange the steps and the spray rails more efficiently to minimise the drag.

From this we learned that no design could be the same and each one would depend on the target top speed, the cruising speed, the planing threshold, the sea state, the LCG, the drive system, the hull weight etc, etc. For racing boats, the best one was the boat that finished first, while for cruising boats it may be that the low planing speed is more important. So, all our hulls are different due to different requirements. Today, we use Computer Fluid Dynamics if we feel we need it and we have developed our own Speed Prediction program, which works just fine. We have a huge register of hull designs that we have made over the years and I think we know pretty well today how to design a good hull for a specific client, although we are always searching to develop hulls that perform better.

For racing boats, we also look at the aerodynamics, not only to reduce air drag but also to help stabilise the boat at high speeds. A rounded nose is important as a starting point to reduce drag and then we try to recess everything on the foredeck, such as cleats and rails, to smooth the flow of air. We try to get the transom as low as possible, sometimes so that the deck here is underwater when stopped, and to minimise the roll and pitching we place some aerodynamic stabilisers as far back as possible. These things will raise the moment of inertia and the boat will be more stable at high speeds. We test the aerodynamics by CFD and also by adding wool tufts on the real boat to check the airflow.

The stepped hull designs we have developed for racing have given us the experience that means they can be used on many series production boats with great success. They have approximately 8–12 per cent higher speeds than comparable boats and are also very fuel-efficient. They are easy to drive and need almost no trim help from the driver.

Ted Mannerfelt, my son, has now worked for 12 years in the company and is the Chief Exterior Designer and the Managing Director of the Mannerfelt Design Team.

This traditional steering wheel is fine for standing at the helm but not very practical when seated.

CREW COMFORT AND SAFETY

In recent years, there has been a distinct change in the focus of boats – both fast and slow. A decade ago, it tended to be the boat that was the weak point in the combination of crew and boat. Now this has changed and it is the crew, or at least the people on board the boat, who tend to be the vulnerable party. For this reason, designers and boatbuilders have to give much more consideration to the safety and comfort of the people on board. This applies to both displacement and planing boats; crews of displacement boats often having to spend longer hours at the helm, whereas the crews of planing boats possibly have to endure greater pounding from the ride in waves. Either way, comfort is important.

Having the crew as the weak link is in fact a good safety feature, because in more extreme conditions it will be the crew who give up first and hopefully moderate the ride or take steps to mitigate the problem, before the boat breaks down. That said, this crew/boat combination should be a happy marriage and not a battleground. Designers can and should do a lot to make the ride comfortable and safe, but ultimately the crew have to play their part; much of the safety, particularly for a fast boat, is in their hands.

HANDHOLDS

One of the basic requirements for crew safety is to have handholds so that the crew can move about the boat safely. These need to be strong because the crew may put their whole weight on them when the boat lurches unexpectedly. This seems obvious and reasonable, yet when I look around many modern motor cruisers on the market it is becoming increasingly rare to find any handholds at all in the saloon or around the cockpit area, which means passengers and crew are left to cling on to the edge of tables or seats if they want to move about when at sea. This lack of handholds is a sad reflection on modern boating; I get the feeling that salespeople fear that if handholds were fitted then they'd give potential buyers the impression that the boat might shift about at sea and people might get hurt.

You see the same approach in many other aspects of modern design, such as the lack of upturned edges on tables, which may not look as sleek but stop things falling off; the absence of secure stowages for small items; and a dearth of fiddles around the galley hob to keep the pots and pans in place. It may be that people only go to sea in fine weather but there is always the wash of other boats to consider and, even at anchor, boats can and do roll in the wash of passing boats. Strangely, when you do see handholds fitted they tend to be on displacement boats rather than faster planing ones, aboard which the movements can be more violent and sudden.

I suspect that things will change in the future if people get injured on a boat because they cannot hold on securely and sue both the owner of the boat and possibly the boatbuilder and designer, this may wake up people to the risks involved.

This helm seat provides comfort, but the large vertical wheel is more traditional than practical.

Duty of care

These days, there are health and safety issues that have to be considered. An employer has a duty of care towards his employees, including the crews of commercial and military boats, and the same is true of masters aboard pleasure boats.

This duty of care means there is a requirement to provide adequate protection for the crew to reduce the risk of injury, although with boats it is not always easy to say where that risk exists. The safest boat is probably one that does not go to sea... In reality, the operating environment of boats can expose crews to risk and on commercial and military boats it can be especially challenging to find the balance between crew safety and getting the job done efficiently.

SHOCK MITIGATION IN PLANING BOATS

One area where there is now a focus in planing boat design is shock mitigation: reducing the chance of injury through impact loadings as the boat operates in waves. EC legislation regarding the duty of care of boat operators towards their boat crews has set out limits for the shock loadings that crews can be exposed to, and this can in part be ameliorated by special seating to reduce the impact on crews.

There are a number of specialised boat seats on the market that offer a varying degree of support and springing – and we cover these in more detail later on in this chapter. There is no doubt about the effectiveness of many of these seats – objective and subjective measurements have shown their efficacy – but installing sprung seating is only part of the story. You are finding a solution to a problem that has been created by both the design of the boat and the way the boat is being operated, so why not consider trying to remove or at

A simple helm layout but the compass could be affected by the electronic systems.

This shiny dash could cause severe reflection in bright, strong sunshine.

least reduce the problem by limiting the impacts on the hull in the first place?

What I am proposing is that a more holistic approach could offer a much better solution. If you reduce the chance of impacts occurring as the boat makes fast progress in waves, there is less of a demand to introduce springing and other solutions to protect the crews.

The question of shock mitigation was developed initially in RIBs, the performance of which outweighed the capability of crews to withstand the impacts, but it has now extended to most fast boats. This can be a challenging area for the designers of performance leisure craft and, as we have seen earlier in this book, the way that the boat is driven can have a major impact on the shock loadings that the crew experience.

The deep-vee hull does a great job of reducing the shock loadings as a boat leaves the water and then re-enters, the vee angle of the hull providing the cushion of a more gradual re-entry. It is only when the deep-vee heels over

that the boat lands more on the flat of one side of the vee, causing the hull to lose part of its cushioning, which results in high impacts. So, if you can stop the boat heeling over or if you can prevent the boat leaving the water when operating in waves, you will be a long way down the line to reducing the shock loadings.

Running the boat on autopilot is a good starting point for keeping the boat upright and avoiding shocks. If you don't want to use the autopilot, then at least use only small movements of the steering wheel to correct the course. Designers should avoid using a wide chine, since this flat surface can impact the water with considerable force even when the boat is upright. Instead of installing a single wide chine, perhaps use a two-stage one, which might reduce the impact loadings. With RIBs that have inflatable tubes there can also be an element of bounce in the tube when it is inflated too hard, which can make the ride harsher. This can result in impacts in waves when the boat heels over and the tube bounces, causing quite violent lateral movements. Once it has been identified, this issue can be easily solved, as we explored earlier in the book, by reducing the air pressure in the tube.

As discussed previously, having a fine entry at the bow enables the hull to slice through waves rather than riding over them and this can help to reduce the pitching

One hand on the wheel and one on the throttles for RIB driving.

motions of the hull. It also reduces the chance of the hull 'flying' off the top of a wave, which can create heavy impact loadings when landing. There are some wave-piercing designs being tried and maybe these will help to smooth the path of fast boats, though a narrow hull will tend to heel over more readily than a wider one.

So, it should be possible to achieve a reduction in the wave impacts by a combination of hull design and considerate driving. The gung-ho driver who bangs and crashes his way through the waves trying to impress should have no place in fast boats, particularly those used for serious commercial or military operations; the considerate driver will probably make just as rapid progress and still have a crew and passengers who can enjoy the ride and the exhilaration of high speed on the water. The so-called thrill rides have a lot to answer for!

SEATING

Now we can look at seating for shock mitigation, because even the best driver is not going to be able to maintain the concentration needed to avoid all wave impact, and the more this can be minimised the better. There are three main types of seating to be considered for shock mitigation:

» sprung seats that have an up-and-down movement but do not provide much lateral support

» saddle seating that was developed for the early RIB, which uses foam padding to reduce the impacts

» larger and more embracing sprung seats that can provide some lateral support (in my experience, this is important since fast boats move from side to side just as much as they move up and down).

SPRUNG AND FOAM SEATING

I have tried a lot of these alternatives and I have discovered that I am not a fan of sprung seating. This is because unless the damping system is carefully tuned you can find yourself going up when you should be coming down, since the springing is not in tune with the varying movement of the boat. Having said that, some of the modern sprung saddle seating is much better and the designers are starting to realise that it is not so much the softer impacts that need absorbing, but the really hard bangs. So, you feel the seat 'give' when there is a hard bang but then they can 'bottom out' once the limit of the springing is reached. The springing does not seem to be progressive, though, which is what is needed, with it ultimately being stiff enough so there is not a terminal bang.

There is so much unnecessary clutter at this patrol boat helm which can be distracting.

Damping out the impacts on a boat is never going to be easy because of the huge variation in the direction and strength of the impacts and, in addition, with mechanical springing there will always be the question of wear and tear as the equipment gets older.

The alternative to mechanical springing is foam and this has been the cushioning of choice for many builders because it is relatively cheap. However, foam has had a bad reputation, mainly I think because of a poor choice of the foam used. Today, however, there are so many different types of foam available that it is possible to pick the right one for the job although, obviously, it has to be of closed-cell type so that it does not absorb water.

My ideal seat

What I propose for boat seating is a form of progressive foam with, say, three layers, each having different characteristics. The top layer in contact with the body would be a relatively soft foam that would deform under normal body weight, mainly to make

the person comfortable in the seat. The middle layer would be much stiffer, perhaps starting to deform under loadings of around 5G, which is somewhere near the point at which the impact starts to hurt the body. This would be a thicker layer and would absorb most of the normal impacts. The final bottom layer would be very stiff, perhaps starting to deform at around 8–10G, and would provide the final impact absorption to protect the body from the worst of the impacts. In theory, with such a seat there would be no bottoming out and the body would be protected progressively from even the worst of the impacts.

SADDLE SEATING

Having seen what a difference saddle seating made in the early days of RIBs, I believe this is still a viable solution, although it only offers limited support against the lateral movement of the boat. As the vee of the hulls of fast boats has got deeper, so there is a great tendency for the boat to heel over further, and this has generated much more lateral movement. This can

The cockpit of a four-engined racing powerboat designed for multiple person operation.

This high dash makes for poor visibility from the helm and the white finish will reflect the sun.

cause great discomfort and in a wheelhouse boat can bring the head very close to the sides of the wheelhouse structure. The saddle seat helps to locate the bottom half of the body, which is fine except that most of the body weight is concentrated in the upper half of the body, which remains unsupported. Widely spaced handholds can help with lateral support, although a seat with good side support might be a more effective solution. An angled footrest can also be a useful addition to any seating in fast boats since it can help you to brace against the movement of the boat.

EMBRACING SEATING

In its simplest form, saddle seating provides support around the hips, but in a more embracing form there is support around the shoulders as well. This side-support seating is now being offered by many seat manufacturers, which is perhaps a recognition of the problem of lateral movement. Some seats of this type also have a squab that is sprung and that can be raised or lowered under electric control, so that there is the option of standing or sitting, or a bit of both. These features are all well and good, but they are by no means light: the weight of sprung seats can be 15–20kg (33–44lb), with much of it mounted quite high in the boat. Add in the weight of the crew, who are also mounted quite high, and you have a considerable weight high in

the boat, which can accentuate the lateral movements of the boat and increase the shock loadings.

Another problem is that some of the sprung seats on the market are hinged at their forward end with the rear of the seat allowing the required movement. This means that the seat's occupant is moving backwards and forwards as well as up and down, which can make it difficult to use the throttles sensitively since it is likely that the throttle hand will also be going backwards and forwards.

Poorly situated throttle levers and unmarked flap and trim controls.

190

Other considerations when it comes to seating are whether or not they enable you to stand; so often it can be helpful to have the choice of sitting or standing in a fast boat. Seating with a squab that can be lowered offers this option while still providing support, but many of the sprung seats on the market do not allow room for standing at the helm or in other positions in the boat, so you are stuck with what you have got. If you are going to be doing long passages, you should also consider fitting seat belts. These not only meet duty of care requirements, but they also allow the user to relax and not feel the need to hang on tightly the whole time. We have used seat belts on most record attempts I have done and I believe they are worth their weight in gold.

WAYS TO IMPROVE DISPLACEMENT BOATS

We talk here mainly about the need for shock mitigation in fast boats, but comfort and support can be just as important in displacement boats. Despite this, there does seem to be a lot less focus on the ergonomics in these boats and tradition often dictates a vertical wheel, which is fine if you are standing at the helm but uncomfortable if you are sitting. The normal seating found on trawler yachts and the like is the big captain's chair, which works well and usually gives a commanding view out of the windows but often renders all the controls out of reach.

On most displacement boats the layout of the controls and displays could be greatly improved; many leave a lot to be desired, particularly in terms of night lighting and convenience. For instance, electronic displays need to be protected from the sun so that you can see them clearly – something that is very much not the norm. Dashboards are often cluttered up with rows of switches that can make it hard to find the right one, especially in the dark. Also, removing lights from the helm at night would help to improve what you can see through the window and retain night vision; so often it is the navigation displays that are the worst culprits at night. In some wheelhouses, it can be challenging to keep a proper lookout, as required by the Colregs, because of the wide window mullions, which could obscure a super-tanker in the distance. Even smeary glass can affect visibility, although this is easier to remedy than the wide mullions.

The moulded mullions at this helm severely obstruct the view.

A complex helm layout that could lead to mistakes being made at night.

For the controls, the angle of the wheel should be adjustable to make it convenient to use. Throttle/ gear levers need to be angled so that the sector that controls the ahead throttle setting is near the vertical position because that is the bit that you use at sea. So often on boats, both fast and slow, it appears that the layout of the helm is left to the boatyard workers who simply look for the most convenient spot in which to install equipment, and even when some thought is given to the layout, the designers rarely understand

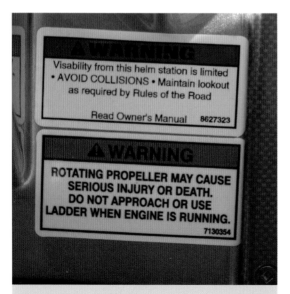

Putting a notice up is no substitute for not providing good visibility from the helm.

the needs of the boat driver or navigator. As a result, helm stations tend to be fine for use in harbour but rarely meet the needs of the crew out at sea in lively conditions or at night.

Coping with seasickness

Seasickness is something that needs to be considered in both fast and slow powerboats. I have been a lifetime sufferer and find that I can handle it if I take one of the proprietary medicines, but you do need to take these at least half an hour before you go to sea; take them when you start to feel sick and they tend to return the way they went down before they can become effective. The stick-on patches also work well for me and can be effective even after the first symptoms show, but they are not always easy to get and require a prescription in some countries.
It is thought that seasickness is caused by the different messages the brain gets from eyes and the balancing system when the boat is moving, so looking at the view outside can help, as can keeping occupied. I have heard stories that sprung seats can exacerbate seasickness when the boat stops after a run in waves because of the change in motion, but I do not have personal experience of this. Whatever the remedy, if any of the crew is suffering then take extra care of them because seasickness can be very debilitating and sufferers can more or less lose the will to live. Also, if you ever have the misfortune to have to take to a liferaft then everyone should take a seasickness pill because I can guarantee that even the hardiest seaman will suffer under these conditions.

CONCLUSION

Driving any powerboat can be challenging because not only are you on the lookout for other boats and ships, but you also have to work out where you are and where you are heading. On a fast boat, in which you may be covering a mile in two minutes or faster, the navigation alone can be a full-time job. Even on boats where life has been made easier by the presence of instant and constant position fixing achieved by GPS and electronic charts, you still can't just relax: concentration is still

A comfortable helm, but that long row of switches could lead to confusion.

key to successful powerboat driving. The other factor is good and well thought-out design. It is therefore my feeling that many designers need to get a lot closer to the powerboat experience to help develop successful designs that not only look and perform well, but which are also a pleasure to drive.

A lifeboat helm station with so many controls and displays.

FRANK KOWALSKI, SAFEHAVEN MARINE

"Primarily, Safehaven Marine specialises in the design and manufacture of all-weather pilot, patrol and SAR vessels. As such, an important part of the R&D involved in new designs is the sea trials that are carried out to ensure the boats are 'fit for purpose'. Operational requirements demand that they are capable of dealing with very heavy weather – a fact that means testing our boats in extreme conditions is very much part of our philosophy. I have always believed that if you are claiming your designs are capable of operating in heavy-weather conditions, then the only way of ensuring this is to have the confidence and experience to head out into a storm in your own vessels. It is only by operating in heavy weather that you can ever gain the experience to understand the dynamics involved when helming in heavy seas. It also allows one to appreciate the extreme stresses that such conditions place on the boat's hull, equipment and of course its crew. When I hand over a SAR boat that may one day have to go out into a storm to save lives, I want to ensure the boat as a design, and as built, is safe for her eventual crew. I am not going to say, 'Here you go, I think the boat is designed and built OK,' I want to know it is and not depend on the crew finding out at night in a storm whether or not that is the case.

As such, we have ventured out into some pretty extreme conditions: force 11–12 with wind speed of 100 knots and wave heights of up to 10m (33ft). However, it's not so much just the wind strength, or indeed the height of the waves, that determines the severity of the prevailing conditions, it's the steepness of the waves and how heavily they are breaking; without doubt, it's a breaking wave that presents the greatest hazard. We are fortunate to be based on Cork Harbour, where very violent wind-over-tide conditions prevail in the entrance when the ebb tide meets big swells. The entrance also has a shallow shoal called the Harbour Rock. When waves exceed 7m (23ft) in height they break very heavily, like surf on a beach, over the rock. We only ever head out into extreme conditions when we have a second boat in attendance so that we are capable of looking after ourselves in the event of any incident. Of course, the experience of crew is of paramount importance when venturing out in such conditions; I think I have probably been out in more than 100 storms exceeding force 9.

In heavy breaking seas, ideally you want to time it so that the wave plunges just ahead of you and is then spilling as it hits the boat. Sometimes, though, no matter how well you time it you can get hit hard. Having the wave break right over the boat can be extremely violent; here, you are looking at several tons of water crashing down on to the foredeck and front windows. When you experience the force of impact you appreciate the need for small-area windows with strong mullions and at least 20mm glass. We have seen window wipers ripped clean off and light mountings bent.

Sometimes, avoiding the plunge involves reversing quickly so the wave plunges ahead of you, then quickly gaining forward momentum before the wave hits you. At other times, it can mean accelerating quickly to get past the wave before it plunges. In any event, I find the best way of taking a breaking wave is to basically stop as it approaches and then just before it hits the boat engage gear and give a burst of power. This gives the boat momentum to resist the wave without gaining speed, which would cause you to fly off the wave and become airborne with an inevitable heavy landing. Yes people do often suggest that the best way to navigate these conditions is with speed, but really it's unrealistic to suggest this in a large swell. Yes, you can run at high speed jumping from crest to crest offshore in 2–3m (6.5–10ft) waves in a light race boat, but you can't compare that with these conditions...

Using my method, a quick burst of momentum also ensures that as the boat is engulfed in the breaker and all vision is momentarily lost, you should come out the other side heading in the right direction and angle for the next wave. Whatever the course of action taken, though, when a big breaking wave hits, expect the boat to be bodily moved backwards a boat's length.

Despite this, heading out is generally easier and safer than trying to re-enter the harbour with a following sea.

A rendering of Safehaven's proposed 76-foot (23 metres) record-breaking trimaran.

At least with a breaking head sea you can to an extent control the situation by heaving-to. If you do run in with a following sea then once you are committed, you can't really stop. The trick is to try to stay either on the back of the wave in front or at least in the trough, ready to accelerate away from the wave behind if it breaks – or at least that's the theory. The reality is often somewhat different: sometimes in a confused sea state with spray and poor visibility you can't tell where one wave ends and another starts. In this situation, you are just at the mercy of the elements and very much depending on the boat being well found and able to look after you. I have been picked up by a breaker and surfed forwards with the engines in full reverse at 25 knots, completely helpless to do anything other than wait for events to unfold. At times like this, you have no control over the boat and that is why running in through big breakers is so dangerous.

Extreme testing of a Safehaven pilot boat.

In my experience, aside from the debate from a hull design point of view, the one single factor that will ensure the boat will survive or handle in a safe manner in this situation is a very low centre of gravity, coupled with a reasonable amount of displacement to resist the force of the wave. A low CG reduces the amount of heel angle the boat assumes, which in turn limits the amount of yaw that develops; this then reduces the likelihood of broaching. And any boat, no matter how good, can broach if the breaking wave is big and violent enough and catches the boat at a bad angle. The trick is surviving the broach, and this is where a low CG counts.

Of course, self-righting is a reassuring feature, and luckily most of our vessels incorporate it, but I can't say I've ever been rolled even close to the point of capsize, at least not on a Safehaven vessel. Then again, I've never put the boat beam-on, and for sure I've gone through plenty of waves that if taken on the side would have resulted in a roll-over. Just don't get it wrong!

On the subject of boat design, I have designed quite a few different types, including semi-displacement, deep-vee planing, catamaran and, recently, wave-piercing boats. All offer advantages and compromises to various extents. For the extreme conditions described previously you can't beat a fairly heavy displacement, semi- or full-planing deep-vee hull with a full weather deck, low CG and a self-righting capability.

195

Few builders would expose their designs to this sort of extreme testing.

Recently, I developed designs based upon wave-piercing concepts. These are designed for high speed (50 knots or more) and up to a point they offered amazing capabilities in rough weather and could run at 40 knots through a 2m (6.5ft) steep head sea condition with amazing crew comfort. Any high-speed design by necessity has to have an LCG well aft and for wave-piercing this means that you are depending on the very high angle of waterline entry at the bow to cleave through the wave, which primarily happens through the boat's forward momentum and speed. In big waves over 4m (13ft), inevitably you have to slow down. Normal hull designs depend on deadrise and a more forward LCG to allow the hull to ride over the wave, tipping forwards over the wave crest around

midships, and depending on a high deadrise to soften the landing. This can't by nature happen on very high-speed designs as at slow speeds the point of tipping is aft of midships. This means that when forced to slow down, because of the aft LCG, the wave-piercing benefit can't be utilised to the same extent as when running at high speed. This in turn causes the boat to ride primarily only on its deep-vee midship sections, and as such it then behaves very much like a normal deep-vee hull.

The point at which this occurs can be extended by a bow ballast tank of sufficient size to significantly move the LCG forwards, with the caveat that the ballast tank is emptied for running in following seas. Here, you want the bow to be light. Surprisingly, the very fine wave-piercing bow doesn't have the negative effect one would expect in following seas. This is because the keel rises up towards the bow and at normal running trim the stem is not deeply immersed – it only interacts with the crest of the waves, and the hull pushes through the wave with very little deceleration and without bow steer, contrary to what one might expect from looking at the design.

On wave-piercing designs the running trim is a critical aspect to the boat's handling and is controlled through drive angle (with surface drives) and large flaps to allow extreme depression of the bow-to-zero running trim to cleave waves without leaving the water, as this eliminates

Testing to extremes.

It is unlikely that a boat would have to face up to these conditions when on service.

the possibility of slamming occurring. In following seas, it allows you to lift and fly the bow.

Catamarans are fabulous in many ways, especially seakeeping in following and beam seas, and they also offer excellent transverse stability. However, if you are running directly into a head sea, once the waves reach a certain height and steepness and it is necessary to slow down, they can suffer as slamming on the flat surfaces of the bridge deck can occur. Compare this to the capabilities of the traditional deep-vee monohull in head seas, whereby the hull remains level so that when it impacts after passing through the wave, it lands with its vee sections cushioning the impact. The problem is that

so often an interaction will occur, either by a cross sea or steering input, that causes the boat to heel and rotate as it leaves the wave, resulting in the hull landing not level on its vee sections but rather on the flat surface of the vee hull. Mostly, this does not occur with a catamaran hull as its excellent transverse stability ensures a much lower degree of roll and heel and the hull lands level.

Now imagine if one could have a hull with all the excellent dynamic transverse stability and deck space of a catamaran and the head sea abilities of the deep-vee hull. This is what I tried to achieve with XSV 20, a hybrid design that seamlessly fuses a catamaran hull with the bow of a wave-piercing deep-vee monohull. Although simple in concept, its execution proved complex; managing the interaction between the three hulls involved determining the best proportion of load distribution between the cat sections and the monohull, and the complex configuration of the height and shape of the bridge deck to reduce interaction and drag from the monohull wake. However, the end result is a high-speed hull design that offers excellent high-speed seakeeping. What's more, the combined fuel load and water ballast system allows optimisation of the LCG for prevailing sea conditions and speed, effectively marrying the excellent rough-weather capabilities of traditional designs with high-speed capabilities.

Most boats would need to go into survival mode in these harsh conditions.

Speed is now an important factor in lifeboat design which puts more emphasis on the safety of the boat lying in the hands of the driver.

THE BOAT FOR THE JOB

You would have thought that by now the best type of hull design for a job would have been determined and all boats would have followed this concept, and to a certain extent this is the case. The differences in hull design from most of the major motor cruiser builders are quite small, and the same is true in the faster sports boat sector. You can possibly see the differences in the deadrise angle and perhaps in the chine line, but most follow a similar pattern.

In such production boats, you find that designers tend to play it safe, and it is not hard to see why when you realise the considerable sums that have to be invested in the creation of the mould and the detailed design work that has to be done before a prototype can be tested on the water. You see the same thing happening with car design, for which there is great similarity between the shapes, styling and handling in a particular sector because the same solution works for all of them.

Look a little deeper, however, and you'll realise just how many options there are beyond the basic principles. Even if you just consider monohulls, for example, there are countless variations – some subtle, some major – and of course this is what keeps designers in business. For the most part, these differences are evident in the styling – the part of the boat above water – and this is where the design focus tends to be these days. However, even here there is not a vast amount of difference between the designs from different builders , because the basic solution to optimising the layout is much the same for everyone. I often wonder if I were in the market for a motor cruiser how I would choose the one for me, and have concluded that my decision would probably be based on what the interior looked like.

THE ALL-IMPORTANT HULL

In terms of ride comfort, though, it's the underwater shape of the hull that is important when you are out at sea. So, while the full hull shapes of the majority of motor cruisers maximise the interior volume, they make the boats more sensitive to waves and give them a more lively motion. Of course, as already discussed, this is not really a problem if you only go out in fine conditions. It does have a knock-on effect on the rest of the boat, however, since in order to control these hull motions automatic trim systems, stabilisers and gyro systems are being introduced to reduce the rolling.

With faster sports cruisers, the hull lines tend to be finer and the bow shape may have a reduced volume to help in waves, since for these boats the design emphasis is more on the performance than the luxury, although even here the priorities are getting blurred. Yes, I know that for many people going to sea should be a pleasure and not a punishment, but you do wonder sometimes if we have not gone too far down the luxury route with boat design at the expense of good and practical seamanship.

It is not all doom and gloom in the leisure sector in terms of hull design, though, and we see some seamanlike hull shapes in the trawler market, which comprises boats that have been designed for serious cruising. There is a huge difference between just going out to sea for a few hours knowing that you can run to harbour if the weather changes and setting out on a long voyage that might last 24 hours or more, or even a cruise that could take weeks or months. These trawler yachts may still be based on moderate-vee hulls because that shape is now so well proven, but you see much more attention being paid to the bow shape to ensure a seaworthy hull that can cope with adverse conditions. While there is still an emphasis on the interior, because you need comfort if you are going to spend days rather than hours on board, this tends to be a practical comfort designed so that you can live on board both at sea and at harbour. There is also far less emphasis on speed and performance because for long voyages you want economy rather than speed.

With this in mind, we are seeing a resurgence in the market for displacement motor yachts that operate at low speeds in considerable comfort, and that don't require you to rush to the refuelling dock every time you enter harbour. With this growth in the displacement yacht market it is thought the wheel has gone full circle and we are back to the type of boating of 100 years ago, although with a lot more quality and dignified style. The quest for 'going green' may also hasten a greater emphasis on displacement hulls, although we are not seeing any signs of this among the major motor cruiser builders.

Some of the best seaworthy hull designs in the leisure sector are seen in the American style of sports fishing boats. These are boats designed to get out and back to distant fishing grounds offshore often in adverse conditions and at considerable speed, and the hull designs reflect this. Most are based on the ubiquitous deep-vee hull, but with a different bow shape comprising a fine entry at the waterline with the bow widening out with a significant flare to deflect the spray away from the hull.

This flare is a feature that has virtually disappeared from modern leisure boat design except on these sports fishing boats, in the interests, once again, of maximising the interior hull volume. One place where you *can* see flare and more seaworthy hull designs being introduced into hull shapes is in those boats designed to work at sea, such as those for commercial or military use. Here, there tends to be a much greater emphasis on the performance of the hull and the contrast between these designs and most of those used in the leisure sector is very noticeable. For these boats, there is a finer entry and a growing trend towards a double-chine configuration so that the buoyancy in the bow increases as the bow becomes submerged in a wave. The accent for these commercial designs is on practical seaworthiness because, unlike leisure boats, they are expected to continue to work in adverse conditions.

It is sad to see this difference but it does reflect how powerboat hulls can be tailored to the specific work that they have to do and the conditions in which they are expected to operate. Some builders of production boats are looking in a bit more depth about their hull designs and how they perform at sea. Fairline, a British builder of production fast boats, turned to the Dutch design group Vripack to develop a deep-vee hull with reduced pitching motions, and by manipulating the weight distribution and making small alterations in the bow shape they have produced a hull that shows significant improvements. This shows the subtlety of hull design and that it is more than just the shape that is important.

CHOOSING AND BUYING A BOAT

When choosing a new boat, there is a wide range of options available and hopefully the guidance in this book will enable a more informed choice to be made. I do wonder, though, if there is any significance in the fact that the underwater parts of the hulls of many of the powerboats exhibited at boat shows are carefully hidden from view by drapes or coverings. It looks as though the salespeople want potential buyers to concentrate on the styling and the luxury and to forget about the working parts of the boat. You are expected to take those for granted. These days, I doubt that there is a 'bad' boat out there on the market, but certainly I have tested a few boats over the years that have not

A modern sports cruiser has to combine comfort in harbour and performance at sea.

been of an acceptable standard if you judge them as a practical seagoing boat.

Factors to consider when selecting a boat

1. Speed requirements
2. Engine type
3. Propulsion system
4. Construction material
5. Accommodation
6. Operational area
7. Berthing (marina, anchorage, trailer, size of boat etc)
8. Use of boat (leisure, commercial, fishing)
9. Price
10. Range (how fast is it and how far does it need to travel)

Factors to consider when buying a boat

1. Condition survey
2. Suitable for requirements (suitable engine and helmsmen position; check the controls)
3. Second hand or new
4. Finance
5. Comfort on board
6. Safety (grab rails, handholds etc)
7. Sea trial
8. Speed and seaworthiness
9. Noise levels
10. Engine and fuel

Just as a subtle change in the hull shape and weight distribution can have a significant effect on the sea-going ability of a hull, so small changes at the helm can also make a considerable improvement to the way that a helmsman can control his boat and so improve the sea-going experience.

CONCLUSION

Boat designers are always trying to push the boundaries – boundaries that might be imposed by overall length and cost, but often also by performance and rules and regulations. These rules and regulations can often have a negative effect on design, well away from what they were originally intended for, so creative thinking is required to work within the limitations and still produce an exciting and innovative concept. This is something that few designers are prepared to do, however, since there is a distinct reluctance among the leisure boat-buying public to invest in untested innovation, so the tried-and-tested solutions remain the predominant choice. Innovation comes in many forms and whilst the obvious ones are concepts such as hydrofoils, hovercraft and SWATHs, there are more subtle innovations such as modern electronic systems that can make navigation safer, can monitor everything that is going on onboard and can even help you to trim the boat and dock it in the marina safely. The skills of boat driving are changing but the human element is still the most vital part of any powerboat.

Few builders are prepared to test their designs to the limit, unlike this Safehaven pilot boat.

When you take a look at the powerboat market there is a huge range of designs out there and the fact that there are so many ideas suggest that the design and development of powerboats is still very much alive and there are always exciting new concepts arriving on the market. There was a time when many boats started to look the same. I know that much of the market is now focussed on style rather than performance but this only reflects the fact that performance is now taken for granted when a new design hits the market. Beauty is in the eye of the beholder and as a traditionalist I do find it hard to accept some of the new boats that have appeared recently but they sell and their owners appreciate the style. There are the owners who love the luxury of modern boat interiors and I have to admit that going to sea in a yacht that combines luxury with a capable sea-going performance is still one of the joys in life. Today boats are somewhat like cars in that you want something that not only performs well but also looks good. It is a challenge for designers to achieve this

combination but there are many powerboats out there that can meet both of these criteria and these will be the ones that will stand the test of time.

People own powerboats for a wide variety of different reasons and use them in a wide variety of different ways. Today we are seeing boats that are developed for specific markets instead of having a 'one size fits all' approach. If the thrill of high performance is what excites you – and it certainly does me – then there are some wonderful boats out there that can not only give you high speeds but can also manage this with much greater safety. If you are into sports fishing, then the particular demands of this sport are met by some very capable designs. Long range cruising is catered for by the trawler type of yacht that looks more towards economy and seaworthiness rather than top speeds. Comfort and luxury can be found in all these sectors, whilst for those working at sea, the accent will be more on rugged seaworthiness and practical operations.

The next stage is fully automated boats. There are many of these around already designed for specific tasks such as surveying.

Boating can take you away from the cares of life ashore and as the seamen of old used to say, 'shaking off the shackles of the shore' can be a wonderful experience. Whilst you may say goodbye to the highly regulated world onshore, you switch this for a world where you take responsibility for your actions and where you are in charge. The modern powerboat can contribute to this new-found freedom but the boat alone is only part of the story. No boat is going to work effectively without a driver who knows what he or she is doing, and each and every boat needs this combination. The sea can provide a challenging environment but the rewards of being out there, of completing a safe passage in good order, are immense. Thanks to the skill and dedication of designers and builders and – dare I say it – investors, you can take pleasure in such a rewarding experience as messing about in boats. Sixty years on and I still love it!

Unmanned powerboats are likely to feature more and more in the future.

Running level and true – a well designed sports cruiser.

This deep-vee hull is running level and true even in a tight turn.

THE THEORY: BASIC HULL DESIGN & STABILITY

Boat design is a complex subject involving countless different parts, forces and factors, many of which are so specialised as to be beyond the scope of this book. However, it is nevertheless useful to have a basic grasp of the theory of boat design because it will enable you to better understand what is going on on the boat, and what you should do in response. One of the key areas to explore are the various forces that act on the hull of a boat, particularly in the open sea.

A long, thin hull can extend the speed potential of displacement hulls.

FORCES THAT ACT ON A BOAT

First, there is the weight of the boat itself. This acts vertically downwards under the force of gravity, through the centre of gravity (CG). This CG is found by adding up all the weights in the boat and their location and finding the point at which they balance. This is a fixed point no matter what the boat does, and it only moves when a weight on the boat moves. You can see this on a small boat when a crew member moves to one side and the boat heels over correspondingly. It will also move when fuel is used up on passage, and the weight decreases, which is why designers tend to locate the fuel tank somewhere close to the CG so that there is not too much change of trim as this occurs. When weights are added to the boat, the CG moves towards that weight and when weights are removed, it moves away. So, for example, if you fill up with water, the CG will move towards the point where that water tank is installed. On most leisure boats there will be little change in the CG, but on some commercial craft that carry passengers or cargo, there can be significant changes that could affect the trim of the boat.

Balanced against this force of gravity and keeping the boat afloat is the upward thrust from the buoyancy, which acts vertically upwards through the centre of buoyancy (CB). This CB is the geometric centre of the underwater part of the hull, so all the parts located underwater, such as the propeller, contribute to the buoyancy even though they might be much heavier than the water. It is the volume that they occupy that counts. When the boat is at rest in still water, the CG and the CB are on the same vertical line with the CG below the CB so that the downward thrust of gravity is balanced by the upward thrust of buoyancy.

Two events can alter this state of equilibrium: a movement of the CG or a movement of the CB. As we have seen, the CG only moves if a weight on board is moved or changed. Taking the earlier example, if a crew member moves to one side then the CG will move to that side and to compensate the boat will heel towards that side. This in turn will increase the underwater volume on that side, which results in the CB also moving accordingly. In effect, there is an automatic compensation system that tries to maintain the boat in balance at all times. This compensation system works both in the transverse and the fore and aft direction, although the effect is not so noticeable in the fore and aft direction because of the much greater stability of the hull in this plane.

Out at sea, the CG stays in virtually the same place but now the underwater part of the hull is continually changing shape as the boat encounters waves, and so the CB is also constantly changing position as waves pass under the hull. With the CG remaining constant, the movement of the CB creates a turning moment as the CB moves towards the point of the hull that is most deeply immersed. This creates an upward force to lift the hull at this deepest point, so that there is a constant force wanting to keep the boat in equilibrium in waves, trying to bring the CG and the CB in line.

Generally speaking, in the transverse plane on a boat with a full hull form, the righting levers created by the force of buoyancy acting upwards and that of gravity acting downwards will produce a strong righting moment to keep the boat upright, as a small angle of heel will create a significant change in the buoyancy.

As well as a full hull form, another way to improve the transverse stability is to increase the vertical distance between the CG and the CB, which usually means lowering the CG. This is an area where designers have to compromise because a righting lever that is too powerful can cause the rolling movements of the boat to become quicker and more uncomfortable thanks to a pendulum movement, which can be very tiring.

In the fore and aft direction, the boat is much more inherently stable due to the length of the boat compared to the beam, and here the problem is not so much to ensure stability but to ensure that there is adequate buoyancy at the ends of the hull for the boat to lift over waves and not go through them. If the bow has very fine lines there will be reduced buoyancy because of the smaller change in the CB, and the bow could easily bury in a wave before there is enough buoyancy generated to lift over it. Most boats designed for rough-sea operations tend to have full bow shapes to ensure a generous amount of lift, but again the designer has to find a delicate balance between too much and too little buoyancy to give a comfortable ride. That is easy to say but hard to do because the shape and height of waves are constantly changing. The designer also has to bear in mind that the boat will be moving forwards, so that the amount of the bow that is being immersed can change very rapidly. The shape of the stern also needs to be considered because you don't want a boat with a fine bow and a full stern, particularly in a following

A deep-vee hulled patrol boat built in stainless steel, a material that is too expensive for general use.

A mini sharp-angled bulbous bow on this planing hull helps to extend the waterline length at lower speeds.

A deep-vee cruiser running with a bow up attitude.

sea. What the designer should be looking to achieve is a balanced hull with comparable bow and stern shapes, and full – but not too full – transverse shapes.

The above comments apply to boats that are operating at displacement speeds at which there is little lift generated from the progress through the water. You can certainly get a change of trim with a displacement hull by varying the speed and that might help to match the hull to the prevailing conditions, but generally the attitude of the hull will be dictated by the waves. With planing hulls, however, the designer has a much bigger challenge because not only does s/he have to produce a hull shape that will work and be balanced at displacement speeds, but it also has to work at higher planing speeds. Now we have a third force coming into play on the hull, the dynamic lift.

DYNAMIC LIFT

Dynamic lift is generated by the interaction of the hull of the boat moving through the water, which creates a lifting force that bodily elevates the hull. As the hull lifts, the force of buoyancy is reduced because there is less of the hull in the water – a loss that is compensated for by the force of the dynamic lift. However, with three forces now in action on the hull, the designer's job becomes a bit more complex.

This dynamic lift is focused at a point just aft of where the hull meets the water when the boat is on the plane. This means that its position will vary fore and aft as the hull encounters waves. This point of dynamic lift is

then matched to the lift from the buoyancy with the CB moving aft because this is the only part of the hull in the water. Both the CB and the point of dynamic lift will vary and they should automatically find or at least strive to find a point of balance, which is why you will see the boat constantly pitching in the waves. In a head sea, when the bow encounters a wave, both of the points of application of these two forces will move forwards, allowing the bow to lift to the wave, and then they will move aft as the wave passes under the hull. So, to a large extent the balance between the forces of gravity, buoyancy and lift are self-adjusting, but not always to the benefit of a comfortable ride.

There is a generous flare on this bow above a fine entry.

When looking at dynamic lift, the point at which this is acting will vary according to the beam of the boat. The boat needs a certain area of the hull in contact with the water to generate the lift that allows it to plane. On a boat with a wide beam, this lift area will be further aft than on a boat with a narrow beam, and will be exaggerated on a boat with a shallow-vee hull that generates more lift. This means that the dynamic lift is concentrated and acts through a point further aft, with less of the longitudinal length of the hull generating the lift. The result is that a smaller change in hull trim can mean quite a big change in the position of the dynamic lift and this is what can cause the hull to 'porpoise', with the bow moving up and down as it seeks to find a comfortable balance. If you find the boat doing this, you can probably cure it by: adjusting the speed so that more of the hull is in the water; using the flaps/interceptors to lower the bow and get more of the hull in the water; or adjusting the power trim, again to lower the bow. There should be no porpoising problems for boats with a narrow hull, and with stepped hulls, porpoising is virtually eliminated. A stepped deep-vee hull also offers the benefit of a more level motion because it is riding on two main points rather than the single point of a non-stepped hull.

HULL SHAPE AND REMAINING UPRIGHT

A boat hull needs to have stability. In sailing boats, this is provided by a heavy keel, whereas powerboats rely mainly on the shape of the hull. As we have discussed, for a hull to be stable in the transverse direction the first step is to keep the CG below the CB. It will vary from hull to hull, but this relationship will remain in place until the boat is heeled over to a considerable angle, perhaps around 70 degrees. This situation usually changes once the deck level becomes immersed, at which point the righting lever generated by the CB in its relationship to the CG starts to get smaller, and with most hulls the righting lever will disappear at quite a severe angle of heel and the boat will capsize. In normal boat operations you will never get to this stage and the boat will have a more than adequate range of stability, but some boats, such as lifeboats and many RIBs, need to be self-righting if this critical angle of heel is exceeded and the boat capsizes.

The secret to making a boat self-right after a capsize is to make it unstable when it is upside down. In the main, this is done by having a watertight superstructure that provides buoyancy in the upside-down position. With RIBs and open boats, this is not normally possible; thanks to their tubes, RIBs can be notoriously stable upside-down. Here, the solution is to have an inflatable bag, usually mounted on a raised frame over the engines aft, which can be inflated either automatically or manually in the event of a capsize. This gives enough buoyancy to right the boat. Of course, having this inflatable bag and its support frame adds weight high up in the boat and will make it more prone to capsize, but it is justified because operators have a duty of care to their boats' crews and the self-righting capability gives crews one more chance of survival if things go wrong. The capsizes that I know about have mainly been RIBs that were operating in heavy breaking waves in which they had been going too slowly, resulting in the breaking crest being able to catch up with the boat and capsize it. Capsize is rare in normal boat operations.

Going back to that righting lever between the CG and the CB that keeps the boat stable: if it is too long the boat will tend to adopt a short, sharp roll that can be very tiring and uncomfortable. If it is too short, the rolling will be much slower and you may wonder if the roll is going to keep going. To a large extent, the shape of the hull will determine the type of roll: full hull shapes with a sharp turn at the bilge are likely to roll more sharply than a more rounded hull shape. On planing

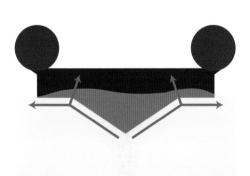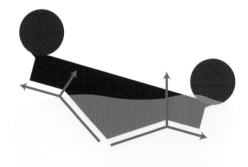

A diagram showing how the chines generate extra lift when the boat heels to bring the boat back upright.

Two deep-vee hulls running at different trim angles.

boats, the lift comes into the stability equation and the transfer of lift from being equally shared between each side of the hull to just one side of the hull as the boat heels will help to keep the boat upright. Wide chines will also help to right the hull if it heels over, but of course too much lift will make the motions of the boat harsh and uncomfortable. With RIBs, additional stability is also provided by the inflatable tube.

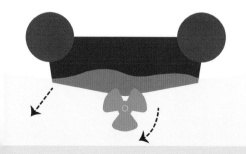

How the torque from a single propeller can cause a boat to heel.

We looked earlier in the book at how the use of fast-acting interceptors can be coordinated to keep the boat upright with planing hulls, but for displacement hulls, stabilising fins can work well. These fins are operated hydraulically or electrically and vary their angle to generate or cancel lift to reduce the rolling of the hull under the control of a motion sensor. They work very well, but you can sense jerkiness in the motions of the hull as they try to counteract the wave-induced motions. Gyro stabilisers do much the same thing, but here it is a heavy spinning flywheel that generates the forces required to keep the boat upright. See Chapter 11 for further information about interceptors, flaps and gyros.

Finally, a word of warning. In most cases, both fast- and slow-boat hulls have adequate stability for the type of operations that they are designed for, but there is one situation in which the stability of a hull can be significantly reduced. This mainly applies to displacement hulls and it can occur when they are operating in a following sea and the waves are travelling at or close to the speed of the boat, in which case the boat can find itself sitting on the crest of a wave for some time. In this situation, the stability of the hull can be significantly reduced because the normal waterline does not extend for the full length of the hull and the bow and stern are largely unsupported. On boats where the righting lever for the stability may be quite short anyway, this could lead to the boat capsizing. That said, I have only ever heard of this happening to a ship. The solution is simply to slow or increase the speed of the boat so that it is not matching that of the waves. You may have wondered why your boat rolled so much in following seas when waves were passing under the hull. This is the reason, and it should act as a warning sign.

CONSTRUCTION MATERIALS

In recent years, there has been a transformation in the way that boats are built. This is partly the result of more intensive production systems using advanced composites, but also due to the requirement to reduce weight. As we have seen, weight can be important to performance; the demands for a reduction in the weight of the mouldings used for boat construction are likely to be the result of designers having to compensate for the increased weight that comes with more sophisticated interiors. However using lighter materials also often brings with it a cost increase.

The Icelandic Rafnar hull moulding showing the embryo keel amidships.

In the days of heavy displacement boats, when wood and steel were the main construction materials, the shape of the hull was dictated to a certain extent by the materials being used: we saw wooden hulls accommodate the shape that can be developed by the wood's ability to bend. Steel hulls tended to have hard chines and be angular, although some steel hulls used plating that had been specially shaped to accommodate double curves in a demonstration of the skills of the builder. Welded construction gave these builders more flexibility in the way that hulls could be developed.

More advanced systems used wood in the form of cold-moulded plywood, whereby the shape was developed over a temporary mould using thin strips of wood that allowed double curves to be utilised. The resin glues used for this construction were similar to the resins now found in composite construction. In metal, the arrival of computer-controlled cutting systems allowed the metal plates to be produced with very high accuracy and this led to more sophisticated construction, with all the pieces fitting together very precisely.

It was the advent of composite construction that changed the face of boat design and construction. For the first time, the designer was largely freed from the constraints of the material being used and could develop the optimum shape for the job that had to be done. Composites had a lot of growing pains as experience with the materials and the ways they could be used developed, and boats tended to be either overbuilt or underbuilt because designers were never sure of the characteristics of the materials.

Early composites used glass fibres and mainly polyester resins, but a modern hull may now include Kevlar and carbon fibres, utilising the tensile strength of Kevlar and the compression strength of carbon to engineer a structure with minimum weight and maximum strength. Construction systems such as vacuum bagging and oven baking also allow more consistent and high-quality finished laminates. The fact that composites are now also used in the construction of cars and aircraft demonstrates just how important this development is and how much it has and will influence the future design and performance of all powerboats.

INDEX

ACKNOWLEDGEMENTS

In writing this book, there are many people I need to thank. First of all, there are those people who have given me the opportunity to drive boats to their limits. These include the RNLI where, for a period, I was testing and evaluating new designs for lifeboats and going to sea in extreme conditions. They also allowed me to help develop the first RIB. Then, there is Fabio Buzzi with whom I raced in offshore powerboat racing for over 25 years at the extremes of fast boat performance, and who allowed me to drive his single seater three-pointer to speeds of 150 mph.

There are many others who gave me the opportunity to go to the limits with fast boats including people such as Richard Branson and Paolo Vitelli who employed me as a navigator and weatherman for Atlantic record attempts.

I must say a very grateful thank you to those designers, naval architects and others who have contributed to this book by giving their views on an array of powerboat design topics, contributions which have added greatly to the depth of experience and thought in powerboat design.

PHOTO CREDITS

THE AUTHOR

AUTHOR

Dag Pike has been a freelance author, journalist and broadcaster for over 40 years. He is the author of over 50 mainly nautical books and contributes to magazines in the US, Europe, Asia and the UK. He was awarded the first Yachting Journalist's Association Lifetime Achievement award in 2009. Pike has 40 years of experience in offshore powerboat racing and record breaking and is one of the most experienced fast boat navigators in his field. He also works as a marine consultant and does expert witness work, having been involved in several high profile trials. Pike was involved in developing the first RIB in the world and in other pioneering developments. He has sailed in every ocean around the world and continues to explore new frontiers.